极 简 语 法

——从零基础到破解 TOEFL/SAT/ACT 长难句

熊志卉　著

上海交通大学出版社

内容提要

本书内容主要包括英语阅读时必备的基础语法知识点以及托福、SAT 及 ACT 阅读中常见的长难句的分析与解析。本书适合托福、SAT 及 ACT 阅读的备考学员用来解决长句理解的准确度和速度问题,对于其他想要解决阅读中句子层面的学员也同样适用。

图书在版编目(CIP)数据

极简语法:从零基础到破解 TOEFL/SAT/ACT 长难句/
熊志卉著. —上海:上海交通大学出版社,2022.9
ISBN 978 - 7 - 313 - 27042 - 9

Ⅰ.①极… Ⅱ.①熊… Ⅲ.①英语-语法-高等学校
-入学考试-美国-自学参考资料 Ⅳ.①H314

中国版本图书馆 CIP 数据核字(2022)第 117143 号

极简语法——从零基础到破解 TOEFL/SAT/ACT 长难句
JIJIAN YUFA—CONG LINGJICHU DAO POJIE TOEFL/SAT/ACT CHANGNANJU

著　　者:熊志卉
出版发行:上海交通大学出版社　　　　　地　　址:上海市番禺路 951 号
邮政编码:200030　　　　　　　　　　　电　　话:021 - 64071208
印　　制:上海新艺印刷有限公司　　　　经　　销:全国新华书店
开　　本:787mm×1092mm　1/16　　　印　　张:12.25
字　　数:258 千字
版　　次:2022 年 9 月第 1 版　　　　　印　　次:2022 年 9 月第 1 次印刷
书　　号:ISBN 978 - 7 - 313 - 27042 - 9
定　　价:45.00 元

前　言

为什么写这本书

学习一门语言，最为基本的内容莫过于词汇和语法规则了。词汇的重要性不言而喻，但很多学生却经常忽视语法的重要性，尤其是非体制内的学生。笔者在多年的阅读教学过程中发现一个有趣的现象：在托福考试中，大多数国际学校学生最薄弱的环节竟然是阅读。本质的原因就是这些学生没有系统地学过语法，对于他们来说，语感就是语法。但大多数学生靠这种语言沉浸式学习所获得的语感远没有到达母语者的程度，所以他们的语感就处于一种比较尴尬的状况——时灵时不灵。这也是他们托福阅读的分数会上下起伏非常大的主要原因。所以，对于非母语者来说，要想对外语语言有一个精准而稳定的理解，语法是绕不过的、同时也是最高效的路径。

但是，考虑到很多学生可能没有充分的时间将所有的语法规则都掌握，笔者根据多年的教学经验以及教研成果，对阅读所需的语法规则进行提炼和压缩，力求将语法规则的学习过程简单化以及高效化。本书就是在这个方向上不断尝试的结果。

内容安排与使用说明

本书一共分为八个章节，其中第一章至第三章是阅读必备的基本语法规则。这部分内容尽可能避免晦涩的语法术语，力求通过使用简单的规则和例句，帮助学生掌握最基本的语法规则。对于基本没有语法基础的学生来讲，这部分内容必须认真阅读并且完成相应练习。可能所配的例句和练习是你可以轻松看懂的，但这部分的内容不是考查你对于句子的理解，而是通过这些简单的例子去理解和记住最为基本的语法规则。对于已经有一定语法基础的学生，还是建议通读一下这个部分，因为这部分的内容是从纯实用的角度来书写的，可以帮你简化已有的语法体系。

第四章是特殊语法现象的集合，这部分的内容需要理解的规则少，需要记忆的规则多，因此，需要把这些常见的特殊句型和规则牢记于心。

第五章至第七章的内容是关于如何利用前四个章节中的基本规则来分析出国类考试

中阅读部分常见的长难句。这些长难句都是笔者从 TOEFL/SAT/ACT 真题中精挑细选的例句,如果能够轻松熟练地分析理解这些长难句,那么从语法层面上来讲就足以应对这些阅读了。这部分的学习重点是掌握长难句的分析方法,由浅入深分为三个阶段:长难句分析、句子层次及模式化。模式化是长难句阅读的最高境界,也是从语法层面接近母语者状态的必经阶段。希望通过这些针对性的练习,可以帮助各位学生在长难句掌握上有所提高。

第八章为综合练习的章节,分为 9 个单元,每个单元有一个长难句模式的小主题,意在帮助学生专项突破,更清晰地掌握英语的语法模式。

声明

本书中的语法规则源于笔者多年教学过程中对于英语语法的简化与提炼,是从纯实用的角度出发来处理这些规则,与传统的学术语法并不相同,有些部分为了力求"简单好用",弱化了学术角度的严谨性。因此,无需从学术角度对本书内容求全责备。如果读者对本书内容有任何疑惑或者建议,欢迎指出!"取长补短"和"教学相长"一直是笔者在教学过程中不断的追求。

熊志卉

2022 年 3 月 1 日

目　录

句子的主干成分

一 什么是句子主干

句子的主干部分是一个句子不可或缺的部分,也是句子中最重要的信息所在。句子的主干部分我们重点强调主语和谓语部分。**主语就相当于一棵树的树根部分,而谓语就是树的树干部分。**一个句子必须要有主语和谓语,否则就不是一个正确的句子,就像一棵树必须有树根和树干,否则就不是一棵可以存活的树。

二 什么是主语

对于"什么是主语"这个问题,比较学术的定义是"主语是句子陈述或说明的对象,表明句子说的是谁或者什么事,是执行句子行为和动作的主体"。不过,本书不是从学术角度,而是从实用角度出发的,所以接下来我们就从比较实用的角度来讲如何快速识别一个句子的主语。这可能从学术上不是百分之百的严谨,但一定是百分之百的实用。

1. 快速识别主语

主语是:**从句首起,第一个独立的名词或具有名词性质的词或短语。**

1)"从句首起"是很好理解的,就是从句子最左边起第一个单词开始找。

2)"独立"指得是这个名词的前面**没有介词或者动词**与之构成的介词短语或动词短语。例如,在 on the table,in the morning,eating a cake,loving them 这几个短语中,table,morning,cake,them 等都不是独立的名词或代词。

3)"具有名词性质的词或短语"指的是除了名词以外,像代词、数词、动名词、to do 不定式以及"the＋形容词"等这类词或短语,它们整体上也可以表达人、事、物等相当于名词的概念,所以也可以充当句子的主语。不过,最常见的句子主语还是名词或代词。

2. 主语示例

<u>Country music</u> has become more and more popular.

In class,<u>we</u> often speak English.

Up to now,<u>Mr. Scott</u> has sent a great many requests for spare parts.

<u>The rich</u> should help the poor.（the＋形容词,表示一类人或事）

<u>Smoking</u> does harm to the health.（doing 或 doing sth,表示动作的概念）

<u>To go to the park</u> is my plan.（to do 或 to do sth,表示动作的概念）

大多数句子中主语都可以通过上述的原则快速找到,至于不符合上述规律的特殊情况会在后面第四章特殊句型中做整理和分析。

三 什么是谓语

谓语是对主语动作状态或特征的陈述或说明,一般出现在主语后面。这里我们还是抛开学术的定义,直接来看看如何快速识别一个句子的谓语。

1. 快速识别谓语

谓语是跳过主语后面的从句且不是 to do/doing/done 形式的动词。

1）跳过主语后面的从句

从句的级别是低于主句的,所以在快速识别谓语时,如果主语后面有从句的话,要先跳过。如果对于什么是从句不太清楚的话,我们在第三章中会具体展开。例:

<u>The student</u> ~~who wears a pair of big glasses~~ <u>studies</u> very hard.

2）不是 to do/doing/done 形式的动词

我们必须牢记**"谓语一定是动词,但动词并不一定是谓语"**。对于 to do/doing/done 这种形式的动词,它们在句子中只起修饰作用,其地位要比谓语动词低一个级别,**所携带的信息重要性自然要低于谓语动词**,所以一定不能将其与谓语动词搞混,例:

<u>The woman</u> ~~holding a baby in her arms~~ <u>is</u> my aunt.

<u>His ability</u> ~~to solve difficult situation~~ <u>impressed</u> me.

四 谓语的重要特点

1. 时态

英语中的谓语动词,不但能表达动作本身,还能**通过形态的变化来表示这个动作发生**

的时间和状态，下面我们来看看谓语动词的不同形态是如何体现动作的时间与状态的：

发生的时间				
发生的状态	过去	过去将来	现在	将来
一般 翻译：做	**did/was/were**	would do/be	**do/does/am/is/are**	**will do/be**
进行 翻译：正在做	**was/were doing**	would be doing	**am/is/are doing**	will be doing
完成 翻译：已经做	**had done/been**	would have done/been	**has/have done/been**	will have done/been
完成进行 翻译：一直在做	had been doing	would have been doing	**has/have been doing**	will have been doing

　　要牢记每种动词形式所反映的动作发生的时间和状态，比如，was doing 就表示"这个动作是过去发生且当时正在进行"。表格中加粗部分的形态及含义要尤其注意，因为这些时态出现频率是非常高的，例：

　　He **works** hard. 他工作努力。

　　He **is reading.** 他正在阅读。

　　He **has finished** it. 他已经完成了。

　　He **has been writing** it for two hours. 他已经一直写了两个小时了。

　　He **worked** hard. 他过去工作很努力。

　　He **was reading** last night. 他昨晚在阅读。

　　He **had finished** it since you arrived. 在你到达之时他已经完成了。

　　He **had been writing** it. 他过去就已经一直在写了。

　　He **will work** hard. 他将努力工作。

　　He **will be reading.** 他（将）会在阅读。

　　He **will have finished** it by the time of tomorrow. 明天之前他将完成。

　　He **will have been staying** there for ten years by the time of next month 到下个月，他（将）已经一直待在那儿十年了。

　　He **would work** hard. 他过去（将）工作努力。

　　He **would be working** hard. 他过去一段时间在努力工作着。

　　He **would have finished** it by the last month 他到上个月为止就将完成任务。

　　He **would have been staying** there for ten years by the time of last month. 到上个月为止，他（将）已经一直在那里待了十年之久。

2. 语态

就像汉语中的"把"字句和"被"字句来表达动作的主被动一样,英语中也有主被动之分。英语中"被"字句的识别模式是"be + done"的结构,这种结构一律表示被动,例:

The floor **was swept**.

地面**被扫**了。

Knives **are used** for cutting things.

刀**被用来**切东西。

The work **has been done**.

工作已**经被做**了。

The students **were given** some advice by the teacher.

学生**被**老师**给**了一些建议。

3. 过去分词与谓语动词过去式的区别

之前在讲谓语动词的快速辨别时,规则之一是 to do/doing/done 形式的动词一定不是谓语。细心的读者可能会发现,to do 和 doing 形式的动词可以从形态上一眼看出来不是谓语,但是大多数动词的过去分词(done)和过去式(did)的形态是一样的,怎么样去区分一个句子中单独出现的 v-ed 形式的动词到底是过去分词还是谓语动词的过去式呢? 记住以下 2 个原则:

a) 在没有连词的情况下,一个句子只有一个谓语动词。

b) 过去分词是被动关系,而谓语动词过去式是主动关系。因为过去分词(done)其实是被动语态 be done 的结构省略而来的。

下面我们来看一个简单的示例的分析:

The flower **bought** by my friend **attracted** a bee.

分析:首先,这个句子的主语是"The flower",但一眼看去,这个句子里有两个动词,"bought"和"attracted"。这两个动词必然只有一个是谓语动词,另外一个是非谓语。不过,因为两个动词都是过去式,所以无法直接从形态上判断,只能分析这两个动词的主被动关系了。动词 bought 和 the flower 是被动关系,表示"被买"而不是"买",因为花是不可能去执行"买"这个动作的,只能是被买。动词 attracted 和 The flower 应该是主动关系,因为是花吸引蜜蜂而不是花被蜜蜂吸引,这样一来,这个句子的成分分析如下:

The flower bought by my friend attracted a bee.

= The flower ~~which was~~ bought by my friend attracted a bee.

此外,还有一些快速区分过去分词(done)与谓语动词过去式(did)的小技巧:

- be 动词的各种形式(am/is/are/was/were)一定是谓语;
- 情态动词(can/could/would/should/must 等)所接动词一定是谓语;has/have/had

一定是谓语；

● 第三人称单数的动词一定是谓语。

如果一个句子在没有连词的情况下，既出现 v-ed 形式的动词又有上述特征的动词的话，那么有上述特征的动词一定是谓语，这个 v-ed 形式的动词一定是过去分词。

练一练

下列句子的动词用"＿＿"标记出过去分词（省略的被动语态），用"＿＿"标记出过去式。

1) The public clocks installed in town halls and market squares became the very symbol of a new, secular municipal authority.

2) Another visual signal produced by white-tailed deer is termed a buck scrape.

3) First, the chemicals deposited on the rub provided information on the individual identity of an animal.

4) Field experiments carried out by Charles Krebs and coworkers in 1992 provided an answer.

答案解析

1) The public clocks **installed** in town halls and market squares **became the very symbol** of a new, secular municipal authority.

= The public clocks which were **installed** in town halls and market squares **became** the very symbol of a new, secular municipal authority.

2) Another visual signal **produced** by white-tailed deer **is** termed a buck scrape.

= Another visual signal which is **produced** by white-tailed deer **is** termed a buck scrape.

3) First, the chemicals **deposited** on the rub **provided** information on the individual identity of an animal.

= First, the chemicals which were **deposited** on the rub **provided** information on the individual identity of an animal.

4) Field experiments **carried** out by Charles Krebs and coworkers in 1992 **provided** an answer.

= Field experiments which were **carried** out by Charles Krebs and coworkers in 1992 **provided** an answer.

五　其他的主干成分

我们可能经常听到英语的五大基本句型这一说,即"主＋谓""主＋谓＋宾""主＋系＋表""主＋谓＋双宾""主＋谓＋宾＋宾补"。这五种句型确实是英语句子最为核心的句型结构,不过,从阅读理解的角度来看,没有必要去掌握这么复杂的句型。如果从读懂句子的角度出发,最核心的一点是找到句子的主语和谓语,没有必要具体到是五种基本句型中的哪一种,因为这五大基本句型本质上是不同性质的谓语动词的不同呈现,下面我们就这个点来详细分析一下。

1. 主＋谓

如果谓语部分的动词本身就能把一个动作表达完整,则这个句子的主干就是简单的"主＋谓"结构,无需别的成分了(这类动词的术语叫作"**不及物动词**"),如:

He **runs**.

They **listened**.

The gas has **given out**. (动词短语当做整体来看)

My ink has **run out**.

2. 主＋谓＋宾

如果谓语部分的动词本身不能把一个动作表达完整,则需要出现一个新的成分来把这个动作补充完整(这个新成分的术语叫作"**宾语**",就是这个动作的承受者),这时,这个句子的主干就是"主＋谓＋宾"结构(这类动词的术语叫作"**及物动词**"),如:

I **saw a film**.

They **found their home**.

They **built a house**.

They have **taken good care of the children**.

You should **look after your children**.

3. 主＋谓＋双宾或主＋谓＋宾＋宾补

如果谓语部分的动词加了一个宾语不能把一个动作表达完整,还需要另一个宾语或者宾语的补语来把这个动作补充完整,那么这个句子的主干结构就是"主＋谓＋双宾"或"主＋谓＋宾＋宾补"(这类动词叫作"**双宾动词**"和"**宾补动词**")。这两个结构好像听起来挺复杂的,但是其实并没有那么可怕。这类动词我们在学习它们的时候就倾向以固定搭配的形式来记,所以阅读时我们只要知道这类动词的固定搭配就可以理解了,不需要记住"主＋谓＋双宾"或"主＋谓＋宾＋宾补"这么复杂的结构,如:

He **gave me a book.**　　　give sb sth

He **brought me a pen.**　　buy sb sth

He **offered me his seat.**　offer sb sth

They **made the girl angry.**　make sb/sth adj

I **made her smile.**　　　make sb/sth do

I **heard the glass broken.**　make sb/sth done

4. 主＋系＋表

如果谓语部分的动词不是一般的表示动作的动词,而是像 be 动词这种表示状态的动词(术语叫"**系动词**"),那么它的后面也一定要有其他成分来把这个句子的意思补充完整(这个补充的成分术语叫做"**表语**"),这种句子的主干就是"主＋系＋表",如:

They **are my students.**

She **is my friend.**

经过上面的分析之后不难发现,对于理解一个句子来讲,只要找到主语和谓语就可以了(be 动词这类动词也归到谓语这个概念里去)。如果我们认识这个动词,自然知道这个动词后面是否需要宾语之类的其他主干成分;相反,如果我们不认识这个动词,就算我们知道这个句子属于五种结构中的哪一种,对我们的理解也没有太大的帮助。

练一练

用"＿＿"标记出主语,用"＿＿"标记出谓语部分(包括谓语动词和其宾语等)。

1) Detailed field studies of thick rock formations containing fossils provide the best potential tests of the competing theories.

2) North and South America species migrating across the Isthmus now came into competition with each other.

3) A conspicuous sign indicating the presence of white-tailed deer in a woodlot is a buck rub.

4) Also，the availability of jobs in railway construction attracted many rural laborers accustomed to seasonal and temporary employment.

5) The simple motifs found at Panaramitee are common to many rock-art sites across Australia.

6) In the 1990s，enough electricity to meet about half the needs of San Francisco was being generated there.

7) Artists，often reluctantly，were forced to accept the evidence provided by the camera.

8）The ability to talk about one's past represents memory of a different level of complexity than simple recognition or recall.

9）The accidental effects obtained by photographers were soon being copied by artists such as the French painter Degas.

10）Prices of spices delivered by ship from the eastern Mediterranean came to equal those of spices transported by Portuguese vessels.

11）The physical structure of species competing for resources in the same ecological niche tends to gradually evolve in ways that allow territories no longer overlap.

12）The marks of abrasion caused by foot binding testify to early herding of domestic stock.

答案解析 ....

1）<u>Detailed field studies</u> of thick rock formations containing fossils <u>provide the best potential tests</u> of the competing theories.

2）<u>North and South America species</u> migrating across the Isthmus now <u>came into competition</u> with each other.

3）<u>A conspicuous sign</u> indicating the presence of white-tailed deer in a woodlot <u>is a buck rub.</u>

4）Also，<u>the availability of jobs</u> in railway construction <u>attracted many rural laborers</u> accustomed to seasonal and temporary employment.

5）<u>The simple motifs</u> found at Panaramitee <u>are common</u> to many rock-art sites across Australia.

6）In the 1990s，<u>enough electricity</u> to meet about half the needs of San Francisco <u>was being generated</u> there.

7）<u>Artists,</u> often reluctantly，<u>were forced to accept the evidence</u> provided by the camera.

8）<u>The ability</u> to talk about one's past <u>represents memory</u> of a different level of complexity than simple recognition or recall.

9）<u>The accidental effects</u> obtained by photographers <u>were soon being copied</u> by artists such as the French painter Degas.

10）<u>Prices</u> of spices delivered by ship from the eastern Mediterranean <u>came to equal those</u> of spices transported by Portuguese vessels.

11）The physical structure of species competing for resources in the same ecological niche tends to gradually evolve in ways that allow territories no longer overlap.

12）The marks of abrasion caused by foot binding testify to early herding of domestic stock.

第 二 章

修饰成分

一 什么是修饰成分

如果我们把句子的主干比喻为树的树根和树干的话,那么修饰成分就像树的枝条、叶子、花朵、果实之类。虽然它们不像树根树干那么必不可少,但是如果一个句子完全没有修饰的话,那也是很奇怪的。

句子常见的修饰成分有两种:名词的修饰(术语为"**定语**")和非名词的修饰(术语为"**状语**")。下面我们来详细了解这两种修饰成分。

二 名词的修饰成分——定语

1. 什么是定语

"定语"这个概念虽然对我们来说比较陌生,但是它的例子我们一定很熟悉。比如我们会说"美丽的花朵""快乐的小鸟",这些表示"……的"的描述其实就是定语。

2. 定语的位置

在汉语中,定语的位置一般就只在它所修饰的名词前面,但是英语中不一样,它既可以在被修饰的名词前面,也可以在被修饰的名词后面,具体的规则如下:

1) 一个单词修饰名词的话,一般放在被修饰的名词的前面(术语是"前置定语"),如:"beautiful flowers""happy birds";

2) 短语或从句修饰名词时,一般放在被修饰名词的后面(术语是"后置定语"),如:"these flowers on the table""the birds that rest on a tree"

前置的定语我们在这里不再赘述,因为与汉语的定语相似,所以只要单词认识基本就不会给理解造成问题,按顺序翻译即可。**但是,后置的定语我们需要高度重视**,一来是因为汉语中很少会有这种表达方式,这会影响我们对于句子的理解或者影响我们的阅读速度;二来,大多数非常复杂的句子的"罪魁祸首"基本上是后置定语。

3. 后置定语

1)短语

a. 形容词短语做后置定语

It is a method wonderfully efficient.
　　　　名词　　后置定语

It is a condition unfavorable to the enterprise.
　　　　名词　　　后置定语

A man often forgetful of his promise will never succeed.
名词　　　后置定语

This is a book good enough to teach us morals.
　　　名词　　　后置定语

b. 介词短语做后置定语

I went to the shop opposite the post office.
　　　　名词　　后置定语

The problem of poverty among children worried him.
　名词　　　后置定语

He has a good idea about how to master Chi.
　　　　名词　　后置定语

c. 现在分词短语做后置定语

The woman holding a baby in her arms is my aunt.
　名词　　后置定语

Anyone driving a lorry must first get a permit.
名词　后置定语

Some planets circling these stars might be similar to Earth.
　名词　　后置定语

d. 过去分词短语做后置定语

This is a letter written in German.
　　　名词　　后置定语

A man satisfied with his lot is happy.
名词　　后置定语

It is a bedroom seldom slept in.
　　　名词　　后置定语

e. 不定式短语做后置定语

His ability to solve difficult situation is impressive.
　名词　　后置定语

There is a sick man to look after.
　　　名词　　后置定语

There are many miserable people to help.
                        名词 后置定语

2）从句

除了短语修饰名词时需要后置之外，从句修饰名词也需要后置（这种从句叫作定语从句）。关于从句我们下个章节会详细介绍，这里先简单地举一些例子：

The girl who won the first prize in the contest is from Zhejiang.
名词   后置定语

The person to whom you just talked is Mr. Depp.
 名词   后置定语

We'll go to the hospital to see the patients，most of whom are children.
                              名词   后置定语

The new house which I have just bought is about six miles away.
  名词   后置定语

I'll never forget the time when we first met in London.
                名词   后置定语

3. 多重后置定语修饰

在短语和从句做后置定语的句子结构中，我们看到的都是相对比较简单的例子，基本只有一个修饰成分来修饰前面的名词。但是在比较复杂的情况下，往往会出现一个名词后面有多个后置的修饰成分，在这种情况下，**分清它们之间的修饰关系**对于准确地理解句子是非常关键的。

对于"名词＋修饰成分"这种结构，这个修饰成分基本上都是修饰前面这个名词，这种情况比较简单。但是，对于**"名词＋修饰成分1＋修饰成分2＋修饰成分3……"**这种结构，修饰成分2、修饰成分3的修饰对象的确定就比较重要了。我们需要记住以下的原则：修饰成分的修饰对象是**距离最近且逻辑合理**的名词。下面我们来看一下具体的示例：

例1：

the increased value placed on the idea of the family
      名词   修饰成分1   修饰成分2

在这个短语中，离修饰成分2最近的名词是"idea"，如果修饰成分2是修饰"idea"的话，其意思为"家庭的观念"，这符合日常逻辑，所以在这个示例中，修饰成分2修饰"idea"。

例2：

a system of complex technique composed of more than 14,000 parts
名词   修饰成分1   修饰成分2

在这个短语中，离修饰成分2最近的名词是"technique"，如果修饰成分2是修饰"technique"的话，其意思为"由超过14 000零件组成的技术"，这不符合日常逻辑，所以在这个示例中，修饰成分2是修饰"system"的，意为"由超过14 000个零件组成的系统"。

例3：

the invention of the visible-light microscope late in the sixteenth century
     名词   修饰成分1   修饰成分2

在这个短语中,离修饰成分 2 最近的名词是"microscope",如果修饰成分 2 是修饰"microscope"的话,其意思为"16 世纪后期的显微镜",这不符合上下文逻辑,所以在这个示例中,修饰成分 2 是修饰"invention"的,意为"16 世纪晚期的发明"。

例 4:

the advantages claimed for organically grown foods over conventionally grown
名词　　　　　　修饰成分1　　　　　　　　　修饰成分2
and marketed food products

在这个短语中,advantage...over 是个固定搭配,所以修饰成分 2 是修饰"advantage"而不是"food"。

其实,"最近且符合逻辑"的原则也是适用于汉语的,比如下面的两个例子:

例 1:

桌子上的 小明的 课本
修饰1　修饰2 名词

例 2:

教室里的 桌子上的 课本
修饰1　　修饰2　名词

例 1 中的修饰 1 是修饰"课本"的,而例 2 中的修饰 1 是修饰"桌子"的,所以无论在汉语还是在英语中,出现多个修饰成分时,每个修饰成分与修饰对象的关系的确立,都是需要建立在对修饰成分信息的理解及上下文或常规逻辑的基础上。唯一不同的是,汉语中的名词修饰语,无论长短,大多是放在名词的前面,而在英语中则是"**短的放前,长的放后**"。

在前面讨论的基础上,我们可以进一步得出英译中的小技巧,就是在英译中的过程中,通常都将英语中名词的后置定语统一提前,放到被修饰的名词的前面,例:

the increased value placed on the idea of the family
名词　　　　　修饰成分1　　　修饰成分2
翻译:家庭的 观念被赋予的 日益增加的价值

a system of complex technique composed of more than 14,000 parts
名词　　　　修饰成分1　　　　　　修饰成分2
翻译:由超过 14 000 个零件组成的 复杂技术的 系统

the invention of the visible-light microscope late in the sixteenth century
名词　　　　　　修饰成分1　　　　　　修饰成分2
翻译:16 世纪晚期的 可见光显微镜的 发明

the advantages claimed for organically grown foods over conventionally grown
名词　　　　　　修饰成分1　　　　　　　　　修饰成分2
and marketed food products
翻译:相较于传统种植与营销的食物产品的 有机种植的食物的 优势

练一练 ....

确定下面每个修饰成分的修饰对象。

1）the reconstruction of the process of seafloor spreading

2）changes in the efficiency of the muscles used for breathing

3）stimulation to the growth of synaptic connections in the brain

4）the story of the westward movement of population in the United States

5）the reconstruction of the geography of continents and of ocean basins in the past

6）changes in lake level not explained by river flows plus exchanges with the atmosphere

7）the development of new areas for the raising of livestock and the cultivation of wheat，corn，tobacco，and cotton

答案解析 ....

第一个修饰成分都是修饰最前面的名词的,答案里就不详细展开了,其他的修饰情况如下：

1）the reconstruction of the process of seafloor spreading

解析: of seafloor spreading 修饰 process

2）changes in the efficiency of the muscles used for breathing

解析: of the muscles 修饰 efficiency；used for breathing 修饰 the muscles

3）stimulation to the growth of synaptic connections in the brain

解析: of synaptic connections 修饰 the growth；in the brain 修饰 synaptic connections

4）the story of the westward movement of population in the United States

解析: of population 和 in the United States 都是修饰 movement

5）the reconstruction of the geography of continents and of ocean basins in the past

解析: continents and of ocean basins 和 in the past 都是修饰 geography

6）changes in lake level not explained by river flows plus exchanges with the atmosphere

解析: not explained 修饰 Changes；by river flows plus exchanges 修饰 explained；with the atmosphere 修饰 exchanges

7) the development of new areas for the raising of livestock and the cultivation of wheat, corn, tobacco, and cotton

解析: for the raising 和 the cultivation 并列,修饰 new areas;of livestock 修饰 raising;of wheat, corn, tobacco, and cotton 修饰 the cultivation

三 非名词的修饰成分——状语

1. 什么是状语

修饰非名词的成分叫作状语。一个句子,除去主干成分之后,剩余的都是修饰成分;除了修饰名词的定语之外,就是修饰非名词的状语了,即修饰句中的动词、形容词、副词或全句。其实,给我们理解造成最大障碍的是前面所讲的后置定语,状语一般不会给中国的学生带来太大的困惑,因为汉语中的状语与英语中的状语其实是非常相似的,我们只要**按照原语序理解即可**。

2. 状语的用途

状语虽然可修饰的对象非常多,但因为语序与汉语较为一致,所以,与后置定语不同,一般不会给我们造成太大的理解障碍。因此,关于状语的修饰对象以及修饰关系的分析就没有太大的必要了。而从状语的具体用途方面来分析,却会给我们理解状语的信息带来很大的帮助。英语中的状语按其用途,可以分为时间状语、地点状语、方面状语、原因状语、结果状语、目的状语、条件状语、让步状语、程度状语、方式状语、伴随状语等 11 种。对于这方面的知识,我们不要求能够完全掌握,只需了解即可。

● 时间状语

She is to be married **next month.**

I'll meet you **at 4 o'clock**.

● 地点状语

I first met him **in Paris**.

The children are swimming **in the river**.

● 方面状语

She is very weak **in physics**.

China is very rich **in natural resources**.

● 原因状语

He succeeded **because of hard work**.

He was sent to prison **for robbery**.

- 结果状语

The box is too heavy for me **to lift**.

It rained heavily, **causing severe flooding in that country**.

- 目的状语

He cupped his ear **to hear better**.

He went to the south **in search of a better life**.

I went to France **not to study French, but to study architecture**.

- 条件状语

With more money, I would be able to buy it.

We must be losing at least a third of our staff **under new technology**.

Weather permitting, we'll have the match tomorrow.

- 让步状语

For all his money, he's a very lonely man.

Carol went to work **in spite of feeling ill**.

- 程度状语

I don't like coffee **very much**.

To a great extent, it is not fair.

- 方式状语

We came **on the bus**.

You must pay the bill **in cash**.

- 伴随状语

I slept **with the window open**.

She said good-bye **with tears in her eyes**.

第 三 章

并列句与从句

前两章我们介绍完了句子的主干成分和修饰成分,不过这些讨论基本都局限在简单句中和简单句中的词或短语的范围内。接下来,我们在简单句的基础上,进到并列句与从句部分的学习。

一 并列句

并列句,顾名思义就是将两个简单的句子通过并列连词连接在一句话中,因此,我们只要掌握常见的并列连词即可。另外,并列句中所并列的句子,从语法上来讲,是平等的地位,同等重要,就像数学和语文一样,是两个独立的科目,没有从属关系。

公式:句子 1 + 并列连词 + 句子 2(and/but/or)

We bought her a birthday present, and she liked it very much.

He has never read the book, and he knows nothing about it.

Tom likes football, but his sister likes music.

You can do it yourself, or I can help you.

二 从句

从句,是由"连词 + 句子"构成的一个非独立的句子成分,它是附属于另一个句子的。从句和主句的关系,就像发动机和汽车的关系一样,它只是其所依附的主句的一部分而已,不能独立存在。

从句作为一个整体,可以充当句子的主干成分,也可以做修饰的成分。我们根据从句在主句中具体功能再进行详细的分类。比如，主语从句就是起到主语作用的从句，以此类推，还有宾（表）语从句、定语从句、状语从句、同位语从句。

对于不同种类的从句，从阅读的角度来讲，需要做到：

1）将从句的信息作为一个整体进行处理，必须清晰地知道每个从句的"起"与"止"。从句的基本结构是"连词＋句子"，因此，只要有连词的地方，一定是一个从句的开始。

2）知道从句和主句的关系。像状语从句和定语从句属于修饰性从句，而主语从句、宾（表）语从句则是主干性从句，其在句中的重要性要远高于修饰性从句。接下来我们就详细介绍一下各种从句的基本特征，以便阅读时识别。

1. 状语从句

状语从句就是从句整体起到状语的作用，状语从句的具体分类和之前状语部分的分类是一样的，按功能分为：条件状语从句、时间状语从句、原因状语从句、结果状语从句、目的状语从句、让步状语从句、方式状语从句、比较状语从句、地点状语从句。

状语从句相对比较简单，重点在于**对于状语从句的连词要烂熟于心**。具体的情况及例句如下：

1）公式：[连词＋句子1]，句子2.

[If you work hard]，you will succeed.
  句子1   句子2

阅读理解时，状语从句的处理一般比较简单，**按语序理解**基本就没有问题，关键是掌握连词的意思，因为状语从句的连词的含义就是两个句子内在的逻辑关系。

2）各种状语从句的常用连词、含义及例句

● 条件状语从句

We can go out for a walk unless you are too tired. 除非

You may borrow my book as long as you keep it clean. 只要

You should take your umbrella in case it rains. 以防……

I can tell you the truth on condition that you promise to keep a secret. 如果

Supposing it rains，we will not continue the sports meeting. 如果

He won't be against us in the meeting provided/providing that we ask for his advice in advance. 如果

You will be successful in the interview once you have confidence. 一旦……就……

● 时间状语从句

When she came in，I stopped eating. 当……的时候

While my wife was reading the newspaper，I was watching TV. 当……的时候

I like playing football while you like playing basketball. 然而

As we were going out，it began to snow. 当……的时候

We always sing <u>as</u> we walk. 一边……一边

Einstein almost knocked me down <u>before</u> he saw me. "在……之前"

<u>After</u> you think it over，please let me know what you decide. 在……之后

I worked <u>until</u> he came back. 直到

Cath hasn't phoned <u>since</u> she went to Berlin. 自从……

<u>As soon as</u> I reach Canada，I will ring you up. 一……就……

He had <u>no sooner</u> arrived home <u>than</u> he was asked to start on another journey.
一……就……

<u>By the time</u> you came back，I had finished this book. 到……时为止

● 原因状语从句

The sweater shrank <u>because</u> it was washed badly. 因为

<u>As</u> we've no money，we can't buy it. 由于

<u>Since</u> you are free today，you had better help me with my mathematics. 既然

● 结果状语从句

There is <u>so</u> rapid an increase in population <u>that</u> a food shortage is caused. 如此……
以至于

They are <u>such</u> fine teachers <u>that</u> we all hold them in great respect. 如此……以至于

It was very cold，<u>so that</u> the river froze. 因此

● 目的状语从句

You must speak louder <u>so that/in order that</u> you can be heard by all. 为了，以便

He wrote the name down <u>for fear that/lest</u> he should forget it. 生怕；以免

You should take more clothes <u>in case</u> the weather is cold. 以免

● 让步状语从句

<u>Although/Though</u> he was worn out，he kept on working. 虽然

Object <u>as</u> you may，I'll go. 虽然（as 只有倒装才有这个用法）

Hard <u>though</u> he works，he makes little progress. 虽然

We'll make a trip <u>even if/though</u> the weather is bad. 即使

You'll have to attend the ceremony <u>whether</u> you're free <u>or</u> busy. 无论是否

<u>No matter</u> who you are，you must keep the law. 无论……

<u>While</u> I like the color，I don't like the shape. 尽管（while 放句首时）

● 方式状语从句

<u>Just as</u> we sweep our rooms，we should sweep backward ideas from our minds.
正如

They completely ignore these facts <u>as if/as though</u> they never existed. 仿佛

Please pronounce the word <u>the way</u> I do. 用……方式

- 比较状语从句

You seem to know music <u>as</u> well <u>as</u> you know astronomy. 与……一样……

She studies more diligently <u>than</u> her classmates. 比

- 地点状语从句

You should have put the book <u>where</u> you found it. ……之处

2. 宾语从句

宾语从句就是从句整体起到宾语作用的从句,主要的连词有 that、whether/if 以及 what、why 等特殊疑问词这三类。宾语从句也是比较简单的从句,也是**按语序理解**即可,但是宾语从句的信息相较于状语从句来讲要更重要,毕竟宾语是属于句子的主干成分。下面是宾语从句的具体情况及示例:

1) 公式 1:<u>主语 + 及物动词做谓语</u> + (that)/whether + 句子 2
   句子1(少宾语)　　　　　　　　　　　句子2

I don't know that you will come to the party.
句子1(少宾语)　　　　　句子2

I don't know whether you will come to the party.
句子1(少宾语)　　　　　　　句子2

公式 2:<u>主语 + 及物动词谓语</u> + <u>陈述语序的特殊疑问句</u>
　　　　句子1(少宾语)　　　　　句子2

I don't know when you will come to the party.
句子1(少宾语)　　　　　句子2

I don't know where they will hold the meeting.
句子1(少宾语)　　　　句子2

上述公式中,句子 2 作为整体,充当了句子 1 的宾语,所以句子 2 部分的从句叫作宾语从句。

注:表语从句基本与宾语从句类似,只是句子 1 的谓语部分不是及物动词,而是像 be 动词这类动词,连词使用规则上基本一致,这里就不加赘述。

2) 宾语从句常见连词、含义及例句

- 连词 that,通常**可以省略,无具体含义**

We believe that he is honest.

The doctor insists that I give up smoking.

I suggest that we should go tomorrow.

- 连词 whether/if,不可省略,表示**"是否"**

I don't know whether he'll arrive in time.

I didn't know whether they liked the place.

He enquired if her parents spoke Spanish.

I wonder if it's large enough.

- 连接代词"who""which"等,不可省略,**单词本义**,如"which"就是"哪一个"

I don't know who you mean.

Please tell me which you like.

I'll do whatever I can do.

You can take whichever you like.

Give it to whoever you like.

You don't know what you are talking about.

- 连接副词"why""when""where"等,不可省略,**单词本义**,如"where"就是"哪里"

He asked why he had to go alone.

You don't know when you are lucky.

I asked how he was getting on.

He knows where they live.

3. 主语从句

主语从句就是从句整体起到主语作用的从句,主要的连词有 that、whether/if 以及 what、why 等特殊疑问词这三类,下面是具体情况及示例:

1) 公式 1：$\underbrace{\boxed{\text{That/Whether}} + 句子 1}_{句子1} + \underbrace{谓语(宾语)}_{句子2(少主语)}$

$\underbrace{\boxed{\text{That}}\ \text{the sun rises in the east}}_{句子1}\ \underbrace{\text{is a fact}}_{句子2}.$

$\underbrace{\boxed{\text{Whether}}\ \text{the school will hold the sport meeting}}_{句子1}\ \underbrace{\text{depends on the weather}}_{句子2}.$

公式 2：$\underbrace{陈述语序的特殊疑问句}_{句子1} + \underbrace{谓语(宾语)}_{句子2(少主语)}$

$\underbrace{\boxed{\text{when}}\ \text{they will come back}}_{句子1}\ \underbrace{\text{has not been decided}}_{句子2}.$

上述公式中,句子 **1** 作为整体,充当了句子 **2** 的主语,所以句子 **1** 部分的从句叫作主语从句。

2) 主语从句常见连词、含义及例句

- 连词 that,**不可省略,无意义**

That he is still alive is a wonder.

That we shall be late is certain.

That he should have ignored the working class was natural.

That she is still alive is a consolation.

That she became an artist may have been due to her father's influence.

That you are coming to London is the best news I have heard this long time.

That she was chosen made a tremendous stir in her village.

- 连词 whether,不可省略,表示"是否"

Whether it will do us harm remains to be seen.

Whether they would support us was a problem.

- 连接代词"who""which"等,不可省略,单词本义,如"which"就是"哪一个"

Who will give the operation to the patient is not decided.

Which student will win the game depends on the final result.

- 连接副词"why""when""where"等,不可省略,单词本义,如"where"就是"哪里"

When we will arrive doesn't matter.

How this happened is not clear to anyone.

How many people we are to invite is still a question.

Where I spend my summer is no business of yours.

主语从句相较于状语从句和宾语从句来讲还是有一定挑战的,但是基本上也还是遵循"知道连词的含义后,按顺序阅读理解即可"。需要注意的是,在主语从句结束后,**要意识到前面的从句信息作为一个整体起到主语的作用,后面的谓语部分是对整个从句的信息进行描述或评价的,而不是从句中的某个单词**。例如,在"Which student will win the game depends on the final result"这个句子中,取决于最终结果的是"Which student will win the game"而不是"the game",因此理解主语从句时,需要**在主语从句结束时有一个切换意识,可以通过加上"这"来体现**,如:

Which student will win the game depends on the final result.

哪个学生将赢得比赛,**这**取决于最终的结果。

4. 定语从句

定语从句就是从句整体起到定语作用的从句,它是所有从句中比较复杂的从句。定语从句和较长的定语一样,都是**放在被修饰的名词后面**。主要的连词有 that/which/who/whom/as、why/when/where 以及介词 + which/whom 这三类,下面是具体情况及示例:

1) 公式:名词+(连词+句子)

The man (whom you are talking to) is our new teacher.

2) 定语从句的连词使用规则

被修饰名词在从句中所起作用	被修饰的名词的性质	连词的选择	
主语/宾语	人	who/whom/that	
	非人	which/that	
状语	时间	when	可用介词 + which/whom 替代
	地点	where	
	原因	why	
定语	不限	whose	

从阅读的角度来看,不一定要记住定语从句连词的使用规则,最重要的还是能够识别出从句的功能是定语,用来修饰其前面的名词。

3）简单句合并为定语从句的具体过程

例1,

A. The boy bought a dictionary yesterday.

B. The boy is wearing a black coat.

句子 B 的 The boy 是主语,表示人,根据上表的连词使用规则把它换成连词 who,然后将整个句子 B 置于被修饰的名词后面,如下：

The boy (who is wearing a black coat) bought a dictionary yesterday.

例2,

A. The noodles were delicious.

B. My mother cooked the noodles.

句子 B 的 the noodles 是宾语,表示物,根据上表的连词使用规则把它换成连词 that 或 which（可省略）,然后将整个句子 B 置于被修饰的名词后面,如下：

The noodles (that my mother cooked) were delicious.

例3,

A. The school was very large.

B. I learned judo in the school.

句子 B 的 [in the school] 是状语,表示地点,根据上表的连词使用规则把它换成连词 where,然后将整个句子 B 置于被修饰的名词后面,如下：

The school (where I learned judo) was very large.

或

句子 B 的 the school 是介词 in 的宾语,表示物,根据上表的连词使用规则把它换成连词 which,然后将整个句子 B 置于被修饰的名词后面,如下：

The school (in which I learned judo) was very large.

例4,

A. The tourist wanted to book a room.

B. The window (of the room) faces south.

句子 B 的(of the room)是定语,换成连词 whose,然后将整个 B 句子置于被修饰的名词后面,如下:

The tourist wanted to book a room (whose window faces south).

或

句子 B 的the room是介词 of 的宾语,表示物,根据上表的连词使用规则把它换成连词 which,将整个句子 B 置于被修饰的名词后面,如下:

The tourist wanted to book a room (the window of which faces south).

从上面的替换过程可以看出以下几个规律:

a) **被修饰的名词与从句中的名词是重合的,但在从句中,该名词被连词所替代**。由此我们可以看出,在定语从句中,连词的意思不是由连词本身的词义决定的,而是取决于它所修饰的名词的意思。

b) **连词基本都是放在从句的最前面**,"介词 + which/whom"结构虽然不是严格意义上的最前面,但是连词所在的整个短语确实也是处在整个从句最前面的位置,因此,连词的出现就是从句出现的标志。

c) 所有从句的连词基本都是固定的那些,但是定语从句中,"介词 + which/whom"也可以整体起到连词的作用。**介词的选用取决于与其搭配的名词或固定搭配的性质,但是 which 和 whom 还是指代前面被修饰的名词。**

4) 定语从句简单例句

The girl who won the first prize in the contest is from Zhejiang.

The person to whom you just talked is Mr. Depp.

We'll go to the hospital to see the patients, most of whom are children.

The new house which I have just bought is about six miles away.

I'll never forget the time when we first met in London.

I'll never forget the time during which we first met in London.

The hotel where we stayed was very clean.

The hotel at which we stayed was very clean.

The reason why she was late was that she missed her plane.

The reason for which she was late was that she missed her plane.

The man with whom she entered the hall was her husband.

He is studying in the classroom now, in front of which stand two trees.

定语从句是所有从句中给阅读带来最大挑战的从句,一方面因为定语从句在句子中的位置与汉语大不相同。汉语的定语在名词的前面而英语定语从句一定在被修饰的名词后面,这给习惯汉语思维的读者会造成很大的理解障碍,尤其是修饰主语的定语从句更是如此,这点我们在后面章节会详细展开。另一方面,只要是名词后面就可以加定语从句,它的使用情况比其他几种从句更为普遍,往往会使句子层次和结构变得非常复杂,这点我们在后面的章节也会详细展开。

另外,还有一种和定语从句非常相似的从句,叫作"同位语"从句。**从阅读角度来讲,我们不需要区分定语从句和同位语从句**,因为它们都是修饰其前面的名词的,并且同位语从句也是放在其解释说明的名词的后面,所以在后面长难句中碰到同位语从句时我们基本就按照定语的方式来处理即可。

特殊的从句连词

至此,基本上所有的从句的类型我们都简单了解了,从阅读的角度来讲,有了这些了解也基本差不多够用了。从前面的介绍我们可以看出,基本上,**从句的关键就在于连词**。大多数的连词用法和含义相对来讲都比较固定,就像单词一样记住即可,但是有些连词它可能有好几个含义甚至可以引导多种从句。阅读中遇到这些连词时,对它们的用法和含义的判断则需要谨慎。这里列出了一些最常见的特殊连词及用法,我们需要熟记它们的各种含义及用法。

1. while

1) 引导时间状语从句,意为"当……时候,和……同时",此时 while 引导的从句可放在主句的前面也可以放在主句的后面。

While I was watching TV, the bell rang.

我看电视时,铃响了。

Mary watched TV while she ate her supper.

玛丽边吃晚饭边看电视。

2) 引导让步状语从句,意为"虽然,尽管",此时 while 引导的从句必须放在主句的前面。

While it was late, he went on working.

虽然很晚了,但他还在继续工作。

While he is in poor health, he works hard.

虽然他身体不好,但他还是努力工作。

3) 表示"对比"关系,意为"然而",此时 while 引导的从句必须放在主句的后面。

He went out for a walk while I stayed at home.

他出去散步了,而我却待在家里。

I like singing while she likes dancing.

我喜欢唱歌，而她喜欢跳舞。

You like sports while I prefer music.

你喜欢体育，而我更喜欢音乐。

2. since

1）引导原因状语从句，相当于 now that，意思是"因为……，既然……，鉴于……"。

Since the rain has stopped, let's go for a walk.

既然雨停了，我们出去散散步吧。

Since we are young, we should not be too afraid of making mistakes.

因为我们还年轻，所以不应该太害怕犯错误。

2）引导时间状语从句，意思为"自从"。

He has studied very hard since he came to our school.

自从来到我们学校，他学习就非常努力。

Great changes have taken place in our school since you left.

自从你离开这里，我们学校发生了很大的变化。

3. as

1）引导时间状语从句，表示"当……时候"，"随着……"，"一边……一边……"。

As she was child, she was sent to six different schools.

当她还是个孩子的时候，她被送到六所不同的学校。

She sang songs as she did her homework.

她一边唱歌一边做作业。

As time went by, we found he was an honest man.

随着时间流逝，我们发现他是一个诚实的人。

2）引导原因状语从句，表示"由于，因为"，从句通常位于主句前面。

As he is a qualified doctor, I trust his advice on medical matters.

因为他是一个有资质的医生，我相信他在药物方面的建议。

3）引导让步状语从句，仅用于倒装结构。

Young as I am, I already know what career I want to follow.

＝Although/Though I am young, I already know what career I want to follow.

虽然我很年轻，但是我已经知道我想从事什么样的职业。

Great scholar as he is, he lacks in common sense.

虽然他是一个伟大的学者，但是他缺乏常识。

Much as I like you, I could not live with you.

虽然我喜欢你,但是我不能和你生活在一起。

4)引导方式状语从句,表示"如,像"。

Just as we sweep our rooms, we should sweep backward ideas from our minds.

正如我们打扫我们的房间一样,我们应该将旧思想从我们的脑海里清扫掉。

Do to others as you would have others do to you.

就像你希望别人对待你一样地对待他人。

5)引导定语从句

A. 在定语从句中,如果被修饰的名词前有 same 或者 such 的,则连词只能用 as,此时 as 无固定含义,指代前面被修饰的名词。

There is such an unforgettable experience as they have.

＝There is a very unforgettable experience that they have.

他们有如此难忘的经历。

Nobody will obey such a rule as prevents us from free.

＝Nobody will obey a rule like this that prevents us from free.

没有人会遵守这项阻止我们追求自由的规定。

B. as 在定语从句中也可以指代整个句子,此时 as 引导的从句需用逗号与主句隔开,as 可翻译为"正如",类似于 as 引导的方式状语从句。

Thanksgiving Day has been an international festival, as we know.

正如我们所知道的那样,感恩节已经成为一个国际性的节日。

As is a successful man, he makes a brilliant speech.

他正如一个成功男士般发表了精彩的讲话。

6. what

1)具有疑问性质,意为"什么"。如:

I don't know what she needs.

我不知道她需要什么。

2)不具有疑问性质,相当于"something that"或者"名词＋that",用"什么"这个意思翻译不通时,可以考虑句中的 what 是否是这个用法。此时的 what 无具体含义,指代上下文语境中合适的某一名词。

What happened after that was interesting.

＝Something that happened after that was interesting.

后来发生的事挺有意思。

China is not what used to be.

＝China is not the China that used to be.

中国不再是过去的中国了

The boy dived into water and after what seemed to be a long time，he came up again.

= The boy dived into water and after the time that seemed to be a long time，he came up again.

男孩跳进水里，似乎过了很久之后，他才又从水里出来。

7. 介词＋which/whom

"介词＋which/whom"是定语从句的连词，在阅读理解时，一定要把"介词＋which/whom"当作一个整体来看待，如"in which""at which""on which""during which"等。对于这种连词连接的定语从句一般有两种处理方法：

1）直接将从句提前，翻译为"……的"，例：

The rate *at which the flowing water overcomes this resistance* is related to the permeability of rock.

翻译：流水克服这种阻力**的速度与岩石的渗透性有关**。

Cases *in which many species become extinct within a geologically short interval of time* are called mass extinctions.

翻译：许多物种在地理上很短的时间间隔内灭绝**的情况称为大灭绝**。

2）将 which/whom 替换成前面被修饰的名词，拆成两句话理解，例：

The water table is the underground boundary *below which all the cracks and pores are filled with water*.

= The water table is the underground boundary；*below this boundary* all the cracks and pores are filled with water.

翻译：地下水位是地下边界，**在这个界限的下面**所有裂缝和孔隙都充满水。

It is held there by the force of surface tension *without which water would drain instantly from any wet surface*，*leaving it totally dry*.

= It is held there by the force of surface tension；*without this tension* water would drain instantly from any wet surface，*leaving it totally dry*.

翻译：它被表面张力保持在那里；**没有这个张力**，水会立即从任何潮湿的表面排出，使其完全干燥。

Some scientists speculate that Mars may have enjoyed an extended early period *during which rivers*，*lakes*，*and perhaps even oceans adorned its surface*.

= Some scientists speculate that Mars may have enjoyed an extended early period；*during this period rivers*，*lakes*，*and perhaps even oceans adorned its surface*.

翻译：一些科学家推测，火星可能经历了一个漫长的早期时期；**在这个期间**，河流、湖泊，甚至海洋点缀着它的表面。

练一练 ···

要求：用"___"画出句子主干,用"（）"标记出从句并翻译句子,注意连词"介词＋which"的处理。

1）Above the water table is the vadose zone，through which rainwater percolates.

2）However，more recent data imply that at least some parts of the planet did in fact experience long periods in the past during which liquid water existed on the surface.

3）Ir is found in high concentrations in some meteorites，in which the solar system's original chemical composition is preserved.

4）These episodes of rapid evolution are separated by relatively long static spans during which a species may hardly change at all.

5）A planetarium is essentially a theater with a domelike ceiling onto which a night sky can be projected for any night of the year.

6）When one considers the many ways by which organisms are completely destroyed after death，it is remarkable that fossils are as common as they are.

7）Without predators，the species that is the best competitor for food，shelter，nesting sites，and other environmental resources tends to dominate and exclude the species with which it competes.

8）Alternatively，stability can be defined as the speed with which an ecosystem returns to a particular form following a major disturbance，such as a fire.

9）It is hypothesized that the primordial cloud of dust and gas from which all the planets are thought to have condensed had a composition somewhat similar to that of Jupiter.

10）The residence time is the average length of time that any particular molecule of water remains in the lake，and it is calculated by dividing the volume of water in the lake by the rate at which water leaves the lake.

11）Geothermal energy is in a sense not renewable，because in most cases the heat would be drawn out of a reservoir much more rapidly than it would be replaced by the very slow geological processes by which heat flows through solid rock into a heat reservoir.

12）However，studies of the textures of inclusions reveal that the order in which the minerals appeared in the inclusions varies from inclusion to inclusion，and often does not match the theoretical condensation sequence for those metals.

13) When broken open，Allende stones are revealed to contain an assortment of small，distinctive objects，spherical or irregular in shape and embedded in a dark gray matrix（binding material），which were once constituents of the solar nebula—the interstellar cloud of gas and dust out of which our solar system was formed.

答案解析 ....

1）Above the water table is the vadose zone，（*through which rainwater percolates*）.

翻译：地下水位以上是渗流区，雨水通过这个区域渗透。

2）However，more recent data imply（that at least some parts of the planet did in fact experience long periods in the past）（*during which liquid water existed on the surface*）.

翻译：然而，最近的数据表明，这个星球至少有一些地方在过去确实经历过**液态水存于表面的**长时期。

3）Ir is found in high concentrations in some meteorites，（*in which* the solar system's original chemical composition is preserved）.

注：Ir is found in high concentrations in some meteorites，*in which* the solar system's original chemical composition is preserved.

＝Ir is found in high concentrations in some meteorites，*in these meteorites* the solar system's original chemical composition is preserved.

翻译：铱被发现存于高浓度的陨石中；在这些陨石中，太阳系的原始化学成分被保存了。

4）These episodes of rapid evolution are separated by relatively long static spans（*during which a species may hardly change at all*）.

注：These episodes of rapid evolution are separated by relatively long static spans *during which a species may hardly change at all*.

＝These episodes of rapid evolution are separated by relatively long static spans；*during these long static spans a species may hardly change at all*.

翻译：这些快速进化的阶段被相对较长的静态跨度隔开，**在此期间**，一个物种几乎不会发生任何变化。

5）A planetarium is essentially a theater with a domelike ceiling（*onto which a night sky can be projected for any night of the year*）.

注：A planetarium is essentially a theater with a domelike ceiling *onto which a night sky can be projected for any night of the year*.

= A planetarium is essentially a theater with a domelike ceiling; *onto this ceiling a night sky can be projected for any night of the year*.

翻译: 天文馆本质上是一个有着圆顶状天花板的剧院；**在这个天花板上**, 一年中任何夜晚的星空都可以在上面呈现出来。

6) (When one considers the many ways (by which organisms are completely destroyed after death)), it is remarkable (that fossils are as common as they are).

翻译: 当我们考虑**生物体在死亡后被完全摧毁的**多种方式时, 化石这种普遍现象是值得注意的。

7) Without predators, the species (that is the best competitor for food, shelter, nesting sites, and other environmental resources) tends to dominate and exclude the species (*with which it competes*).

翻译: 如果没有捕食者, 食物、住所、筑巢地点和其他环境资源的最佳竞争者往往会支配和排斥**与其竞争的**物种。

8) Alternatively, stability can be defined as the speed (*with which an ecosystem returns to a particular form following a major disturbance, such as a fire*).

翻译: 或者, 稳定性可以定义为**生态系统在遭受重大干扰(如火灾)后恢复到特定形态的**速度。

9) It is hypothesized (that the primordial cloud of dust and gas (*from which all the planets are thought to have condensed*) had a composition somewhat similar to that of Jupiter.)

翻译: 据推测, **所有行星都被认为是由**尘埃和气体组成的原始云层中凝结而来, 这种云的成分与木星的成分有些相似。

10) The residence time is the average length of time (that any particular molecule of water remains in the lake), and it is calculated by dividing the volume of water in the lake by the rate (*at which water leaves the lake*).

翻译: 停留时间是任何特定的水分子在湖中停留时间的平均值, 其计算方法是将湖中的水量除以**水离开湖的**速率。

11) Geothermal energy is in a sense not renewable, (because in most cases the heat would be drawn out of a reservoir much more rapidly) (than it would be replaced by the very slow geological processes) (*by which heat flows through solid rock into a heat reservoir*).

注：it would be replaced by the very slow geological processes *by which* heat *flows through solid rock into a heat reservoir*.

= it would be replaced by the very slow geological processes；*by these geological processes heat flows through solid rock into a heat reservoir*

翻译：地热能在某种意义上是不可再生的，因为在大多数情况下，热量从储层中排出的速度要比被非常缓慢的地质过程所取代的速度快得多，**通过这种地质过程**，热量通过固体岩石流入储热层。

12）However，studies of the textures of inclusions reveal [that the order（*in which the minerals appeared in the inclusions*）varies from inclusion to inclusion，and often does not match the theoretical condensation sequence for those metals].

翻译：然而，对包含物的质地的研究表明，**包含物中矿物出现的**顺序因包含物而异，并且通常与这些金属的理论冷凝顺序不匹配。

13）When broken open，Allende stones are revealed to contain an assortment of small，distinctive objects，/spherical or irregular in shape/and embedded in a dark gray matrix（binding material），（which were once constituents of the solar nebula）—the interstellar cloud of gas and dust（*out of which our solar system was formed*）.

注：the interstellar cloud of gas and dust out of which our solar system was formed

= the interstellar cloud of gas and dust；out of this interstellar cloud our solar system was formed

翻译：打开阿连德石，发现里面含有各种各样的小而独特的物体，球形的或是不规则形状的，并嵌入深灰色基质中，这些物体曾经是太阳星云的组成部分——**形成我们太阳系的**星际气体和尘埃云。

从句综合练习

要求：用"（）"标记出下列句中所有的从句并圈出连接词，然后判断从句的类型并翻译。

1）In view of the rate at which the radio sources emit energy, they should disappear in a few million years as their electrons slow down and cease producing radiation.

2）Ordinary light，from the Sun or a light bulb，is emitted spontaneously，when atoms or molecules get rid of excess energy by themselves, without any outside intervention.

3）The range of the New York canal system was still further extended when the states of Ohio and Indiana, inspired by the success of the Erie Canal, provided water connections between Lake Erie and the Ohio River.

4）New England still favored wood, though brick houses became common in Boston and other towns, where the danger of fire gave an impetus to the use of more durable material.

5）As the bacteria go about their daily business breaking down lipids, or fatty substances, on the skin, they release volatile substances that usually strike the bloodhound's nose as an entire constellation of distinctive scents.

6）Finally, it set up a system of tariffs that was basically protectionist in effect, although maneuvering for position by various regional interests produced frequent changes in tariff rates throughout the nineteenth century.

7）The quick-drying paint demanded that the artist know exactly where each stroke be placed before the brush met the panel, and it required the use of fine brushes.

8）In Sacramento an excavation at the site of a fashionable nineteenth-century hotel revealed that garbage had been stashed in the building's basement despite sanitation laws to the contrary.

9）Newton's laws of motion assume that the total amount of spin of a body cannot change unless an external torque speeds it up or slows it down.

10）The notion that an artist could or would dash off an idea in a fit of spontaneous inspiration was completely alien to these deliberately produced works.

11）The hard, rigid plates that form the outermost portion of the Earth are about 100 kilometers thick.

12）In the early nineteenth century, the knowledge of the physics of heat, which was essential to a science of refrigeration, was rudimentary.

13）Direct carving—in which the sculptors themselves carve stone or wood with mallet and chisel—must be recognized as something more than just a technique.

14）The process by which the nose recognizes an odor is not fully understood, but there are apparently specific receptor sites for specific odors.

15）For the many small mammals that supplement their insect diet with fruits or seeds, an inability to span open gaps between tree crowns may be problematic, since trees that yield these foods can be sparse.

16）In the seventeenth century the organ, the clavichord, and the harpsichord became the chief instruments of the keyboard group, a supremacy that they maintained until the piano supplanted them at the end of the eighteenth century.

17) Those measures which appeared to bring the desired results were then retained and repeated until they hardened into fixed rituals.

18) This has been called "historical archaeology", a term that is used in the United States to refer to any archaeological investigation into North American sites that postdate the arrival of Europeans.

19) But sculpture as a high art, practiced by artists who knew both the artistic theory of their Renaissance-Baroque-Rococo predecessors and the various technical procedures of modeling, casting, and carving rich three-dimensional forms, was not known among Americans in 1776.

20) Rent controls were spurred by the inflation of the 1970's, which, combined with California's population growth, pushed housing prices, as well as rents, to record levels.

答案解析 ....

1) In view of the rate (⬚at which⬚ the radio sources emit energy), they should disappear in a few million years (⬚as⬚ their electrons slow down and cease producing radiation).

at which 引导定语从句,修饰 rate;as 引导时间状语从句

翻译:考虑到放射源释放能量的速度,它们会在几百万年后消失,随着它们的电子速度减慢,不再产生辐射。

2) Ordinary light, from the Sun or a light bulb, is emitted spontaneously, (⬚when⬚ atoms or molecules get rid of excess energy by themselves, without any outside intervention).

when 引导的时间状语从句

翻译:当原子或分子在没有任何外界干预的情况下自行释放多余能量时,太阳或灯泡的普通光被自发地发出。

3) The range of the New York canal system was still further extended (⬚when⬚ the states of Ohio and Indiana, inspired by the success of the Erie Canal, provided water connections between Lake Erie and the Ohio River).

when 引导时间状语从句

翻译:受伊利运河成功的启发,俄亥俄州和印第安纳州在伊利湖和俄亥俄河之

间建立了水源连接,纽约运河系统的范围得以进一步扩大。

4) New England still favored wood,（though brick houses became common in Boston and other towns）,（where the danger of fire gave an impetus to the use of more durable material）.

though 引导让步状语从句;where 引导定语从句,修饰 Boston and other towns

翻译: 新英格兰仍然青睐木材,尽管砖房在波士顿和其他城镇变得很普遍(在波士顿和其他城镇火灾的危险促使人们使用更耐用的材料)。

5)（As the bacteria go about their daily business breaking down lipids, or fatty substances, on the skin）, they release volatile substances（that usually strike the bloodhound's nose as an entire constellation of distinctive scents）.

as 引导状语从句;that 引导定语从句,修饰 substances

翻译: 当细菌在日常工作中分解皮肤上的脂类或脂肪物质时,它们会释放出挥发性物质,这些物质通常以独特的气味袭击着猎犬的鼻子。

6) Finally, it set up a system of tariffs（that was basically protectionist in effect）,（although maneuvering for position by various regional interests produced frequent changes in tariff rates throughout the nineteenth century）.

that 引导定语从句,修饰 tariff; although 引导让步状语从句

翻译: 最后,它还是建立了一个基本上是保护主义的关税体系,尽管在整个 19 世纪,各地区利益集团为争取地位而采取的策略导致关税率频繁变化。

7) The quick-drying paint demanded（that the artist know exactly（where each stroke be placed）（before the brush met the panel））, and it required the use of fine brushes.

that 和 where 引导宾语从句;before 引导状语从句;and 并列两个主句

翻译: 快干涂料要求艺术家在画笔与面板接触之前准确地知道每一笔的位置,并且使用精细的画笔。

8) In Sacramento an excavation at the site of a fashionable nineteenth-century hotel revealed（that garbage had been stashed in the building's basement despite sanitation laws to the contrary）.

that 引导宾语从句

翻译: 在拉门托对 19 世纪时尚酒店遗址的挖掘中发现:尽管违反了卫生法,垃圾仍被藏在大楼的地下室里。

9) Newton's laws of motion assume（$\boxed{\text{that}}$ the total amount of spin of a body cannot change）（$\boxed{\text{unless}}$ an external torque speeds it up or slows it down）.

that 引导宾语从句；unless 引导的是状语从句

翻译：牛顿运动定律假定，物体的总自旋量不会改变，除非外部力矩使它加速或减慢。

10) The notion（$\boxed{\text{that}}$ an artist could or would dash off an idea in a fit of spontaneous inspiration）was completely alien to these deliberately produced works.

that 从句修饰 notion（这是一个同位语从句，但这个概念我们不需要掌握，只需要知道这个从句是修饰前面的名词即可）

翻译：一个艺术家自发的灵感中迸发出一个想法的观念，与这些刻意创作的作品观念是完全不同的。

11) The hard, rigid plates（$\boxed{\text{that}}$ form the outermost portion of the Earth）are about 100 kilometers thick.

that 引导定语从句，修饰 plates

翻译：构成地球最外层的坚硬板块厚约 100 公里。

12) In the early nineteenth century, the knowledge of the physics of heat,（$\boxed{\text{which}}$ was essential to a science of refrigeration）, was rudimentary.

which 引导的是定语从句，修饰 knowledge

翻译：19 世纪初，对制冷科学而言至关重要的热物理学知识还很初级。

13) Direct carving—（$\boxed{\text{in which}}$ the sculptors themselves carve stone or wood with mallet and chisel）—must be recognized as something more than just a technique.

in which 引导的是定语从句，修饰 carving

翻译：直接雕刻——雕刻家自己用木槌和凿子雕刻石头或木头——不仅仅是一种技术。

14) The process（$\boxed{\text{by which}}$ the nose recognizes an odor）is not fully understood, $\boxed{\text{but}}$ there arc apparently specific receptor sites for specific odors.

by which 引导定语从句，修饰 process；but 是并列连词，并列两个主句

翻译：鼻子识别气味的过程还不完全清楚，但对于特定的气味，明显有特定的接受点。

15）For the many small mammals (that supplement their insect diet with fruits or seeds), an inability to span open gaps between tree crowns may be problematic, [since trees (that yield these foods) can be sparse].

that 引导定语从句,分别修饰 mammals 和 trees;since 引导状语从句

翻译: 对于许多以水果或种子补充昆虫食物的小型哺乳动物来说,无法跨越树冠之间的空隙可能是个问题,因为生产这些食物树木的树枝可能很稀疏。

16）In the seventeenth century the organ, the clavichord, and the harpsichord became the chief instruments of the keyboard group, a supremacy (that they maintained) (until the piano supplanted them at the end of the eighteenth century).

that 引导定语从句,修饰 supremacy;until 引导状语从句

翻译: 在 17 世纪,风琴、古钢琴和大键琴成为键盘乐器的主要成员,它们一直保持着至高无上的地位,直到 18 世纪末钢琴取代了它们。

17) Those measures (which appeared to bring the desired results) were then retained and repeated (until they hardened into fixed rituals).

which 引导定语从句,修饰 measures;until 引导状语从句

翻译: 那些能带来预期效果的措施随后被保留和重复,直到它们变成固定的仪式。

18) This has been called "historical archaeology", a term (that is used in the United States to refer to any archaeological investigation into North American sites) (that postdate the arrival of Europeans).

均为定语从句,第一个定语从句修饰 term,第二个定语从句修饰 sites

翻译: 这被称为"历史考古学",一个在美国用来指代对(在欧洲人到来之后)的北美遗址进行的任何考古调查的术语。

19) But sculpture as a high art, practiced by artists (who knew both the artistic theory of their Renaissance-Baroque-Rococo predecessors and the various technical procedures of modeling, casting, and carving rich three-dimensional forms), was not known among Americans in 1776.

定语从句,修饰 artists

翻译: 但是雕塑作为一门由艺术家实践的高级艺术(这些艺术家既了解文艺复兴-巴洛克-洛可可时期的艺术理论,又了解各种三维形式的雕刻成型的技术流程),在 1776 年时的美国并不为人所知。

20）Rent controls were spurred by the inflation of the 1970's，（which，combined with California's population growth，pushed housing prices，as well as rents，to record levels）.

定语从句,修饰 inflation

翻译：房租管制被 1970 年代的通货膨胀刺激了——1970 年代的通货膨胀,结合加州的人口增长,使房价和房租都达到了创纪录的水平。

第 四 章

特殊现象

 it 做形式主语或形式宾语

1. 形式主语

在英语句子中,主语部分通常不能太长,这样可以保持句子的平衡,避免头重脚轻。一般来讲,这并不是难事,毕竟主语部分基本上都是名词、代词等,基本不会太长。但是,有一些特殊的主语,比如前面我们所提到的"to do","doing"以及主语从句做主语时,经常就会导致主语部分太长。在这种情况下,通常会用"it"来替代它们,而将真正的主语放在句尾。在这种句式中,充当主语的"it"叫形式主语,因为它没有实际意义,放置句尾的真正主语才是它的内涵。我们也可以将 it 理解为指代后面真正的主语。下面来看具体的示例:

1) <u>Whether he can come to Jenny's birthday party or not</u> is uncertain.
       主语从句

  <u>It</u> is uncertain <u>whether he can come to Jenny's birthday party or not</u>.
 形式主语   真正主语

2) <u>That you missed the exciting football match</u> is a pity.
     主语从句

  <u>It</u> is a pity <u>that you missed the exciting football match</u>.
 形式主语   真正主语

3) <u>To master two foreign languages</u> is necessary.
    to do做主语

  <u>It</u> is necessary for the young <u>to master two foreign languages</u>.
 形式主语   真正主语

4) <u>Reading without understanding</u> is no good.
    doing做主语

<u>It</u>　　is no good　<u>reading without understanding.</u>
形式主语　　　　　　　　真正主语

 练一练 ···

划出下面句子中的形式主语和真正主语。

1) It is not decided who will give the operation to the patient.

2) It is unwise to give the children whatever they want.

3) It seemed selfish not to share his dictionary with others.

> **答案解析** ··
>
> 1) <u>It</u> is not decided <u>who will give the operation to the patient</u>.
>
> 2) <u>It</u> is unwise <u>to give the children whatever they want</u>.
>
> 3) <u>It</u> seemed selfish <u>not to share his dictionary with others</u>.

2. 形式宾语

我们在句子主干那一章节提到,有些动词加上宾语之后还是不能把意思表达清楚,必须再补充一些成分才能把意思表达清楚,这种动词我们一般当做固定搭配来记,比如:

The police found a cell phone hidden under a sofa.

固定搭配:find...*adj.*/doing/done　发现……(处于)……(状态)

Grace makes Jenny happy.

固定搭配:make...*adj.*/doing/done　使……(处于)……(状态)

当这些动词的宾语部分是较长的 to do/doing 或者宾语从句时,为了平衡句子,避免由于较长的宾语导致动词和宾补部分距离太远,通常会用 it 来代替 to do/doing 或者宾语从句,将真正的宾语放置句尾。这里的 it 叫作形式宾语,和上面的形式主语一样,没有任何实际的意义,指代后面真正的宾语。

They found　<u>it</u>　pleasant　<u>that they worked with us.</u>
　　　形式宾语　　　　　　真正宾语
他们发现他们和我们共事很愉快

I don't feel　<u>it</u>　difficult　<u>to understand English.</u>
　　　形式宾语　　　　　真正宾语
我觉得理解英语不困难。

 练一练 ···

划出下面句子中的形式宾语和真正宾语。

1) He makes it a rule never to borrow money.

2) I think it no need talking about it with them.

3) I leave it to your own judgement whether you should do it.

4) We owe it to you that there was not a serious accident.

5) The ability to take up sulfides and convert them to sulfate makes it easier for the grass to colonize marsh environments.

6) High farms price makes it easy to repay loans when they felt due.

7) The continued proliferation of banks made it easier for those without cash to negotiate loans in paper money.

答案解析

1) He makes <u>it</u> a rule <u>never to borrow money</u>.

2) I think <u>it</u> no need <u>talking about it with them</u>.

3) I leave <u>it</u> to your own judgement <u>whether you should do it</u>.

4) We owe <u>it</u> to you <u>that there was not a serious accident</u>.

5) The ability to take up sulfides and convert them to sulfate makes <u>it</u> easier for the grass <u>to colonize marsh environments</u>.

6) High farms price makes <u>it</u> easy <u>to repay loans when they felt due</u>.

7) The continued proliferation of banks made <u>it</u> easier for those without cash <u>to negotiate loans in paper money</u>.

 倒装句

英语句子的主干成分一般都是按照"主语 + 谓语"的顺序,但是偶尔也会有少数的句子并不是严格按照"主语 + 谓语"的方式来排列的,这种句子我们叫作倒装句。倒装的原因一般是:**1)平衡句子结构,将较长的主语部分放到句尾 2)起到强调的作用**。倒装有两种形式,主语和谓语顺序完全颠倒的叫做"完全倒装",主语与谓语顺序部分颠倒的叫作"部分倒装",下面我们来详细看一下这两种情况。

1. 完全倒装

1) 谓语 + 主语

<u>Here</u> <u>comes</u> <u>the bus</u>.
　3　　2　　　1

<u>In south of the river</u> <u>lies</u> <u>a small factory</u>.
　　　　3　　　　　　　2　　　1

From the valley came a cry.
　　　3　　　　2　　1
Present at the party were Mr. Green and many other guests.
　　　3　　　　　2　　　　　　　1
Seated on the ground are a group of young men.
　　　3　　　　　2　　　　　1

按照１２３的顺序来看,就是这个句子非倒装的正常语序了。

2) 完全倒装句型的处理技巧

当我们按照"句首起第一个独立的名词或代词"的原则来找主语时,在没有找到主语之前却先找到了谓语动词时,则表明我们遇到了全部倒装的情况,这时,整个句子的主语就是紧接着谓语动词后面的那个名词,我们可以通过复原句子的语序来帮助理解句子的意思。

不过,大多数的倒装句并不会给我们的理解造成太大的障碍,阅读时完全可以按照原来的语序直译理解,只有当这种方法行不通时,我们再通过句子分析,找到句子主干并还原为正常语序。

练一练

将下面完全倒装的句子调整为正常语序,并翻译句子。

1) Of importance is the fact that it was produced rapidly in large amounts, most likely by specialists in a central location.

2) So admired were these pieces that they encouraged the development of earthenware made in imitation of porcelain and instigated research into the method of their manufacture.

3) Missing until recently were fossils clearly intermediate, or transitional, between land mammals and cetaceans.

4) Consistent with this idea, according to the investigators, is the fact that the art of the cultural period that followed the Upper Paleolithic also seems to reflect how people got their food.

5) Interbedded with the salt were thin layers of what appeared to be windblown silt.

6) Out of the demes were created 10 artificial tribes of roughly equal population.

7) From the demes, by either election or selection, came 500 members of a new council, 6,000 jurors for the courts, 10 generals, and hundreds of commissioners.

答案解析
倒装句一般不会给我们的理解造成太大的障碍,所以解析中给出的翻译是尽可能按照倒装语序进行的,我们可以体会一下,英文的倒装语序和汉语的语序没有太大的冲突,所以不会产生太大的问题,重点还是处理好主语的修饰成分。

1) 正常语序:The fact that it was produced rapidly in large amounts, most likely by specialists in a central location is of importance.

翻译:很重要的是:它被快速地大量生产,极有可能是由身处中心位置的专家生产的。(知识点:of importance＝important)

2) These pieces were so admired that they encouraged the development of earthenware made in imitation of porcelain and instigated research into the method of their manufacture.

翻译:这些作品非常受推崇以至于促进了仿瓷器的发展并刺激了对其生产方法的研究。

3) 正常语序:Fossils clearly intermediate, or transitional, between land mammals and cetaceans were missing until recently.

翻译:直到最近,陆地哺乳动物和鲸目类之间过渡的化石才消失。

4) 正常语序:The fact is, according to the investigators, consistent with this idea that the art of the cultural period that followed the Upper Paleolithic also seems to reflect how people got their food.

翻译:根据研究人员的说法,事实是与这个观念一致的,即旧石器时代晚期之后的文化时期的艺术也反映了人们如何获取食物。

5) 正常语序:Thin layers of what appeared to be windblown silt were interbedded with the salt.

翻译:与盐镶嵌在一起的似乎是被风吹来的淤泥的薄层。

6) 正常语序:10 artificial tribes of roughly equal population were created out of the demes.

翻译:从当地人口里涌现出了大约10个人口数量相近的人为部落。

7) 正常语序:500 members of a new council, 6,000 jurors for the courts, 10 generals, and hundreds of commissioners came from the demes, by either election or selection.

翻译:从当地人口里,通过选举或筛选的方式,产生了500名新理事会成员,6 000名法院陪审员,10个将军和数百名委员。

2. 部分倒装

部分倒装指的是,谓语部分只有助动词被提到了主语的前面,主要的动词还是在主语的后面。对于部分倒装的情况,我们只需能够识别并理解以下几种特殊的句型即可:

1）含有否定意义的副词或短语如：few，little，never，not，nowhere，rarely，seldom，at no time，by no means，in no case 等放在句首时,需用部分倒装。

Little does he know about the news.

By no means can he catch up in such a short time.

He is active in personality，and seldom does he stay indoors.

Not until yesterday did John change his mind.

2）"only＋状语（或状语从句）"放在句首时,句子用部分倒装。

Only in this way can you learn English well.

Only if he has time will he come here.

Only after being asked three times did he come to the meeting.

对于1）和2）这两种情况,阅读时可以直接把这些助动词去掉或者还原到谓语动词之前,基本不会影响理解。

3）If＋主语＋were/should/had……，主句

＝Were/Should/Had＋主语……，主句

If they were here now，they could help us.

＝Were they here now，they could help us.

If you had come earlier，you would have met him.

＝Had you come earlier，you would have met him.

If it should rain，the crops would be saved.

＝Should it rain，the crops would be saved.

4）在"so/such...that"结构中,将 so/such 放句首时,句子倒装。

So terrible was the storm that the whole roof was blown off.

＝The storm was so terrible that the whole roof was blown off.

Such a clever boy was Jack that he was able to work out all these difficult problems.

＝Jack was such a clever boy that he was able to work out all these difficult problems.

5）"n/*adj.*/*adv.*/分词＋as/though＋主语＋谓语"或

"谓语＋as/though＋主语＋辅助动词"

Brave as/though they were，the danger made them afraid.

＝Though they were brave，the danger made them afraid.

Child as/though he is，he knows a lot of things.

＝Though he is a child，he knows a lot of things.

Try as/though she might，she couldn't get the door open.

= Though she might try，she couldn't get the door open.

注：as 从句只有在倒装的时候才能表示让步。

对 3)、4)、5)这三种情况，我们需要牢记这些句型，做到看到之后就能识别并调整语序。

 三　强调句

1. 强调句公式

It＋is/was＋强调部分＋that/whom＋剩余部分,翻译为"正是……"

2. 示例

$\underline{\text{Mary}}$ saw a black cat in the street yesterday.
　主　　谓　　宾　　　状1　　　状2

It was Mary that saw a black cat in the street yesterday.

强调主语：正是玛丽昨天在街上看到了一只黑猫。

It was a black cat that Mary saw in the street yesterday.

强调宾语：玛丽昨天在街上看到的正是一只黑猫。

It was yesterday that Mary saw a black cat in the street.

强调状语：正是昨天玛丽在街上看到了一只黑猫。

It was in the street that Mary saw a black cat yesterday.

强调状语：昨天正是在街上玛丽看到了一只黑猫。

3. it 形式主语与强调句的区别

我们之前讲过,当主语部分是从句时,可以用 it 做形式主语,将真正的主语放到句尾,如：

That the sun rises in the east is a fact.

＝It is a fact that the sun rises in the east.

it 做形式主语的这个句子,乍一看是不是与强调句很像呢？

It is a fact that the sun rises in the east.

It was yesterday that Mary saw a black cat in the street.

那我们如何快速区分是形式主语还是强调句呢？ 记住下面两个区别：

1) 强调句中,去掉 **it is/was. . . that** 之后,这个句子仍然是完整的句子,而形式主语并非如此。

~~It is~~ a fact ~~that~~ the sun rises in the east（×）

~~It was~~ yesterday ~~that~~ Mary saw a black cat in the street.（√）

2）强调句中, it 没有任何意义, 而形式主语 it 指代后面的真正主语。

It is a fact that the sun rises in the east.

it = that the sun rises in the east

It was yesterday that Mary saw a black cat in the street.

it 无意义

练一练 ··

分辨下面的句子是强调句还是形式主语, 并翻译句子。

1）It was this that made the organization of irrigation, particularly the building of canals to channel and preserve the water, essential.

2）It is likely that in the near future geothermal energy can make important local contributions

3）It is at the boundaries between plates that most of Earth's volcanism and earthquake activity occur.

4）it is doubtful that complete eradication of Spartina from nonnative habitats is possible

5）It was these conditions that allowed an elite to emerge, probably as an organizing class, and to sustain itself through the control of surplus crops.

答案解析 ···

1）强调句

~~It was~~ this ~~that~~ made the organization of irrigation, particularly the building of canals to channel and preserve the water, essential.

翻译: 正是这个使得灌溉组织, 尤其是建造运河来输送和保存水, 变得必不可少。

2）形式主语

It is likely that in the near future geothermal energy can make important local contributions

翻译: 在不远的未来, 地热能可以为当地做出重大贡献——这是可能发生的。

3）强调句

~~It is~~ at the boundaries between plates ~~that~~ most of Earth's volcanism and earthquake activity occur.

翻译: 正是在板块的边界处, 地球大多数的火山和地震活动发生。

4）形式主语

<u>It</u> is doubtful <u>that complete eradication of Spartina from nonnative habitats is possible</u>

翻译：从非本土栖息地完全根除互花米草是可能的这件事值得怀疑。

5）强调句：

~~It was~~ <u>these conditions</u> ~~that~~ allowed an elite to emerge，probably as an organizing class，<u>and to sustain itself</u> through the control of surplus crops.

翻译：这些情况允许精英出现，可能作为一个管理阶层，并且通过对剩余农作物的控制来维持自己。

四 并列结构

我们在前面第三章的时候学习了并列句，就是用并列连词连接两个简单的句子。并列连词除了能够连接两个句子之外，也能够连接句子内部的相同的两个成分，比如：

<u>Sue</u> and <u>I</u> left early. 并列主语

He <u>quit</u> the job and <u>started</u> his own business. 并列谓语

I like <u>fruits</u> and <u>vegetables</u>. 并列宾语

The owner of the house <u>whose wife is dead</u> and <u>whose son works in New York</u> is willing to sell the house at a low price. 并列定语

Israel offers automatic citizenship to all Jews, <u>whatever color they are</u> and <u>whichever language they speak</u>. 并列状语

当然这些都比较简单，但是，当一个句子中出现多个并列结构的时候，每个并列连词的并列对象就有些复杂了，例：

The rapid technical development of photography—the introduction of lighter and simpler equipment，and of new emulsions that coated photographic plates，film，and paper and enabled images to be made at much faster speeds—had some unanticipated consequences.

我们如何确定较为复杂的并列关系呢？在并列结构中，and 后面的那项通常是所有并列项当中的最后一项，因此在确定并列对象时，我们一般先确定 and 后面的那个并列项，然后根据最后一个并列项的特征，往前寻找其他并列项。在确定其他并列项时，我们需要遵循以下的原则：

1）距离最近

2）语法性质一致

3）逻辑合理

下面我们用刚才的例子来说明：

The rapid technical development of photography—the introduction of lighter and₁ simpler equipment，and₂ of new emulsions that coated photographic plates，film，and₃ paper and₄ enabled images to be made at much faster speeds—had some unanticipated consequences.

分析：

and₁ 并列 lighter 和 simpler 两个是比较简单的

and₂ 后面的一项是个介词短语，往前寻找距离最近的介词短语是 of lighter and simpler equipment，因为 of lighter and simpler equipment 是修饰 the introduction 的，所以如果 of new emulsions 和 of lighter and simpler equipment 并列的话，那么它也一定是修饰 the introduction。the introduction of new emulsions（新的乳胶的引入）和 the introduction of lighter and simpler equipment（更轻更简单的的设备的引入）是合理逻辑的并列，因此是 and₂ 并列 of new emulsions 和 of lighter and simpler equipment 的。

and₃ 并列 photographic plates，film 和 paper 这三个名词也是比较简单的。

and₄ 后面的一项是 enabled 这个过去式，那么和它并列的一定是个动词的过去式，往前找离它最近的过去式是 coated，如果 enabled 和 coated 并列的话，意思为"覆盖照相底片、胶卷、纸并且使图片可以以更快的速度被制作的新乳胶的引入"，这句话的逻辑没有奇怪之处，因此 and₄ 是并列 enabled 和 coated 的。

我们再来看一个例子：

The war chief led the men in fighting during occasional conflicts that broke out with neighboring villages and directed the men in community building projects.

这个句子中的 and 后面并列的是 directed 这个动词过去式，离它距离最近的过去式是 broke out，但是如果 directed 和 broke out 并列的话，这个并列结构部分的意思就是"与邻村爆发的并且在社区建造项目中指导人们的偶尔的冲突"。我们一看便知这句话的逻辑是有问题的，因为冲突怎么能在社区建造项目中指导人们呢？所以我们必须继续往前找另外的动词过去式，下一个就是 led。如果 directed 和 led 并列的话，这句话的意思是"战争领袖带领人们在与邻村爆发的偶尔的冲突中战斗，并且在社区建造项目中指导人们"。这是符合逻辑的，所以这句话中的 and 并列了 directed 和 led 这两项。

 练一练 ··

要求：用相同的符号标记出同一并列成分并翻译。

例：Spartina establishes itself on substrates ranging from sand and silt to gravel and cobble and is tolerant of salinities ranging from that of near freshwater（0.05 percent） to that of salt water (3.5 percent).

翻译：互花米草建立在从沙子和淤泥到砾石和鹅卵石的基质上，并且能承受从接近淡水(0.05%)到盐水(3.5%)的盐度。

1) As the seaweed and marsh grass leaves die, bacteria break down the plant material, and insects, small shrimplike organisms, fiddler crabs, and marsh snails eat the decaying plant tissue, digest it, and excrete wastes high in nutrients.

2) The problem is that competition ordinarily cannot be observed directly but must be inferred from the spread of increase of one species and the concurrent reduction or disappearance of another species.

3) It would appear that the instability of the climatic conditions led populations that had originally been nomadic to settle down and develop a sedentary style of life, which led in turn to population growth and to the need to increase the amount of food available.

4) They therefore permit the reconstruction of the process of seafloor spreading, and consequently of the geography of continents and of ocean basins in the past.

5) Among the superbly preserved Messel fossils are insects with iridescent exoskeletons, frogs with skin and blood vessels intact, and even entire small mammals with preserved fur and soft tissue.

6) The new candid photography—unposed pictures that were made when the subjects were unaware that their pictures were being taken—confirmed these scientific results, and at the same time, thanks to the radical trimming of images that the camera often imposed, suggested new compositional formats.

7) A few chondrules contain grains that survived the melting event, so these enigmatic chondrules must have formed when compact masses of nebular dust were fused at high temperatures—approaching 1,700 degrees Celsius—and then cooled before these surviving grains could melt.

8) Water containing dissolved silica, calcium carbonate, or iron may circulate through the enclosing sediment and be deposited in cavities such as marrow cavities and canals in bone once occupied by blood vessels and nerves.

9) Leaves and tissue of soft-bodied organisms such as jellyfish or worms may accumulate, become buried and compressed, and lose their volatile constituents.

10) A rotary engine attached to the steam engine enabled shafts to be turned and machines to be driven, resulting in mills using steam power to spin and weave cotton.

11) Few of the cultural traditions and rules that today allow us to deal with dense populations existed for these people accustomed to household autonomy and the ability

to move around the landscape almost at will.

12）Attack by scavengers and bacteria, chemical decay, and destruction by erosion and other geologic agencies make the odds against preservation very high.

13）In Europe as a whole, the exceptional reduction in the population and the related fall in demand for grain since the beginning of the seventeenth century had caused the price of agricultural products to fall.

14）Many complex factors led to the adoption of the new economies, not only at Abu Hureyra, but at many other locations such as Ain Ghazal, also in Syria.

15）They possess drought-resisting adaptations: loss of water through the leaves is reduced by means of dense hairs covering waxy leaf surfaces, by the closure of pores during the hottest times to reduce water loss, and by the rolling up or shedding of leaves at the beginning of the dry season.

16）Merchants complained that the privileges reserved for Venetian-built and owned ships were first extended to those Venetians who bought ships from abroad and then to foreign-built and owned vessels.

17）Although aragonite has the same composition as the more familiar mineral known as calcite, it has a different crystal form, is relatively unstable, and in time changes to the more stable calcite.

答案解析 ....

1）As the seaweed and marsh grass leaves die, bacteria break down the plant material, and insects, small shrimplike organisms, fiddler crabs, and marsh snails eat the decaying plant tissue, digest it, and excrete wastes high in nutrients.

翻译：随着海藻和沼泽草叶子的死亡,细菌分解植物材料,昆虫、小虾类生物、招潮蟹和沼泽蜗牛吃掉腐烂的植物组织,消化它们,并排出高营养的废物。

2）The problem is that competition ordinarily cannot be observed directly but must be inferred from the spread of increase of one species and the concurrent reduction or disappearance of another species.

翻译：问题是,竞争通常不能直接观察到,而必须从一个物种的增长扩散和另一个物种的同时减少或消失中推断出来。

3）It would appear that the instability of the climatic conditions led populations that had originally been nomadic to settle down and develop a sedentary style of life, which led in turn to population growth and to the need to increase the amount of food available.

翻译：似乎是气候条件的不稳定性导致原本是游牧民族的人定居下来并且形成了久坐的生活方式,这进而导致人口增长和食物量求的增加。

4) They therefore permit the reconstruction of the process of seafloor spreading, and consequently of the geography of continents and of ocean basins in the past.

翻译：因此,它们可以允许海底扩张过程的重建,还有过去大陆和海洋盆地地理的重建。

5) Among the superbly preserved Messel fossils are insects with iridescent exoskeletons, frogs with skin and blood vessels intact, and even entire small mammals with preserved fur and soft tissue.

翻译：在保存完好的梅塞尔化石中,有外骨骼呈彩虹色的昆虫、皮肤和血管完好无损的青蛙,甚至还有皮毛和软组织保存完好的小型哺乳动物。

6) The new candid photography—unposed pictures that were made when the subjects were unaware that their pictures were being taken—confirmed these scientific results, and at the same time, thanks to the radical trimming of images that the camera often imposed, suggested new compositional formats.

翻译：新的抓拍的摄影——在被拍对象不知道自己的照片被拍摄时拍摄的未摆姿势的照片——证实了这些科学结果,同时,由于相机经常对图像进行大幅裁剪,表明了新的构图格式。

7) A few chondrules contain grains that survived the melting event, so these enigmatic chondrules must have formed when compact masses of nebular dust were fused at high temperatures—approaching 1,700 degrees Celsius—and then cooled before these surviving grains could melt.

翻译：一些球粒中含有在熔化后幸存下来的颗粒,因此这些神秘的球粒一定是在星云尘埃的致密物质在接近1700摄氏度的高温下熔化,并且在这些幸存的颗粒熔化之前冷却而形成的。

8) Water containing dissolved silica, calcium carbonate, or iron may circulate through the enclosing sediment and be deposited in cavities such as marrow cavities and canals in bone once occupied by blood vessels and nerves.

翻译：含有溶解的二氧化硅、碳酸钙或铁的水可能在封闭的沉积物中循环,并且沉积在被血管和神经占据的骨髓腔和骨管等腔中。

9) Leaves and tissue of soft-bodied organisms such as jellyfish or worms may accumulate, become buried and compressed, and lose their volatile constituents.

翻译： 软体生物如水母或蠕虫的叶子和组织可能会积聚，被掩埋和压缩，并失去其挥发性成分。

10）A rotary engine attached to the steam engine enabled shafts to be turned and machines to be driven, resulting in mills using steam power to spin and weave cotton.

翻译： 附在蒸汽机上的旋转发动机可以使轴转动并驱动机器，从而使纺织厂利用蒸汽动力将棉花纺纱和织布。

11）Few of the cultural traditions and rules that today allow us to deal with dense populations existed for these people accustomed to household autonomy and the ability to move around the landscape almost at will.

翻译： 今天能让我们应对稠密人口的文化传统和规则已经很少了，对于这些习惯于家庭自治和可以随意四处走动的人来说。

12）Attack by scavengers and bacteria, chemical decay, and destruction by erosion and other geologic agencies make the odds against preservation very high.

翻译： 受到食腐动物和细菌的攻击、化学腐蚀、侵蚀和其他地质作用都会使得破坏的几率变得非常大。

13）In Europe as a whole, the exceptional reduction in the population and the related fall in demand for grain since the beginning of the seventeenth century had caused the price of agricultural products to fall.

翻译： 在整个欧洲，自 17 世纪初以来，人口的锐减和与此相关的粮食需求的下降导致了农产品价格的下降。

14）Many complex factors led to the adoption of the new economies, not only at Abu Hureyra, but at many other locations such as Ain Ghazal, also in Syria

翻译： 许多复杂的因素导致新经济的采用，不仅在阿布胡雷拉，也在许多其他地方，如艾因加扎尔和叙利亚。

15）They possess drought-resisting adaptations: loss of water through the leaves is reduced by means of dense hairs covering waxy leaf surfaces, by the closure of pores during the hottest times to reduce water loss, and by the rolling up or shedding of leaves at the beginning of the dry season.

翻译： 它们具有抗旱的适应能力：通过覆盖蜡质叶表面的浓密毛发；通过在最热的时候关闭气孔以减少水分流失；通过在旱季开始时卷起或脱落叶片来减少叶片的水分流失。

16) Merchants complained that the privileges reserved for <u>Venetian-built and owned</u> ships were first extended <u>to</u> those Venetians who bought ships from abroad <u>and then to</u> foreign-built and owned vessels.

翻译：商人抱怨说，为威尼斯人建造和拥有的船只所保留的特权首先扩大到那些从国外购买船只的威尼斯人，然后扩大到外国建造和拥有的船只。

17) Although aragonite has the same composition as the more familiar mineral known as calcite, it has a different crystal form, is relatively unstable, and in time changes to the more stable calcite.

翻译：虽然文石的成分与人们更熟悉的矿物方解石相同，但它的晶体形态不同，相对不稳定，而且随着时间的推移会变成更稳定的方解石。

五 并列省略

在并列结构中，不仅可以省略意思明显的主语和谓语等成分，还可以省略连接词。在并列结构中，后一个分句与前一个分句中相同的句子成分可以省略。

省略前：Its scientists were the world's best and its workers were the most skilled.

省略后：Its scientists were the world's best, its workers the most skilled.

省略前：Failing hips can be replaced, clinical depression can be controlled, and cataracts can be removed in a 30-minutes surgical procedure.

省略后：Failing hips can be replaced, clinical depression controlled, cataracts removed in a 30-minutes surgical procedure.

省略前：It is said that in England death is pressing, in Canada death is inevitable and in California death is optional.

省略后：It is said that in England death is pressing, in Canada inevitable and in California optional.

省略前：If the moderate end of the legal community has its way, the information on products might actually be provided for the benefit of customers and the information on products might not be provided as protection against legal liability.

省略后：If the moderate end of the legal community has its way, the information on products might actually be provided for the benefit of customers and not as protection against legal liability.

练一练 ....

要求：还原句中被省略的部分。

1）While rock between two consistent strata might in one place be shale and in another sandstone，the fossils in that shale or sandstone were always the same.

2）The Greeks were wedded to the sea；the Romans，to the land.

3）Limestone may be found in the Cambrian or in the Jurassic strata but a Cambrian trilobite will never be found in Jurassic strata，nor a dinosaur in the Cambrian.

答案解析 ....

1）While rock between two consistent strata might in one place be shale and might in another place be sandstone，the fossils in that shale or sandstone were always the same.

2）The Greeks were wedded to the sea；the Romans were wedded to the land.

3）Limestone may be found in the Cambrian or in the Jurassic strata but a Cambrian trilobite will never be found in Jurassic strata，nor a dinosaur will be found in the Cambrian.

六 宾语后置

及物动词和其宾语的位置在英语中一般来讲也是相对比较固定的,如果有修饰该及物动词的修饰成分(修饰动词的成分叫状语)或宾语的补充成分(叫作宾补,我们一般当做动词固定搭配来记),一般都放在宾语的后面,例如：

I put the book on the desk.

但是,有一种情况例外：如果宾语本身被很长的后置定语修饰的话,为了保持句子结构的平衡,会将整个宾语及其修饰成分放到状语或宾补的后面,例如：

I put on the desk the book which Jack gave me as a birthday present and which I like most among all the books.

处理这种情况需要我们具备以下两种能力：1)对于及物动词和动词的固定搭配要非常熟悉,预判该动词一定需要宾语　2)有很强的意群意识,不能将宾语划入状语或宾补的意群。

练一练 ....

要求：识别出下列句中被分离的动词和其宾语。

1）The society retained as parts of their oral tradition the myths that had grown up around the rites.

2）The doorways and windows are made possible by placing over the open spaces thick stone beams that support the weight from above.

3）These roads made possible a reduction in transportation costs.

4）Economic exchange was clearly very important as the Roman army brought with it very substantial spending power.

5）The impulse toward liberation enabled them to see with fresh eyes untried possibilities for arranging images on paper.

答案解析 ....

1）The society retained the myths ~~that had grown up around the rites~~ as parts of their oral tradition.

2）The doorways and windows are made possible by placing thick stone beams ~~that support the weight from above~~ over the open spaces.

3）These roads made a reduction in transportation costs possible.

4）Economic exchange was clearly very important as the Roman army brought ~~very substantial~~ spending power with it.

5）The impulse toward liberation enabled them to see untried possibilities ~~for arranging images~~ on ~~paper~~ with fresh eyes.

七 同位语

一般来讲，在一个句子中，除了主干成分以外，剩余的部分无论是从句还是短语，都是起修饰作用。只要确定这些修饰成分的修饰对象，句子理解基本就没有太大问题了。一般起到修饰作用的成分都是从句、非谓语短语、介词短语等，不过名词的修饰成分中有一种比较特殊的修饰作用，就是名词或名词短语本身来修饰名词，我们叫作同位语。其实这个名词和其修饰的名词，指的都是同一个事物，只是用不同的名称，方便我们更好地理解该事物，例：

My brother，Tom，was born in 1992.

这句话里,My brother 和 Tom 指得都是同一个人,只是用这种方式给我们补充了更多关于 My brother 的信息。

 练习一 ···

找出下列句中的同位语和其所修饰的名词。

1) Marilyn Monroe，a famous movie star，committed suicide.

2) London，the capital of Great Britain，lies astride the Thames in South Central England.

3) Most colonies were developed to export products such as fish，sugar，and furs，some of the most valuable resources to people at the time.

4) In 1524，Francis sent Italian-born Giovanni da Verrazano to explore the region between Florida and Newfoundland，a very large expanse of land，for a route to the Pacific Ocean.

5) Later，in 1534，Francis sent Jacques Cartier on the first of the three voyages to explore the coast of Newfoundland and the St. Lawrence River，uncharted territory at the time.

6) In 1565，the Spanish attacked and destroyed the fort，a short-lived French presence.

7) In 1608，he created a fur trading post that would grow into the city of Quebec，a city that would continue to prosper.

答案解析 ··

1) Marilyn Monroe, | a famous movie star |, committed suicide.

修饰 Marilyn Monroe

2) London，| the capital of Great Britain |, lies astride the Thames in South Central England.

修饰 London

3) Most colonies were developed to export products such as fish，sugar，and furs，| some of the most valuable resources to people at the time |.

修饰 products such as fish, sugar, and furs

4) In 1524，Francis sent Italian-born Giovanni da Verrazano to explore the region between Florida and Newfoundland，| a very large expanse of land |, for a

route to the Pacific Ocean.

修饰 the region between Florida and Newfoundland

5）Later，in 1534，Francis sent Jacques Cartier on the first of the three voyages to explore the coast of Newfoundland and the St. Lawrence River， uncharted territory at the time .

修饰 the coast of Newfoundland and the St. Lawrence River

6）In 1565，the Spanish attacked and destroyed the fort， a short-lived French presence .

修饰 the fort

7）In 1608，he created a fur trading post that would grow into the city of Quebec， a city that would continue to prosper .

修饰 Quebec

偶尔,如果同位语修饰的名词是句子的主语时,也可以放在被修饰的名词的前面,这时需要区分出哪个是真正的主语。其实分辨起来也很简单,一般来讲,同位语如果放在句中的话一定是用两个逗号隔开的,试比较:

One of the most striking of the transparent glass buildings in the world， the Rose Center for Earth and Space marks a new age in glass architecture.

The Rose Center for Earth and Space， one of the most striking of the transparent glass buildings in the world， marks a new age in glass architecture.

 练习二 ....

写出下列句子中的同位语,并用"____"划出句子主干。

1）In Death Valley，California，one of the hottest，most arid places in North America，there is much salt.

_____ ≈ _____

2）They usually do not get rabies（狂犬病），a nasty disease，because of the temperature of their blood.

_____ ≈ _____

3）In both areas，there was a well-established ground stone tool technology，a method of pounding and grinding nuts and other plant foods.

_____ ≈ _____

4）Monarchs, figureheads（有名无实的领袖）without real power in most countries, are usually kings and queens coming from the same family.

<u>　　　　　　　　　　</u> ≈ <u>　　　　　　　　　　</u>

5）Shortly after 1 400, shipbuilders began developing a new type of vessel designed to operate in rough, open water: the caravel.

<u>　　　　　　　　　　</u> ≈ <u>　　　　　　　　　　</u>

6）There are two kinds of crust, a lower and denser oceanic crust and an upper, lighter continental crust found over 40 percent of the Earth's surface.

<u>　　　　　　　　　　</u> ≈ <u>　　　　　　　　　　</u>

7）The traditional view of the first terrestrial organisms is based on mega fossils（大化石）-relatively large specimens of plants and animal.

<u>　　　　　　　　　　</u> ≈ <u>　　　　　　　　　　</u>

8）Around the time, the largest of these centers, Cuicuilco, was seriously affected by a volcanic eruption, with much of its agricultural land covered by lava（岩浆）.

<u>　　　　　　　　　　</u> ≈ <u>　　　　　　　　　　</u>

9）From the Middle East the Chinese acquired a blue pigment, a chemical unobtainable at that time in China containing only a low level of manganese.

<u>　　　　　　　　　　</u> ≈ <u>　　　　　　　　　　</u>

答案解析 ....

1）In Death Valley, California, one of the hottest, most arid places in North America, <u>there is much salt</u>.

<u>Death Valley</u>≈<u>one of the hottest, most arid places in North America</u>

2）<u>They usually do not get rabies</u>（狂犬病）, a nasty disease, because of the temperature of their blood.

<u>rabies</u>≈<u>a nasty disease</u>

3）In both areas, <u>there was a well-established ground stone tool technology</u>, a method of pounding and grinding nuts and other plant foods.

<u>a well-established ground stone tool technology</u>≈<u>a method of pounding and grinding nuts and other plant foods</u>

4）<u>Monarchs</u>, figureheads（有名无实的领袖）without real power in most countries, <u>are usually kings and queens</u> coming from the same family.

<u>Monarchs</u>≈<u>figureheadswithout real power in most countries</u>

5）Shortly after 1 400, <u>shipbuilders began developing a new type of vessel</u>

designed to operate in rough, open water: the caravel.

a new type of vessel≈the caravel

6) There are two kinds of crust, a lower and denser oceanic crust and an upper, lighter continental crust found over 40 percent of the Earth's surface.

two kinds of crust≈a lower and denser oceanic crust and an upper, lighter continental crust found over 40 percent of the Earth's surface

7) The traditional view of the first terrestrial organisms is based on mega fossils（大化石）—relatively large specimens of plants and animal.

mega fossils≈relatively large specimens of plants and animal

8) Around the time, the largest of these centers, Cuicuilco, was seriously affected by a volcanic eruption, with much of its agricultural land covered by lava（岩浆）.

the largest of these centers≈Cuicuilco

9) From the Middle East the Chinese acquired a blue pigment, a chemical unobtainable at that time in China containing only a low level of manganese.

a blue pigment≈a chemical unobtainable at that time in China containing only a low level of manganese

八 非谓语动词

1. 逻辑主语

既然 to do/doing/done 这三种动词不能做谓语成分，那么它们在句子中的作用是什么呢？这里我们只需牢记一条规则：**只要不是主干成分，剩余的一定是修饰成分。**

对于不做谓语动词的 to do/doing/done 的处理原则很简单，就是**找到这些动词的逻辑主语**，这些动词都是修饰其逻辑主语的。那什么是逻辑主语呢？其实也很简单，虽然 to do/doing/done 不做谓语动词，但它们本质上仍然是个动词。既然是动词，那么这个动作一定是有其发出主体的。谓语动词的动作发出主体一定是主语，而 to do/doing/done 这些动词不是谓语，所以其动作的发出者不一定是主语。我们把这些动词的动作执行主体叫作逻辑主语，即从逻辑上来讲的动作执行主体。

寻找逻辑主语的方法也很简单，就是**向前找逻辑上说得通的名词**；如果 **to do/doing/done 在句首的话，那么它们的逻辑主语基本上就是其所在句子的主语。**

我们来看一组例句：

1) The woman holding a baby in her arms is my aunt.

holding 动作的执行主体是 the woman，所以 the woman 是其逻辑主语

2）Anyone driving a lorry must first get a permit.

driving 动作的执行主体是 Anyone，所以 Anyone 是其逻辑主语

3）Some planets circling these stars might be similar to Earth.

circling 动作的执行主体是 planets，所以 planets 是其逻辑主语

4）Hearing the news, they all jumped with joy.

Hearing 动作的执行主体是 they，所以 they 是其逻辑主语

5）Seeing its mother, the baby smiled.

Seeing 动作的执行主体是 the baby，所以 the baby 是其逻辑主语

6）I stood by the door, not daring to say a word.

daring 动作的执行主体是 I，所以 I 是其逻辑主语

2. 省略的状语从句

在状语从句中，如果主语的主语和从句的主语是同一事物的话，可以将从句的主语省略，并将从句的谓语变为非谓语的形式，状语从句的连词可省可不省，例如：

Because I was asked to work overtime that evening, I missed a wonderful film.

＝Because asked to work overtime that evening, I missed a wonderful film.

＝Asked to work overtime that evening, I missed a wonderful film.

When he was asked for his views about his teaching job, Philip said he found it very interesting and rewarding.

＝When asked for his views about his teaching job, Philip said he found it very interesting and rewarding.

＝Asked for his views about his teaching job, Philip said he found it very interesting and rewarding.

When he was caught by the police again, the thief hung his head.

＝When caught by the police again, the thief hung his head.

＝Caught by the police again, the thief hung his head.

3. 非谓语动词短语与句子的转换

其实本质上，所有做修饰的非谓语动词都是由一个完整的句子降级而来的，就像上面我们所举的例子中，这些做修饰的非谓语动词都是由原来的状语从句按照一定的规则缩减而来。反过来讲，几乎所有做修饰的非谓语动词都可以通过添加连词，复原为一个完整的句子，例如：

1）The boy playing basketball on the playground is our monitor.

＝The boy who is playing basketball on the playground is our monitor.

2）The machine produced last year is very expensive.

= The machine which was produced last year is very expensive.

3）His parents died，leaving him a lot of money.

= His parents died，who left him a lot of money.

4）Many people come to the parks，looking for relaxations and entertainment.

= Many people come to the parks，who are looking for relaxations and entertainment.

5）The man loved by all the students is our headmaster.

= The man who is loved by all the students is our headmaster.

6）Deeply moved by his words，I promised to help him.

= Because I was deeply moved by his words，I promised to help him.

7）Considered as a building material，wood is not very strong.

= When wood is considered as a building material，wood is not very strong.

4. with 的复合结构

在用非谓语动词做修饰时，还有一种比较特殊的结构，叫"with 的复合结构"，其实就是使用介词 with 来将原本的句子缩减为一个词组，此时的介词"with"没有具体意义，表示一种伴随的状态，而且有时也可省略，例如：

Don't speak with your mouth full.

= Don't speak when your mouth is full.

The square looks more beautiful than ever with the lights on.

= The square looks more beautiful than ever when the lights are on.

He was asleep with his head on his arms.

= He was asleep while his head was on his arms.

She felt very nervous with so many people looking at her.

= She felt very nervous when so many people were looking at her.

With the old man leading, the two started toward the mountains.

= When the old man was leading, the two started toward the mountains.

With five minutes to go before the last train left，we arrived here.

= When there was five minutes to go before the last train left，we arrived here

With his matter settled，we left the room.

When his matter was settled，we left the room.

九 插入成分

我们在阅读时,经常会有句子读到一半突然出现一些打岔的信息,如果处理不好的话,这些信息往往会打断我们阅读的思绪,忘记前面阅读的重点。就像我们在和别人聊天时,突然有人插话进来,就会打乱我们前面的节奏。其实这种"打岔"的现象不仅是英文中有,中文中也有,比如"总经理,作为公司的法人代表,可以代表公司与其他单位或个人签署合同"。

这些插入的信息往往是对前面内容的补充说明或解释,通常会用逗号、破折号或括号来与主干信息隔开。也正是因为它有这个特点,我们可以这样巧妙地处理:阅读时,遇到两个逗号、两个破折号及括号里面的信息我们先跳过,之后再来阅读这些信息。这样我们就可以避免其给我们带来的干扰了,例如:

两个破折号

When the choice isn't all or nothing—when people have "even a slight amount" of control—they are more open to automation.

解析:忽略破折号里的信息后,句子简化为,When the choice isn't all or nothing, they are more open to automation.这样一来信息就变得流畅很多。破折号里的插入成分只是用来具体说明什么是"the choice isn't all or nothing",就是"人们有即使是一丁点的控制权",忽略之后也不会影响句子的核心信息。

翻译:当选择不是非此即彼——当人们有"即使是一丁点"的控制权时——他们也能更坦然地接受自动化。

括号

However，unlike the cases of sea otters and pinnipeds（seals，sea lions，and walruses，whose limbs are functional both on land and at sea），it is not easy to envision what the first whales looked like.

解析:忽略括号里的信息后,句子简化为,However，unlike the cases of sea otters and pinnipeds，it is not easy to envision what the first whales looked like.这样一来信息就变得流畅很多。括号里的信息用来解释什么是 pinnipeds,也就是"海豹、海狮和海象,它们的四肢在陆地和海上都有功能"的这样一类动物,忽略之后也不会影响句子的核心信息。

翻译：然而，与海獭和鳍足动物（海豹、海狮和海象，它们的四肢在陆地和海上都有功能）不同的是，很难想象最初鲸鱼的样子。

两个逗号

Before then，I'd allowed the car to steer around gentle turns，with my hands still on the wheel，and to adjust speed in traffic.

解析：忽略两个逗号之间的信息后，句子简化为：Before then，I'd allowed the car to steer around gentle turns and to adjust speed in traffic. 这样一来信息就变得流畅很多。两个逗号之间的信息来补充说明，汽车转弯时，"我的双手仍在在方向盘上"，忽略之后也不会影响句子的核心信息。

翻译：在那之前，我让汽车在平缓的转弯处转向，双手仍放在方向盘上，并在行驶中调整车速。

值得注意的是，因为破折号和括号的功能基本就只有"解释说明"这一个用法，所以处理起来比较简单。但是，逗号的功能除了用来隔开插入成分之外，还有一些其他的用法，比如并列成分，并列句等。因此，**在处理逗号隔开的插入成分时要谨慎，不能看到两个逗号之间的内容就跳过，需要注意其是否真的是插入成分。一个很关键的标准就是看这个逗号出现的位置是否打断了原来的信息流，如果是，则果断先跳过；如果不是，只是并列成分停顿或者其他正常的停顿时则不能盲目跳过**，如：

In the playground，our monitor，Jack，is playing football with his friends.

在上面这个句子中，有三个逗号，Jack 前后的逗号才是标志着插入成分的逗号。第一个逗号是正常的停顿，第二个逗号是插入成分的开始，因为它打断了句中主语和谓语的连贯性，因为正常来讲，主语与谓语作为整体才能表达完整的信息，所以第二和第三个逗号中间的 Jack 就破坏了这个整体，是插入的成分。

当然，这些插入成分也可以放在句尾。不过，当其出现在句尾时，对句子信息的干扰不大，因为此时重点信息已经全部讲完了，所以我们这里就不过多讨论句尾的插入成分了，例：

Recent research suggests that screen-printing techniques can produce lines as thin as 30 micrometers—about the width of the lines Green used for his record solar cells，but at costs far lower than his lithography techniques.

解析：破折号开始之前，核心信息已经完全结束了，所以这个插入信息完全不会造成干扰，按顺序阅读理解即可。

翻译：最近的研究表明，丝网印刷技术可以产生细至 30 微米的线条——其宽度相当于格林用来记录太阳能电池线的宽度，但成本远远低于他的平版印刷技术。

 练习一 ....

找出下列句中的插入成分，并翻译句子。

1) Any driverless crashes will be sensationalized, as has already happened, while we ignore tens of thousands of deaths from human crashes.

2) Its royal tombs, both those underground and the skyward reaching pyramids, are rife with stories of hidden chambers.

3) Several of its internal chambers, including the Queen's chamber, the King's chamber and the Grand Gallery, were robbed in antiquity, and excavated more systematically in the 19th and 20th centuries by various archaeologists

4) Presumably there is, somewhere in the pyramid, a corridor of some sort that leads to the new void.

答案解析

1) Any driverless crashes will be sensationalized, ~~as has already happened,~~ while we ignore tens of thousands of deaths from human crashes.

翻译: 任何无人驾驶导致的车祸都会引起轰动,正如已经发生的那样,而我们却忽略了数以万计的人为事故造成的死亡。

2) Its royal tombs, ~~both those underground and the skyward reaching pyramids,~~ are rife with stories of hidden chambers.

翻译: 它的皇家陵墓,那些地下的和高耸的金字塔,都隐含着密室的故事。

3) Several of its internal chambers, ~~including the Queen's chamber, the King's chamber and the Grand Gallery,~~ were robbed in antiquity, and excavated more systematically in the 19th and 20th centuries by various archaeologists

翻译: 它的几个内室,包括皇后室、国王室和大画廊,在古代遭到抢劫,并在19世纪和20世纪被各种考古学家更系统地挖掘出来。

4) Presumably there is, ~~somewhere in the pyramid,~~ a corridor of some sort that leads to the new void.

翻译: 据推测,在金字塔的某个地方,有一条通向新虚空的走廊。

 **练习二**

找出下列句中的插入成分,并翻译句子。

1) To find out, she and Adler planted 168 Texas gourd vines in an Iowa field and, throughout the August flowering season, made half the plants more fragrant by tucking dimethoxybenzene-treated swabs deep inside their flowers.

2) Instead, the "warm, wet phase" of Mars, when life might have originated, was

actually quite short-lived, lasting less than a billion years, and was followed by a series of extreme conditions unlike any experienced on Earth.

3) And since a third of the planet is already used for agriculture—destroying forests and other wild habitats along the way—anything that could help us produce more food on less land would seem to be good for the environment.

4) Auersperg's observations culminated in a study showing that cockatoos can solve elaborate multistep lock puzzles, without intermediate behavioral reinforcements, and immediately transfer their new knowledge to a novel challenge.

5) If one of them was a transiting planet—dimming the light of its parent star as it passed between the star and Earth—astronomers would see its transit timing vary over multiple orbits, betraying the presence of a companion planet.

6) In a recent study, researchers found that they could isolate and grow individual soil bacteria—including types that can't normally be grown in the laboratory—in soil itself, which supplied critical nutrients and minerals.

7) Add in a little plausible speculation—specifically, that there may be more sedimentary rocks buried beyond Curiosity's reach, or that other rocks may have eroded over the course of time—and the lake's possible lifespan rises to tens of millions of years.

8) McGargill and co-workers envisioned a different role for rapamycin when they set out to explore how the strain-specific influenza vaccines used today—which must be updated each year to keep up with the ever-changing virus—might be transformed into a universal shot.

9) The question of what to do with null results—when researchers fail to see an effect that should be detectable—has long been hotly debated among those conducting medical trials, where the results can have a big impact on lives and corporate bottom lines.

10) Environmentalists disdain the enormous amounts of energy needed and waste created by conventional farming, while organic practices—forgoing artificial fertilizers and chemical pesticides—are considered far more sustainable.

11) But astronomers in a more extreme galactic environment—such as a galaxy undergoing a burst of intense star formation, like M82, or galaxies in the process of merging, like the Antennae—would reach starkly different conclusions.

12) Either way the goal is crops that would tap the main advantage of perennials—the deep, dense root systems that fuel the plants' rebirth each spring and that make them so resilient and resource efficient—without sacrificing too much of the grain yield

that millennia of selection have bred into annuals.

13）Because there are numerous tributaries of the streams in Trinidad，with guppies living in some but not all of them，Reznick realized that he could，as he put it in a 2008 paper，"treat streams like giant test tubes by introducing guppies or predators" to places they had not originally occurred，and then watch as natural selection acted on the guppies.

答案解析

1）To find out，she and Adler planted 168 Texas gourd vines in an Iowa field and，~~throughout the August flowering season，~~ made half the plants more fragrant by tucking dimethoxybenzene-treated swabs deep inside their flowers.

翻译：为了找到答案，她和阿德勒在爱荷华州的一块地里种植了168株得克萨斯葫芦，并且在整个8月份的花期里，把经过二甲氧基苯处理的棉签塞进花朵深处，以使一半的植物更香。

2）Instead，the "warm，wet phase" of Mars，~~when life might have originated，~~ was actually quite short-lived，~~lasting less than a billion years，~~ and was followed by a series of extreme conditions unlike any experienced on Earth.

翻译：相反，火星的"温暖潮湿阶段"，也就是生命可能起源的时候，实际上是相当短暂的，持续时间不到10亿年，并且随之而来的是一系列地球上从未经历过的极端情况。

3）And since a third of the planet is already used for agriculture——~~destroying forests and other wild habitats along the way~~——anything that could help us produce more food on less land would seem to be good for the environment.

翻译：由于地球上三分之一的土地已经被用于农业——破坏了森林和其他野生栖息地——任何能够帮助我们在更少的土地上生产更多食物的东西似乎都对环境有益。

4）Auersperg's observations culminated in a study showing that cockatoos can solve elaborate multistep lock puzzles，~~without intermediate behavioral reinforcements，~~ and immediately transfer their new knowledge to a novel challenge.

翻译：奥斯佩格的观察结果表明，风头鹦鹉可以解决复杂的多步骤解锁难题，不需要中间的行为强化，并可以立即将他们的新知识转移到新的挑战中。

5）If one of them was a transiting planet——~~dimming the light of its parent star as it passed between the star and Earth~~——astronomers would see its transit timing vary over multiple orbits, betraying the presence of a companion planet.

翻译: 如果其中一颗行星是一颗凌日行星——当它经过恒星和地球之间时,它的母恒星的光线会变暗——那么天文学家会看到它过境时间在多个轨道上是不同的,这表明伴星的存在。

6) In a recent study, researchers found that they could isolate and grow individual soil bacteria——including types that can't normally be grown in the laboratory——in soil itself, which supplied critical nutrients and minerals.

翻译: 在最近的一项研究中,研究人员发现,他们可以在土壤中分离和培养个体的土壤细菌,包括在实验室无法生长的细菌,这些土壤本身提供了关键的养分和矿物质。

7) Add in a little plausible speculation——specifically, that there may be more sedimentary rocks buried beyond Curiosity's reach, or that other rocks may have eroded over the course of time——and the lake's possible lifespan rises to tens of millions of years.

翻译: 再加上一点可能的推测——特别是,好奇号无法触及的地方可能埋藏着更多的沉积岩,或者其他岩石可能会随着时间的推移而被侵蚀——湖泊可能达到的寿命会上升到数千万年。

8) McGargill and co-workers envisioned a different role for rapamycin when they set out to explore how the strain-specific influenza vaccines used today——which must be updated each year to keep up with the ever-changing virus——might be transformed into a universal shot.

翻译: 麦克嘉吉和他的同事们设想雷帕霉素将扮演一个不同的角色,他们开始探索如何将目前使用的流感疫苗——这些疫苗必须每年更新以跟上不断变化的病毒——转化为通用疫苗。

9) The question of what to do with null results——when researchers fail to see an effect that should be detectable——has long been hotly debated among those conducting medical trials, where the results can have a big impact on lives and corporate bottom lines.

翻译: 如何处理无效结果的问题——当研究人员看不到应该被检测到的效果时——在那些进行医学试验的人中长期以来一直是一个激烈争论的问题,在这些试验中,结果可能会对生命和企业的盈亏底线产生重大影响。

10) Environmentalists disdain the enormous amounts of energy needed and waste created by conventional farming, while organic practices——forgoing artificial fertilizers and chemical pesticides——are considered far more sustainable.

翻译：环保主义者蔑视传统农业所产生的大量能源和废物，而有机做法——放弃人工肥料和化学农药——则被他们认为更具可持续性。

11）But astronomers in a more extreme galactic environment—such as a galaxy undergoing a burst of intense star formation, like M82, or galaxies in the process of merging, like the Antennae—would reach starkly different conclusions.

翻译：但是在一个更极端的星系环境中——比如一个星系正在经历一次强烈的恒星形成爆发，比如 M82，或者一个星系正在合并的过程中，比如触须星系——天文学家会得出截然不同的结论。

12）Either way the goal is crops that would tap the main advantage of perennials—the deep, dense root systems that fuel the plants' rebirth each spring and that make them so resilient and resource efficient—without sacrificing too much of the grain yield that millennia of selection have bred into annuals.

翻译：无论哪种方式，目标都是利用多年生植物的主要优势——深而密的根系，每年春天为植物再生提供燃料，使它们具有如此强的弹性和资源效率——在不过多牺牲千年培育成的一年生作物的粮食产量的情况下。

13）Because there are numerous tributaries of the streams in Trinidad, with guppies living in some but not all of them, Reznick realized that he could, as he put it in a 2008 paper, "treat streams like giant test tubes by introducing guppies or predators" to places they had not originally occurred, and then watch as natural selection acted on the guppies.

翻译：因为特立尼达河有许多支流，有些地方生活着孔雀鱼，但有些地方没有，瑞斯尼克意识到，正如他在 2008 年的一篇论文中所说的那样，"把河流看作是巨型试管一样，通过将孔雀鱼或食肉动物引入"到它们未曾出现过的地方，然后观察自然选择对孔雀鱼所起的作用。

第 五 章

长难句分析与理解

　　随着阅读文本难度的提高,我们遇到长难句的频率也会大大提高。所谓长难句,顾名思义,就是那些句子很长且理解有难度的句子。这种句子信息量大且语法结构复杂,往往一遍读完之后,不知所云。本章的重点就是如何使用基本的语法知识来分析长难句,抽丝剥茧,最终使整个句子的意思清晰明了。

　　长难句的分析可以简单分为以下三个步骤:

第一步　分析语法成分

第二步　分析修饰关系

第三步　直译长难句

一 分析语法成分

　　符号: <u>主句主干</u> （从句） 意群/意群

1. 主句的主干成分用＿＿划出

　　主干成分就是第一章所讲的主语和谓语部分。如果谓语动词是及物动词或有固定搭配的话,则需要将其宾语和固定搭配部分一并划出。

　　主句是相对于从句而言的。打个比方,主句就像一棵树的树干,从句就相当于树权。树权是长在树干上的,从句是依附在主句上的。从形式上而言,**主句的句首没有连词,而从句的句首是一定有连词的**(除部分连词可省略的情况外),例:

The girl （who won the first prize in the contest） is from Zhejiang.
　　　　　 连词

（When she came in,） I stopped eating
　连词

I suggest（that we should go tomorrow.）
　　　　　连词

2. 从句部分用()划出

从句识别需要注意以下几点

1）从句始于连词

2）从句本质上是个句子，所以从句内部必须有谓语动词

3）附属于从句的修饰成分也应包括在内

4）如果从句内部嵌有新的从句时，则用()将其标记出

5）如果从句内部过于复杂，则也用……将其主干标记出

例1：

The hard，rigid plates（that form the outermost portion of the Earth）are about 100 kilometers thick.

例2：

An inability/to span open gaps between trees/may be problematic，（since trees（that yield these foods）can be sparse）.

在以上两个例子中，从句均是从连词开始；每个从句都有谓语动词；例2中 since 引导的从句中又嵌入了一个附属从句，所以也用从句的符号标记；since 引导的从句主干被隔开，所用……标记主干，以便快速理解主干信息。

3. 用/划分剩余的意群

句子除了主干和从句以外，还会有很多修饰性的短语，比如介词短语、to do/doing done 短语等等。这些短语有时非常长，我们可以以意群为单位，用/将其隔开。所谓意群就是**我们能一次性处理的、意思相对完整的单词群**。当一个句子或短语过于复杂的时候，我们往往很难一口气读完并理解，阅读时往往会有一定的停顿来消化已读信息。每个停顿的模块我们就叫作一个意群，恰当的停顿对于我们的阅读理解有非常大的帮助。

每个意群可长可短，取决于我们对于语言的处理能力，比如：Changes in the efficiency of the muscles used for breathing 这个短语，对于语言处理能力较强的人来说，它就是一个整体，可以一口气看完理解，不用停顿。但对于语言处理能力一般的人，也可以看作是两个意群，Changes in the efficiency of the muscles/used for breathing，甚至是三个意群，Changes in the efficiency/of the muscles/used for breathing。

虽然意群停顿相对主观，但也不是完全任意的。错误的停顿不但无助于阅读，反而会给理解带来很大的障碍。在阅读停顿时尤其注意以下两点：1)**介词短语内部不能停顿**。就像刚才 Changes in the efficiency of the muscles used for breathing 这个短语，你可以选择不停

顿,也可以选择在以下几个地方停或不停:Changes/in the efficiency/of the muscles/used for breathing,但绝对不能这样停:in/the efficiency of/the muscles used for/breathing;2)**动词短语内部不能停**。比如,having a dinner with my friend in a fancy resteraunt near my home,不能停成 having/a dinner with my friend in/a fancy resteraunt near my home。

例:

In the seventeenth century/<u>the organ, the clavichord, and the harpsichord/became the chief instruments</u> of the keyboard group,/a supremacy（that they maintained）（until the piano supplanted them/at the end of the eighteenth century）.

分析修饰关系

除了主干以外,句子的剩余部分,无论是从句还是修饰短语,本质上都起修饰作用。长难句理解的最大的挑战是**修饰关系的确定**,这直接决定句子细节上的理解是否准确。另外,修饰关系的确定不仅要考虑到**语法关系**,还需要考虑**上下文或者日常逻辑**。

我们通常只分析名词的修饰成分,如果一个修饰成分不是修饰名词的话,我们通常不用考虑,按照语序顺译即可理解。但名词的修饰成分是不能这样处理的,因为汉语和英语在定语方面的差异,所以在阅读理解中,英语中后置的名词修饰成分需要适当地移位,那确定其修饰对象就显得至关重要了。我们在第二章详细讲过如何确定多个后置定语的修饰关系,这里就不加赘述。例:

Widely reported accounts by figures like the famous traveler from Venice,Marco Polo,of the willingness of people in China to trade with Europeans and of the immensity of the wealth to be gained by such contact made the idea irresistible.

Widely reported <u>accounts</u>/by figures like the famous traveler from Venice/,Marco Polo,/of the willingness of people in China to trade with Europeans/and of the immensity of the wealth to be gained by such contact/<u>made the idea irresistible</u>.

按照**“距离最近且逻辑合理”**的原则,by figures like the famous traveler from Venice、of the willingness of people in China to trade with Europeans 和 of the immensity of the wealth to be gained by such contact 三个意群均是修饰 accounts 的,Marco Polo 修饰 traveler.

三　**直译长难句**

1. 如何直译长难句

长难句的语法和修饰关系分析完之后,基本上句子的意思已经非常清晰了,我们在理解和组织语言时需要注意以下两点：

1）先将主干的信息组织在一起进行理解

2）再添加修饰信息

例：

Widely reported <u>accounts</u>/by figures like the famous traveler from Venice/，Marco Polo，/of the willingness of people in China to trade with Europeans/and of the immensity of the wealth to be gained by such contact/<u>made the idea irresistible</u>.

1）主干信息：描述使这个想法不可抗拒

2）添加修饰：广泛报道的、由像来自威尼斯马可波罗这样著名旅行家所提供的、关于中国人愿意与欧洲人进行贸易的以及通过这样的接触将获得巨大财富的描述使这个想法不可抗拒。

3）这个句子的后置定语比较复杂，也可以拆成两句，单独处理名词的修饰成分：广泛报道的描述使这个想法不可抗拒；这些描述是由像来自威尼斯马可波罗这样著名的旅行家所提供的、关于中国人愿意与欧洲人进行贸易的以及通过这样的接触将获得巨大财富的描述。

2. 各种句式直译小技巧

1）主干部分和非修饰名词的成分，按语序直接翻译

Although the potential is enormous，it is likely that in the near future geothermal energy can make important local contributions only where the resource is close to the user and the economics are favorable，as they are in California，New Zealand，and Iceland.

（Although the potential is enormous），it is likely（that in the near future

　　虽然　　　潜能　　是 巨大的，　这是可能的 但在 不远的　未来

geothermal energy can make important local contributions）（only where the

地热的能量　　　可以 创造　重要的 当地贡献　　　　　仅　 在

resource is close to the user and the economics are favorable），（as they are in

这个资源　靠近　　　用户　　且在　经济上　是 有利的地方，正如它们在

California，New Zealand，and Iceland.）

加利福尼亚、新西兰和冰岛一样。

2）后置定语提前至被修饰的名词前面

● 汉语中没有后置定语，所以英语的后置定语翻译成汉语时一定要提前。

the book on the desk　桌上的书

the student who studies very hard　学习很努力的学生

● 对于名词后面有多个修饰成分的，基本可按由远及近的顺序。

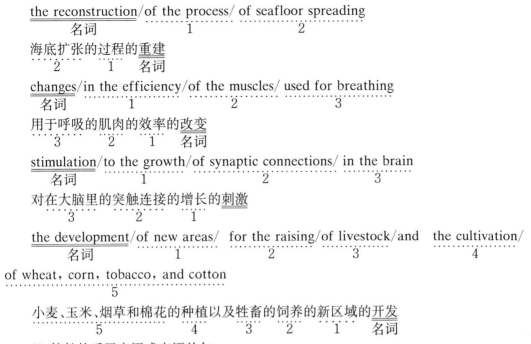

the reconstruction/of the process/ of seafloor spreading
名词　　　　　　1　　　　　　　2
海底扩张的过程的重建
　　　2　　　1　　名词

changes/in the efficiency/of the muscles/ used for breathing
名词　　　　1　　　　　　2　　　　　　3
用于呼吸的肌肉的效率的改变
　3　　　2　　　1　　名词

stimulation/to the growth/of synaptic connections/ in the brain
名词　　　　1　　　　　　2　　　　　　3
对在大脑里的突触连接的增长的刺激
　　3　　　　2　　　1　　名词

the development/of new areas/ for the raising/of livestock/and　the cultivation/
名词　　　　1　　　　　　2　　　　3　　　　　4
of wheat，corn，tobacco，and cotton
　　　　　5
小麦、玉米、烟草和棉花的种植以及牲畜的饲养的新区域的开发
　　5　　　　4　　　　3　　2　　　1　　名词

3）较长的后置定语或定语从句

● 如果后置定语较长，直接全部移至名词前面有点拗口的话，可以拆成两句，单独处理名词的修饰。

● 定语从句拆分为两句话时，可将连词换为前面被修饰的名词。

例1　This cooperation allowed people to contend with a patchy environment in which precipitation and other resources varied across the landscape.

＝This cooperation allowed people to contend with a patchy environment；in this patchy environment precipitation and other resources varied across the landscape.

例2　The solar nebula is the interstellar cloud of gas and dust out of which our solar system was formed.

＝The solar nebula is the interstellar cloud of gas and dust；out of the interstellar cloud our solar system was formed.

例3　The green algae would have been subjected to environmental pressures that resulted in adaptations that enhanced their potential to give rise to land-dwelling or organisms.

＝The green algae would have been subjectcd to environmental pressures；these environmental pressures resulted in adaptations that enhanced their potential to give rise to land-dwelling or organisms.

4）主语从句

先翻译主语从句部分，然后再用"这……"来指代主语从句部分，承接句子剩余部分。

That she became an artist may have been due to her father's influence.
　　　　主语从句

翻译：她成为一个艺术家,这可能是受她父亲的影响。

To what extent competition determines the composition of a community and the density of particular species has been the source of considerable controversy.

翻译：竞争在多大程度上决定了一个群体的组成及特定物种的密度,这一直是许多争议的起源。

四　长难句分析、翻译与解析

1) In addition to finding an increase of suitable browse，like huckleberry and vine maple，Arthur Einarsen，longtime game biologist in the Pacific Northwest，found quality of browse in the open areas to be substantially more nutritive.

难句解析

In addition to finding an increase of suitable browse,/like huckleberry and vine maple,/Arthur Einarsen,/longtime game biologist in the Pacific Northwest,/found quality of browse/in the open areas/to be substantially more nutritive.

修饰关系分析: like huckleberry and vine maple 修饰 suitable browse；longtime game biologist in the Pacific Northwest 修饰 Arthur Einarsen；in the open areas 修饰 browse。

翻译：除了寻找像越橘和藤槭这样适宜的牧草外,太平洋西北部的长期猎物生物学家亚瑟·埃纳森发现,开阔地区的牧草质量大体上更有营养。

2) Estimates indicate that the aquifer contains enough water to fill Lake Huron, but unfortunately，under the semiarid climatic conditions that presently exist in the region，rates of addition to the aquifer are minimal，amounting to about half a centimeter a year.

难句解析

Estimates indicate（that₁ the aquifer contains enough water to fill Lake Huron）, but unfortunately，under the semiarid climatic conditions（that₂ presently exist in the region）, rates of addition to the aquifer are minimal，amounting to about half a centimeter a year.

修饰关系分析：第一个 that 从句是宾语从句,可以直接按顺序理解翻译即可;第二个从句是定语从句,修饰 conditions,翻译时提前;amounting to 的逻辑主语是 rates,修饰 rates。

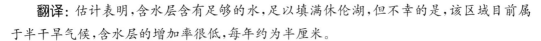

翻译：估计表明，含水层含有足够的水，足以填满休伦湖，但不幸的是，该区域目前属于半干旱气候，含水层的增加率很低，每年约为半厘米。

3）Contrary to the arguments of some that much of the Pacific was settled by Polynesians accidentally marooned after being lost and adrift，it seems reasonable that this feat was accomplished by deliberate colonization expeditions that set out fully stocked with food and domesticated plants and animals.

难句解析

Contrary to the arguments of some（that 1 much of the Pacific was settled/by Polynesians/accidentally marooned after being lost and adrift），<u>it seems reasonable</u>（that 2 this feat was accomplished by deliberate colonization expeditions）（that 3 set out fully stocked with food and domesticated plants and animals）.

修饰关系分析：第一个 that 从句修饰 arguments，说明 arguments 的具体内容；第二个 that 从句是主语从句，前面的 it 是形式主语，翻译时可以直译；第三个 that 是定语从句，修饰 expeditions。这些比较长的名词的修饰成分，如果提前至名词前面翻译使句子过于冗长，可以另起一句说明。

翻译：与一些人的论点相反，这些人的观点是太平洋大部分地区被在迷路和漂泊后意外被困的波利尼西亚人所定居，似乎合理的是，这项壮举是通过精心的殖民探险完成的，这些探险队出发时有充足的食物和驯化的动植物。

4）Unlike in the Americas，where metallurgy was a very late and limited development，Africans had iron from a relatively early date，developing ingenious furnaces to produce the high heat needed for production and to control the amount of air that reached the carbon and iron ore necessary for making iron.

难句解析

Unlike in the Americas，（where metallurgy was a very late and limited development），<u>Africans had iron</u>/from a relatively early date，developing ingenious furnaces/to produce the high heat/needed for production and to control the amount of air（that reached the carbon and iron ore necessary for making iron）.

修饰关系分析：where 从句修饰 Americas；developing 的逻辑主语是 Africans；to produce...与 to control...并列，是目的状语，按顺序直译即可；needed for production 修饰 high heat；that 从句修饰 air，翻译时从句提前。

翻译：与冶金发展非常晚、发展有限的美洲相比，非洲人从相对早期开始就有了铁，并开发出精巧的熔炉，以生产所需的高热量，来控制达到炼铁所需的碳和铁矿石的空气量。

5）Most engravings，for example，are best lit from the left，as befits the work of right-handed artists，who generally prefer to have the light source on the left so that the shadow of their hand does not fall on the tip of the engraving tool or brush.

难句解析

Most engravings，for example，are best lit from the left，（as befits the work of right-handed artists），（who generally prefer to have the light source on the left）（so that the shadow of their hand does not fall on the tip of the engraving tool or brush）.

修饰关系分析: as 从句修饰主句, 这里的 as 等同于 which；who 引导的从句修饰 artists；so that 引导的状语从句, 按顺序直译就好。

翻译: 例如, 大多数雕刻品最好从左边方向照明, 这与惯用右手的艺术家的作品很相配, 他们通常更喜欢把光源放在左边, 这样他们手的影子就不会落在雕刻工具或者画笔的顶端。

6）This "atmospheric engine," invented by Thomas Savery and vastly improved by his partner，Thomas Newcomen，embodied revolutionary principles，but it was so slow and wasteful of fuel that it could not be employed outside the coal mines for which it had been designed.

难句解析

This "atmospheric engine," invented by Thomas Savery and vastly improved by his partner，Thomas Newcomen，embodied revolutionary principles，but it was so slow and wasteful of fuel（that it could not be employed outside the coal mines）（for which it had been designed）.

修饰关系分析: so...that 引导的状语从句；for which 修饰 the coal mines。

翻译: 这种由托马斯·萨弗里发明, 并由他的合作伙伴托马斯·纽科曼进行了极大改进的"大气发动机"体现了革命性的原理, 但它速度慢, 燃料浪费严重, 因此不能在它为之设计的煤矿之外使用。

7）Numerous seeming exceptions to this law have since been found，but they can usually be explained as cases in which the two species，even though competing for a major joint resource，did not really occupy exactly the same niche.

难句解析

Numerous seeming exceptions to this law have since been found，but they can usually be explained as cases（in which the two species，even though competing for a major joint resource，did not really occupy exactly the same niche）.

修饰关系分析: in which 从句修饰 cases, 这种"介词＋which"引导的长定语从句, 可以将 which 换成被修饰的名词, 转化为, in these cases the two species，even though competing for a major joint resource，did not really occupy exactly the same niche.

翻译: 许多看似不符合这一规律的例外情况自此被发现了, 但它们通常可以解释这样

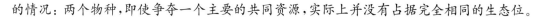

的情况：两个物种，即使争夺一个主要的共同资源，实际上并没有占据完全相同的生态位。

8) Continued sedimentation—the process of deposits' settling on the sea bottom—buries the organic matter and subjects it to higher temperatures and pressures, which convert the organic matter to oil and gas.

难句解析

Continued sedimentation—the process of deposits' settling on the sea bottom—buries the organic matter and subjects it to higher temperatures and pressures,（which convert the organic matter to oil and gas）.

修饰关系分析：两个破折号之间的内容修饰前面的名词；which 从句修饰高温高压或者整句都说得通。

翻译：持续沉积作用——沉积物在海底的沉积过程——将有机物掩埋并使其承受更高的温度和压力，从而将有机物转化为石油和天然气。

9) The growing power of the elite, who controlled the economy, would give them the means to physically coerce people to move to Teotihuacan and serve as additions to the labor force.

难句解析

The growing power of the elite,（who controlled the economy）, would give them the means/to physically coerce people/to move to Teotihuacan and serve as additions to the labor force.

修饰关系分析：who 从句修饰 elite；to physically coerce people 修饰 means；to move 和 to serve 并列，与动词 coerce 构成固定搭配，coerce sb to do sth 威胁某人做某事。

翻译：控制着经济的精英力量不断增长，这使他们有办法迫使人们搬到特奥蒂瓦坎，并作为劳动力的补充。

10) As a result of crustal adjustments and faulting, the Strait of Gibraltar, where the Mediterranean now connects to the Atlantic, opened, and water cascaded spectacularly back into the Mediterranean.

难句解析

As a result of crustal adjustments and faulting, the Strait of Gibraltar,（where the Mediterranean now connects to the Atlantic）, opened, and water cascaded spectacularly back into the Mediterranean.

修饰关系分析：where 从句修饰 the Strait of Gibraltar。

翻译：由于地壳的调整和断层作用，相连地中海与大西洋的直布罗陀海峡，打开了，海水壮观地泻回到地中海。

11）Over long periods of time，substances whose physical and chemical properties change with the ambient climate at the time can be deposited in a systematic way to provide a continuous record of changes in those properties over time，sometimes for hundreds or thousands of years.

难句分析

Over long periods of time，<u>substances</u>（whose physical and chemical properties change with the ambient climate at the time）<u>can be deposited in a systematic way</u>/to provide a continuous record of changes/in those properties over time，/sometimes for hundreds or thousands of years.

修饰关系分析：whose 从句修饰 substance；to provide... 是状语，按顺序直译即可；in those properties 修饰 changes。

翻译：在很长一段时间内，其物理和化学性质随当时环境气候变化的物质可以系统地沉积下来，以提供这些性质随时间变化的连续记录，有时长达数百年或数千年。

12）In order for the structure to achieve the size and strength necessary to meet its purpose，architecture employs methods of support that，because they are based on physical laws，have changed little since people first discovered them—even while building materials have changed dramatically.

难句分析

In order for the structure to achieve the size and strength/necessary to meet its purpose，<u>architecture employs methods</u> of support（that，~~because they are based on physical laws~~，have changed little）（since people first discovered them）—（even while building materials have changed dramatically）.

修饰关系分析：necessary to... 修饰 size 和 strength；that 从句修饰 methods；because、since、while 引导的都是状语从句，按顺序直译即可；需要注意的是，because 连接的状语从句插在了 that 从句的主谓之间，可以先忽略它，先将从句主干连在一起理解。

翻译：为了使结构达到实现其目的所需的尺寸和强度，建筑采用了支撑方法，因为这些方法是基于物理定律的，自从人们第一次发现它们以来，这些方法几乎没有变过，即使建筑材料发生了巨大的变化。

13）The possibility that mass extinctions may recur periodically has given rise to such hypotheses that a companion star with a long-period orbit deflected other bodies from their normal orbits，making some of them fall to Earth as meteors and causing widespread devastation upon impact.

难句分析

<u>The possibility</u>（that mass extinctions may recur periodically）<u>has given rise to such</u>

<u>hypotheses</u>（that a companion star/with a long-period orbit/deflected other bodies from their normal orbits，making some of them fall to Earth as meteors and causing widespread devastation upon impact）.

修饰关系分析：第一个 that 从句修饰 possibility；第二个 that 从句修饰 hypotheses；with a long-period orbit 修饰 star；making 和 causing 的逻辑主语是"伴星使其他天体轨道偏离"这整个句子。

翻译：大规模灭绝可能周期性地重现，这一点已经产生了这样的假设：一颗有长周期轨道的伴星使其他天体偏离其正常轨道，使其中一些天体以流星的形式坠落到地球，并在撞击时造成广泛的破坏。

14）The fact that some societies domesticated animals and plants，discovered the use of metal tools，became literate，and developed a state should not make us forget that others developed pastoralism or horticulture（vegetable gardening）but remained illiterate and at low levels of productivity.

难句分析

<u>The fact</u>（that some societies domesticated animals and plants，discovered the use of metal tools，became literate，and developed a state）<u>should not make us forget</u>［that others developed pastoralism or horticulture（vegetable gardening）but remained illiterate and at low levels of productivity］.

修饰关系分析：第一个 that 从句修饰 fact；第二个 that 从句是宾语从句，按顺序直译即可；多项并列时，and 总是在最后一项的前面，and developed 的并列关系如上高亮部分所显示。

翻译：一些社会驯养动物和植物，发现并使用金属工具，变得有文化，并发展了国家，这一事实不应使我们忘记，其他社会发展了畜牧业或园艺（蔬菜园艺），但仍然不识字且生产力水平低下。

15）Changes in lake level not explained by river flows plus exchanges with the atmosphere must be due to the net difference between what seeps into the lake from the groundwater and what leaks into the groundwater.

修饰关系分析：

<u>Changes</u> in lake level/not explained by river flows plus exchanges with the atmosphere/<u>must be due to the net difference</u> between（what seeps into the lake from the groundwater）and（what leaks into the groundwater）.

修饰关系分析：in the lake 及 not explained by...均修饰 changes；两个 what 从句是 between A and B 中的两个并列项，直译即可；这里的 what = something that，无具体意义。

翻译：湖泊水位不能用河流流量加上与大气的交换来解释的变化一定是由于地下水渗入湖泊和(湖泊)漏入地下水之间的净差异造成的。

16）The frequency with which certain simple motifs appear in these oldest sites has led rock-art researchers to adopt a descriptive term.

难句分析

The frequency（with which certain simple motifs appear in these oldest sites）has led rock-art researchers to adopt a descriptive term.

修饰关系分析：with which 从句修饰 frequency

翻译：某些简单的图案出现在这些最古老的遗址中的频率使得岩画研究人员采用了一个描述性的术语。

17）Learning appropriate social behaviors is especially important for species that live in groups，like young monkeys that needed to learn to control selfishness and aggression and to understand the give-and-take involved in social groups.

难句分析

Learning appropriate social behaviors is especially important/for species（that live in groups），like young monkeys（that needed to learn to control selfishness and aggression and to understand the give-and-take/involved in social groups）.

修饰关系分析：两个 that 从句分别修饰 species 和 monkeys，involved...修饰 the give-and-take；并列关系见高亮部分。

翻译：学习适当的社会行为对于群居的物种尤其重要,比如幼猴,这些猴子需要学习控制自私和攻击性以及理解社会群体中的给予和索取。

18）The growth of the electric-power industry was the result of a remarkable series of scientific discoveries and developments in electro-technology during the nineteenth century，but significant changes in what we might now call hydro（water）technology also played their part.

难句分析

The growth/of the electric-power industry/was the result of a remarkable series of scientific discoveries and developments/in electro-technology/during the nineteenth century/，but significant changes/in what we might now call hydro（water）technology）/also played their part.

修饰关系分析：of the electric-power industry 修饰 growth；in electro-technology 和 during the nineteenth century 修饰 discoveries and developments；in what we might now call hydro（water）technology 修饰 changes,其中 what 引导的从句是介词 in 的宾语,整体是个介词短语,不表示疑问的 what 无具体含义,这里也是如此。

翻译：电力工业的发展是19世纪电气技术一系列重大科学发现和发展的结果,但我们现在称之为水力(水)技术的重大变化也发挥了作用。

19) But detractors maintain that the terraces could also have been created by geological activity, perhaps related to the geologic forces that depressed the Northern Hemisphere far below the level of the south, in which case they have nothing whatever to do with Martian water.

难句分析

But detractors maintain （that the terraces could also have been created by geological activity,/perhaps related to the geologic forces）（that depressed the Northern Hemisphere far below the level of the south）,（in which case they have nothing whatever to do with Martian water）.

修饰关系分析：第一个 that 是宾语从句,按顺序直译即可;第二个 that 从句修饰 forces; in which 从句修饰 that 引导的宾语从句整句; perhaps related to the geologic forces 修饰 geological activity。

翻译：但批评者坚持认为,这些梯田也可能是由地质活动造成的,这些地质活动可能与将北半球压得远远低于南半球的地质力有关,在这种情况下,它们与火星水没有任何关系。

20) It is significant that the earliest living things that built communities on these islands are examples of symbiosis, a phenomenon that depends upon the close cooperation of two or more forms of life and a principle that is very important in island communities.

难句分析

It is significant （that the earliest living things （that built communities on these islands） are examples of symbiosis）, a phenomenon （that depends upon the close cooperation of two or more forms of life） and a principle （that is very important in island communities）.

修饰关系分析：第一个 that 从句是主语从句,it 是形式主语,指代后面 that 从句所引导的真正的主语;后面三个 that 分别修饰 living things、phenomenon 及 principle; phenomenon 和 principle 是同位语,用来解释说明 symbiosis。

翻译：重要的是,在这些岛屿上建立社区的最早生物是共生的例子;共生是取决于两种以上生命形式的密切合作的现象,也是在岛屿社区中非常重要的原则。

21) Though it may be difficult to imagine from a later perspective, a strain of critical opinion in the 1920s predicted that sound film would be a technical novelty that would soon fade from sight, just as had many previous attempts, dating well back

before the First World War, to link images with recorded sound.

难句分析

(Though it may be difficult to imagine from a later perspective), <u>a strain of critical opinion</u> in the 1920s <u>predicted</u> (that sound film would be a technical novelty) (that would soon fade from sight), (just as had many previous attempts, dating well back before the First World War, to link images with recorded sound).

修饰关系分析: though 引导让步状语从句;第一个 that 是宾语从句,直译即可;第二个 that 引导定语从句修饰 novelty;just as 引导方式状语从句,直译即可;dating well... 与 to link... 均修饰 attempts。

翻译: 虽然从后来的角度来看可能很难想象,但 20 世纪 20 年代的一种批判观点预测,有声电影将是一种很快就会从人们的视线中消失的技术创新,就像第一次世界大战前许多人试图将图像与录音联系起来一样。

22) Indeed, stability of the biological clock's period is one of its major features, even when the organism's environment is subjected to considerable changes in factors, such as temperature, that would be expected to affect biological activity strongly.

难句分析

Indeed, <u>stability</u> of the biological clock's period <u>is one of its major features</u>, (even when the organism's environment is subjected to considerable changes in factors, such as temperature,) (that would be expected to affect biological activity strongly).

修饰关系分析: of the biological clock's period 修饰 stability;when 引导的是状语从句,顺译即可;that 引导定语从句,修饰 factors(that 从句不可能修饰 temperature,因为 that 引导定语从句与修饰词之间不能有逗号,这里的 such as temperature 是一个插入成分,可忽略)。

翻译: 事实上,生物钟周期的稳定性是其主要特征之一,即使当生物体的环境受到诸如温度等因素的显著变化时,这些因素预计会强烈影响生物活动。

23) As among tribes people, personal relationships and a careful weighing of character have always been crucial in a mercantile economy with little regulation, where one's word is one's bond and where informal ties of trust cement together an international trade network.

难句分析

As among tribes people, <u>personal relationships and a careful weighing of character have always been crucial</u>/in a mercantile economy/with little regulation, (where one's word is one's bond) and (where informal ties of trust cement together an international trade network).

修饰关系分析：in a mercantile economy 是状语，顺译即可；with little regulation 修饰 economy；两个并列的 where 从句均修饰 economy。

翻译：在一个几乎没有监管的商业经济中，个人关系和谨慎的品格权衡一直是至关重要的，在这个经济体中，一个人的言行是一个人的纽带，非正式的信任关系巩固了一个国际贸易网络。

24）Ramsay then studied a gas that was present in natural gas deposits and discovered that it was helium，an element whose presence in the Sun had been noted earlier in the spectrum of sunlight but that had not previously been known on Earth.

难句分析

Ramsay then studied a gas（that 1 was present in natural gas deposits）and discovered［that 2 it was helium，an element（whose presence in the Sun had been noted earlier in the spectrum of sunlight）but（that 3 had not previously been known on Earth）］.

修饰关系分析：that 1 引导定语从句，修饰 gas；that 2 是宾语从句，顺译即可；whose 和 that 3 的从句是定语从句，修饰 element；an element 是同位语，解释说明 helium。

翻译：拉姆塞随后研究了在天然气矿床中存在的一种气体，发现它是氦，这种元素在太阳光光谱中的存在早就被发现了，但此前在地球上并不为人所知。

25）When broken open，Allende stones are revealed to contain an assortment of small，distinctive objects，spherical or irregular in shape and embedded in a dark gray binding material，which were once constituents of the solar nebula—the interstellar cloud of gas and dust out of which our solar system was formed.

难句分析

（When broken open），Allende stones are revealed to contain an assortment of small，distinctive objects，spherical or irregular in shape／and embedded in a dark gray binding material，（which were once constituents of the solar nebula）—the interstellar cloud of gas and dust（out of which our solar system was formed）.

修饰关系分析：when 引导被省略的状语从句；spherical or irregular in shape 和 embedded in a dark gray binding material 修饰 objects；which 修饰 objects（which 从句的谓语是复数，所以不可能修饰 material）；破折号后面的内容解释说明 solar nebula；out of which 从句修饰 cloud。

翻译：打开阿连德石后，发现里面含有各种各样的小而独特的物体，这些物体是球形或不规则形状的，并嵌入深灰色的结合材料中，这些物体曾经是太阳星云的组成部分——太阳系星云是形成我们太阳系的星际气体和尘埃云。

26）From a plant's evolutionary view point，however，it was also a land of opportunity, free of competitors and predator, and full of carbon dioxide and sunlight (the raw materials for photosynthesis, which are present in far higher concentrations in air than in water).

难句分析

From a plant's evolutionary view point, however, it was also a land of opportunity, free of competitors and predator/and full of carbon dioxide and sunlight (the raw materials for photosynthesis, which are present in far higher concentrations in air than in water).

修饰关系分析: free of competitors and predator 以及 full of carbon dioxide and sunlight 均修饰 land;括号里的内容解释说明 carbon dioxide 和 sunlight。

翻译: 然而,从植物进化的角度来看,它也是一片充满机遇的土地,没有竞争者和掠食者,充满了二氧化碳和阳光(光合作用的原材料,空气中的浓度远远高于水中的浓度)。

27) This was a small cylinder, usually no more than 3 centimeters high and 2 centimeters in diameter, of shell, bone or various types of stones, on which a scene was carved into the surface.

难句分析

This was a small cylinder, usually no more than 3 centimeters high/and 2 centimeters in diameter,/of shell, bone or various types of stones, (on which a scene was carved into the surface).

修饰关系分析: 本句中所有的短语和从句均是修饰 a small cylinder。

翻译: 这是一个小圆柱体,通常不超过3厘米高,直径2厘米,由贝壳、骨头或各种类型的石头制成,上面雕刻着一个场景。

28) A glance at a map of the Pacific Ocean reveals that there are many islands far out at sea that are actually volcanoes—many no longer active, some overgrown with coral—that originated from activity at points in the interior of the Pacific Plate that forms the Pacific seafloor.

难句分析

A glance at a map of the Pacific Ocean reveals (that 1 there are many islands far out at sea) (that 2 are actually volcanoes)—many no longer active, some overgrown with coral—(that 3 originated from activity at points in the interior of the Pacific Plate) (that 4 forms the Pacific seafloor).

修饰关系分析: that 1 是宾语从句,顺译即可;that 2 是定语从句,修饰 islands; that 3 是定语从句,修饰 volcanoes;that 4 修饰 the Pacific Plate;破折号中的内容解释说明 volcanoes。

翻译：只要看一眼太平洋的地图,就会发现在遥远的海面上有许多实际上是火山的岛屿——这些火山有些已经不活跃了,有些长满了珊瑚——这些火山源于形成太平洋海底的太平洋板块的内部活动点。

29) Only the last of these was suited at all to the continuous operating of machines, and although waterpower abounded in Lancashire and Scotland and ran grain mills as well as textile mills, it had one great disadvantage: streams flowed where nature intended them to, and water-driven factories had to be located on their banks whether or not the location was desirable for other reasons.

难句分析

Only the last of these was suited at all to the continuous operating of machines, and (although waterpower abounded in Lancashire and Scotland and ran grain mills as well as textile mills), it had one great disadvantage: streams flowed (where nature intended them to), and water-driven factories had to be located on their banks (whether or not the location was desirable for other reasons).

修饰关系分析：although 引导让步状语从句,顺译即可;where 引导地点状语从句,顺译即可;whether 引导让步状语从句,顺译即可;冒号后面的内容解释说明 disadvantage;at all 是"完全"的意思。

翻译：只有最后一种才适合机器的连续运转,尽管兰开夏郡和苏格兰有丰富的水力资源,并经营着谷物加工厂和纺织厂,但它有一个很大的缺点:溪流在大自然所希望的地方流动,水力驱动的工厂必须建在河岸上,不管这个位置出于其他原因是否合适。

30) Glaciers move slowly across the land with tremendous energy, carving into even the hardest rock formations and thereby reshaping the landscape as they engulf, push, drag, and finally deposit rock debris in places far from its original location.

难句分析

Glaciers move slowly across the land/with tremendous energy, carving into even the hardest rock formations/and thereby reshaping the landscape (as they engulf, push, drag, and finally deposit rock debris in places/far from its original location).

修饰关系分析：with tremendous energy 是状语,顺译即可;carving 和 reshaping 的逻辑主语都是 glacier;as 引导状语从句,顺译即可;far from its original location 修饰 places。

翻译：冰川以巨大的能量缓慢地在陆地上移动,甚至雕刻成最坚硬的岩层,因此当它们吞没、推动、拖曳,最后在远离其原始位置的地方沉积岩屑时,就会重塑地貌。

31) While population estimates are notoriously unreliable, scholars assume that Uruk inhabitants were able to support themselves from the agricultural production of

the field surrounding the city, which could be reached with a daily commute.

难句分析

（While population estimates are notoriously unreliable）, <u>scholars assume</u>（that Uruk inhabitants were able to support themselves from the agricultural production/of the field/surrounding the city）,（which could be reached with a daily commute）.

修饰关系分析: while 引导状语从句, 顺译即可; that 引导宾语从句, 顺译即可; of the field 修饰 production; surrounding the city 修饰 the field; which 引导定语从句, 修饰 field(定语从句不修饰最近的 city 是因为逻辑不符)。

翻译: 虽然人口估量是出了名的不可靠, 但学者们认为乌鲁克居民能够靠城市周围农田的农业生产养活自己, 这些农田可以通过每天的通勤达到。

32）The West had plenty of attractions: the alluvial river bottoms, the fecund soils of the rolling forest lands, and the black loams of the prairies were tempting to New England farmers working their rocky, sterile land and to southeastern farmers plagued with soil depletion and erosion.

难句分析

<u>The West had plenty of attractions</u>: <u>the alluvial river bottoms, the fecund soils/</u> of the rolling forest lands, <u>and the black loams/</u> of the prairies <u>were tempting to New England farmers/</u>working their rocky, sterile land <u>and to southeastern farmers/</u>plagued with soil depletion and erosion.

修饰关系分析: 冒号后面具体解释了 attractions; of the rolling forest lands 修饰 soil; of the prairies 修饰 loams（壤土）; working their rocky, sterile land 修饰 New England farmers; plagued with soil depletion and erosion 修饰 southeastern farmers。

翻译: 西部有很多吸引人的地方: 冲积的河底, 起伏的林地和肥沃的土壤, 以及大草原的黑壤土, 吸引着在多岩石、贫瘠的土地上耕作的新英格兰农民, 也吸引着东南部饱受土壤枯竭和侵蚀之苦的农民。

33）At one time, the animals present in these fossil beds were assigned to various modern animal groups, but most paleontologists now agree that all Tommotian fossils represent unique body forms that arose in the early Cambrian period and disappeared before the end of the period, leaving no descendants in modern animal groups.

难句分析

At one time, <u>the animals/</u>present in these fossil beds/<u>were assigned to various modern animal groups</u>, <u>but most paleontologists now agree</u>（that 1 all Tommotian fossils represent unique body forms）（that 2 arose in the early Cambrian period and disappeared before the end of the period, leaving no descendants in modern animal groups）.

修饰关系分析：present in these fossil beds 修饰 animals；that 1 从句是宾语从句，顺译；that 2 是定语从句，修饰 body forms，翻译时可提前也可另起一句；leaving 的逻辑主语是代指 body forms 的连词 that 2。

翻译：曾经，这些化石层中存在的动物被划分为不同的现代动物群，但现在大多数古生物学家都同意，所有托英特阶化石都代表着独特的身体形态，这些形态出现在寒武纪早期，并在该时期结束前消失，在现代动物群中没有留下后代。

34）Once established，a stand of Spartina begins to trap sediment，changing the substrate elevation，and eventually the stand evolves into a high marsh system where Spartina is gradually displaced by higher-elevation，brackish-water species.

难句分析

（Once established），a stand of Spartina begins to trap sediment，changing the substrate elevation，and eventually the stand evolves into a high marsh system （where Spartina is gradually displaced by higher-elevation，brackish-water species）.

修饰关系分析：once 引导省略的时间状语从句，顺译；changing 的逻辑主语是 Spartina；where 引导定语从句，修饰 system。

翻译：一旦建立起来，一丛米草开始捕获沉积物，改变基层的高度，最终这丛米草演变成一个高沼泽系统，在那里米草逐渐被海拔较高的微咸水物种取代。

35）Many plants and animals disappear abruptly from the fossil record as one moves from layers of rock documenting the end of the Cretaceous up into rocks representing the beginning of the Cenozoic.

难句分析

Many plants and animals disappear/abruptly from the fossil record （as one moves from layers of rock/documenting the end of the Cretaceous up into rocks/representing the beginning of the Cenozoic）.

修饰关系分析：as 引导时间状语从句，顺译即可；from...（in）to 的固定搭配意识要有；documenting...修饰 layers of rock；representing...修饰 rocks；one 在句中如果没有具体的指代关系的话，泛指"人们"。

翻译：当人们从记录白垩纪末的岩层向上移动到代表新生代开始的岩石中时，许多植物和动物突然从化石记录中消失。

36）Fladmark's hypothesis received additional support from the fact that the greatest diversity in native American languages occurs along the west coast of the Americas，suggesting that this region has been settled the longest.

难句分析

Fladmark's hypothesis received additional support/from the fact〔that 1 the greatest diversity in native American languages occurs along the west coast of the Americas，suggesting（that 2 this region has been settled the longest）].

修饰关系分析：that 从句修饰 the fact，可提前也可另起一句；that 2 是宾语从句，顺译即可。

翻译：弗拉德马克的假设从这个事实中得到了更多的支持：美洲土著语言的最大多样性发生在美洲西海岸，这表明人们在这个地区的定居时间最长。

37）The myths that have grown up around the rites may continue as part of the group's oral tradition and may even come to be acted out under conditions divorced from these rites.

难句分析

The myths（that have grown up around the rites）may continue/as part of the group's oral tradition/and may even come to be acted out/ under conditions/divorced from these rites.

修饰关系分析：that 是定语从句，修饰 myths；as part of the group's oral tradition 和 under conditions 是状语，顺译即可；divorced from these rites 修饰 conditions。

翻译：围绕着这些仪式发展起来的神话可能会继续作为该团体口头传统的一部分，甚至可能在脱离这些仪式的条件下被表演出来。

38）When rolled over a soft material—primarily the clay of seals，tablets，or clay lumps attached to boxes，jars，or door bolts—the scene would appear in relief，easily legible.

难句分析

（When rolled over a soft material）—primarily the clay of seals，tablets，or clay lumps attached to boxes，jars，or door bolts—the scene would appear in relief，easily legible.

修饰关系分析：when 连接省略的状语从句；破折号里的内容解释说明 soft material；in relief 是状语，relief 直译为浮雕；easily legible 修饰 scene。

翻译：当在软质材料上滚动时（主要是黏土印章、石碑或黏在盒子、罐子或门闩上的黏土块），场景会以浮雕形式出现，很容易辨认。

39）Will the job disruptions caused by technology be temporary as the workforce adapts，or will we see a science-fiction scenario in which automated processes and robots with superhuman skills take over a broad swath of human tasks?

难句分析

Will the job disruptions/ caused by technology/be temporary（as the workforce adapts），or will we see a science-fiction scenario（in which automated processes and robots with superhuman skills take over a broad swath of human tasks)？

修饰关系分析：caused by...过去分词短语,修饰 disruption；as 引导状语从句,顺译即可；in which 引导定语从句,修饰 scenario；一般疑问句或特殊疑问句的主干也要能快速识别出来,如果觉得有难度,可以还原语序。

翻译：随着劳动力的适应,技术造成的工作扰乱是暂时的呢？还是我们会看到一个科幻小说的场景呢？在这个场景中,拥有超人技能和自动化流程的机器人将接管大量的人类任务。

40）With a fuller understanding of signaling and communication within and among plants，it becomes clear that these sensitive biological organisms actively and competitively forage for limited resources，both above and below ground.

难句分析

With a fuller understanding of signaling and communication/within and among plants，<u>it becomes clear</u>（that these sensitive biological organisms actively and competitively forage for limited resources，both above and below ground.）

修饰关系分析：within and among plants 是个省略结构,还原后应该是 within plants and among plants,修饰 signaling and communication；that 从句是主语从句,it 是形式主语。

翻译：随着对植物内部和植物之间的信号和通信的更全面了解,愈发明显的是这些敏感的生物有机体在地上和地下积极地、竞争性地寻找有限的资源。

41）Atmospheric oxygen，it shows，has fluctuated several times throughout history，rising to 25 percent between 250‑300 million years ago，up from 21 percent today and more than double the estimated 10 percent of the Cambrian explosion.

难句分析

<u>Atmospheric oxygen</u>，it shows，<u>has fluctuated several times throughout history</u>，rising to 25 percent/between 250‑300 million years ago，up from 21 percent today/and more than double the estimated 10 percent of the Cambrian explosion.

修饰关系分析：it shows 是插入成分；rising to...的逻辑主语是 Atmospheric oxygen；up from...以及 more than...两个短语修饰 rising to 25 percent。

翻译：报告显示,大气中的氧气在历史上多次波动,从今天的 21% 上升到 2.5 亿至 3 亿年前的 25%,并且是寒武纪爆炸估计值 10% 的两倍多。

42）The proto-Indo-European language must have split into its daughter languages sometime after this date，the argument goes，since how else could the daughter languages，spoken over an enormous region，all have cognate words for wheel?

难句分析

The proto-Indo-European language must have split into its daughter languages sometime after this date，the argument goes，（since how else could the daughter languages，spoken over an enormous region，all have cognate words for wheel?）

修饰关系分析：the argument goes 是插入成分；since 是原因状语，顺译即可；spoken over...修饰 the daughter languages。

翻译：这个论点认为，印欧语系的原始语言一定是在这个时期之后的某个时候分裂成了它的子语言，因为在一个巨大的区域内使用的子语言怎么会都有表示轮子的同源词呢?

43）After Obama's victory in November 2008，this same voter might look back，see the victory as more predictable than it was before the outcome was known，and conclude that Obama's chances were at least 80% at the time of the convention.

难句分析

After Obama's victory in November 2008，this same voter might look back，see the victory as more predictable（than it was）（before the outcome was known），and conclude（that Obama's chances were at least 80% at the time of the convention）.

修饰关系分析：than 引导比较状语从句，before 引导时间状语从句，that 引导宾语从句，均顺译即可。

翻译：在奥巴马2008年11月的胜利之后，同样的选民可能会回顾过去，认为这场胜利比结果公布前更可预测，并得出结论：奥巴马在大会召开时获胜的机会至少为80%。

44）Conventional agriculture makes use of 171 million metric tons of synthetic fertilizer each year，and all that nitrogen enables much faster plant growth than the slower release of nitrogen from the compost or cover crops used in organic farming.

难句分析

Conventional agriculture makes use of 171 million metric tons of synthetic fertilizer each year，and all that nitrogen enables much faster plant growth/than the slower release of nitrogen/from the compost or cover crops/used in organic farming.

修饰关系分析：than...是比较状语，顺译即可；from the compost or cover crops 修饰 release；used in organic farming 修饰 nitrogen。

翻译：传统农业每年使用1.71亿公吨的合成肥料，所有这些氮使得植物生长速度更快，比有机农业中使用的堆肥或覆盖作物缓慢释放的氮要快。

45）What we need to find out is how their information is gathered and processed，what routes do data take，and how are adaptive responses integrated and coordinated，how are these events "remembered" in order to allow realistic predictions of future using past experiences.

难句分析

（What we need to find out）is（how their information is gathered and processed），

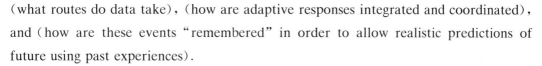

(what routes do data take)，（how are adaptive responses integrated and coordinated），and（how are these events "remembered" in order to allow realistic predictions of future using past experiences）.

修饰关系分析：做主干的从句并列，顺译即可。

翻译：我们需要弄清楚的是,他们的信息是如何收集和处理的,数据采取什么途径,适应性反应是如何整合和协调的,以及这些事件是如何被"记住"的,以便利用过去的经验对未来做出现实的预测。

46）The mtDNA showed genetic markers previously identified as having deep roots in ancient European hunter-gatherer populations，but the Y chromosomes showed the closest affinities to Europeans currently living along the Mediterranean regions of southern Europe，such as Turkey，Cyprus，Portugal，and Italy.

难句分析

The mtDNA showed genetic markers/previously identified as having deep roots in ancient European hunter-gatherer populations，but the Y chromosomes showed the closest affinities to Europeans/currently living along the Mediterranean regions of southern Europe，such as Turkey，Cyprus，Portugal，and Italy.

修饰关系分析：过去分词短语 previously identified as...修饰 genetic markers;现在分词短语 currently living...修饰 Europeans.

翻译：mtDNA 显示了之前被鉴定为与古代欧洲狩猎-采集群体有着很深根源的遗传标记,但 Y 染色体显示出与目前生活在南欧地中海地区(如土耳其、塞浦路斯、葡萄牙和意大利)的欧洲人最接近的亲缘关系。

47）Other studies of guppies in Trinidad have shown evolutionary change in as few as two and a half years，or a little over four generations，with more time required for genetic shifts in traits such as the ability to form schools and less time for changes in the colorful spots and stripes on a male's body.

难句分析

Other studies of guppies in Trinidad have shown evolutionary change/ in as few as two and a half years，or a little over four generations，with more time required for genetic shifts/in traits such as the ability to form schools/and less time for changes/in the colorful spots and stripes on a male's body.

修饰关系分析：in as few as...和 with more time required for genetic shifts...and less time for changes...是状语,顺译即可;in traits such as the ability to form schools 修饰 genetic shifts; in the colorful spots and stripes on a male's body 修饰 changes.

翻译：对特立尼达孔雀鱼的其他研究显示了孔雀鱼在短短两年半的或者说四代多一

点的时间里的进化变化,如形成鱼群能力特征的基因转变需要更多的时间,而雄性孔雀鱼身上彩色的斑点和条纹的变化需要更少的时间。

48) Using these approaches, the researchers could estimate the dates at which the rocks cooled to temperatures between 250℃ and 70℃ , and therefore track the speed at which the rocks rose toward ground level as the overlying strata eroded away.

Using these approaches, the researchers could estimate the dates (at which the rocks cooled to temperatures between 250℃ and 70℃), and therefore track the speed (at which the rocks rose toward ground level) (as the overlying strata eroded away).

修饰关系分析: at which 引导的定语从句分别修饰 the dates 和 the speed;as 引导的从句修饰第二个 at which 的从句。

翻译: 利用这些方法,研究人员可以估计出岩石冷却到 250℃ 至 70℃ 之间的时期,从而跟踪随着上覆地层的侵蚀,岩石上升到地面的速度。

49) Gestural theories on the origin of language contend that spoken language evolved from hand gestures, and cite the fact that non-human primates exclusively use gestures for true communication, merely making vocalizations based on engrained instinct, rather than calculated intention.

难句分析:

Gestural theories on the origin of language contend (that spoken language evolved from hand gestures), and cite the fact (that non-human primates exclusively use gestures for true communication, merely making vocalizations based on engrained instinct, rather than calculated intention.)

修饰关系分析: 第一个 that 从句是宾语从句;第二个 that 从句修饰 the fact;making vocalizations...的逻辑主语是 non-human primates。

翻译: 关于语言起源的手势理论认为,口语是从手势演变而来的,并引用了这样一个事实,即非人类灵长类动物专门使用手势进行真正的交流,仅仅是根据内在的本能发出声音,而不是有计划的意图。

第 六 章

句子层次

长难句的语法分析并不是我们最终要得到的结果,它只是一个过程。语法分析本身是非常耗时的,如果每个句子都进行这样分析的话,无疑会严重影响我们的阅读速度。在有了前面语法分析的基础之后,我们最终需要达到的成果是快速抓住句子的重点信息。尤其是我们需要快速阅读时,最重要的不是吸收句子中所有的信息,而是快速抓住主要信息。

一 句子层次分析

想要快速抓住句子的重点信息,我们需要在长难句语法分析的基础上发展出句子的层次意识。关于句子的层次,我们还是继续用树的结构来类比一个句子。一棵大树,除了树根和树干之外,还有树杈、树枝和树叶。而且越大的树,它的结构就越复杂,每个长在树干上的树杈可能会继续延伸出很多新的树杈,如下图:

同样,句子内部的结构也是如此:

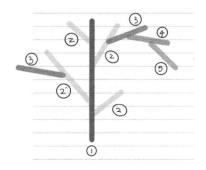

层次①是主句主干部分

修饰层次①的从句或短语属于层次②

修饰层次②的从句或短语属于层次③

依次类推……

可以看出,数字越小的层次越重要,一般来讲最终要的信息都在①②层,越往后层次的信息相对就没那么重要,所以快速阅读时,重点应该放在①层或①②层。

为了更好地体现层次关系,下面我们就通过字体来体现,例如:

The best we can do **is to put the origin of eyes somewhere between the beginning of the Cambrian explosion**,about 600 million years ago,**and the death of the Burgess animals**,some 530 million years ago.

 示例分析

接下来通过更多的示例与解析来提高我们对于核心信息的敏感度。

1) This material gradually coalesced into lumps called planetesimals as gravity and chance smashed smaller pieces together,a chaotic and violent process that became more so as planetesimals grew in size and gravitational pull.

This material gradually coalesced into lumps called planetesimals **as gravity and chance smashed smaller pieces together**,a chaotic and violent process that became more so as planetesimals grew in size and gravitational pull.

翻译:随着引力和偶然性将更小的碎片碰撞在一起,这种物质逐渐凝聚成称为星子的**团块**,这是一个混乱而剧烈的过程,随着星子的尺寸和引力的增大,这种过程变得更加混乱和剧烈。

2) Lighter elements from Earth's interior rose and formed the mantle,a denser layer of silicates around the core,and the crust,a thinner layer of silicates at Earth's surface.

Lighter elements from Earth's interior **rose and formed the mantle**,a denser layer of silicates around the core，**and the crust**，a thinner layer of silicates at Earth's surface.

翻译: 来自地球内部的**较轻元素上升并形成地幔**(地幔是围绕地核的一层较致密的硅酸盐)**和地壳**(地壳是地球表面较薄的一层硅酸盐)。

3）These developments were often so extensive and so interconnected with each other that they effectively fixed the layout of cities well into the eighteenth，and even into the nineteenth century，when walls or open spaces eventually made way for urban redevelopment in the form of parks，railway lines，or beltways.

These developments were often **so extensive and so interconnected** with each other **that they effectively fixed the layout of cities** well into the eighteenth，and even into the nineteenth century，when walls or open spaces eventually made way for urban redevelopment in the form of parks，railway lines，or beltways.

翻译: 这些发展往往**是如此广泛且相互联系以至于它们有效地固定了城市的布局**，直到 18 世纪甚至是 19 世纪，墙壁或开放空间最终以公园、铁路线或环城公路的形式为城市重建让路。

4）It was suggested that Aegean people had visited Iberia in southwestern Europe in search of metal ores and had introduced the idea of collective burial in massive tombs，which then spread northward to Brittany，Britain，North Germany，and Scandinavia.

It was suggested that Aegean people had visited Iberia in southwestern Europe in search of metal ores **and had introduced the idea of collective burial** in massive tombs，which then spread northward to Brittany，Britain，North Germany，and Scandinavia.

翻译: 有人认为，**爱琴海人曾到**欧洲西南部的**伊比利亚寻找金属矿，并引进了集体埋葬在巨大坟墓中的观念**，这个观念向北蔓延到布列塔尼、英国、德国北部和斯堪的纳维亚半岛。

5）Their adoption of agriculture through contact with Neolithic farmers，Renfrew argues，led to a population explosion in the region and consequent competition for farmland between neighboring groups.

Their adoption of agriculture through contact with Neolithic farmers，Renfrew argues，**led to a population explosion** in the region **and consequent competition for farmland** between neighboring groups.

翻译: 伦弗鲁认为，**他们**通过与新石器时代农民的接触而**采用农业，导致**该地区的**人口爆炸，并导致**相邻群体之间**对农田的争夺**。

6）He found that a division of the arable land into territories，each containing one megalith，results in units that correspond in size to the individual farming communities of recent times in the same area.

He found that a division of the arable land into territories, each containing one megalith, results in units that correspond in size to the individual farming communities of recent times in the same area.

翻译: 他发现,将可耕地划分为若干块区域,每一块区域内有一块巨石,导致其大小与同一地区最近的**单个的农业社区**相对应。

7) Gliding has generally been viewed as either a means of escaping predators, by allowing animals to move between trees without descending to the ground, or as an energetically efficient way of traveling long distances between scattered resources.

Gliding has generally been viewed as either a means of escaping predators, by allowing animals to move between trees without descending to the ground, **or as an energetically efficient way of traveling long distances** between scattered resources.

翻译: 滑翔通常被视为一种逃避捕食者的手段,通过允许动物在树木之间移动而不下降到地面,或者作为一种高效的方式在分散的资源之间**长途旅行**。

8) The 1930s that threatened to turn the United States Great Plains into a vast desert was a traumatic experience that led to revolutionary changes in American agricultural practices, such as the planting of tree shelter belts, rows of trees planted beside fields to slow wind and thus reduce wind erosion.

The 1930s that threatened to turn the United States Great Plains into a vast desert **was a traumatic experience that led to revolutionary changes in American agricultural practices,** such as the planting of tree shelter belts, rows of trees planted beside fields to slow wind and thus reduce wind erosion.

翻译: 美国大平原有可能变成一片广袤的沙漠的**20 世纪 30 年代是一次痛苦的经历,这导致美国农业实践发生了革命性的变化**,比如种植防护林带,在田地旁种植成排的树木以减缓风速从而减少风蚀。

9) In the United States, where farmers during the 1990s were required to implement a soil-conservation plan on erodible cropland to be eligible for crop price supports, the no-till area went from 7 million hectares in 1990 to nearly 21 million hectares (51 million acres) in 2000, tripling within a decade.

In the United States, where farmers during the 1990s were required to implement a soil-conservation plan on erodible cropland to be eligible for crop price supports, **the no-till area went from 7 million hectares** in 1990 **to nearly 21 million hectares** (51 million acres) in 2000, tripling within a decade.

翻译: 在 20 世纪 90 年代的,美国农民被要求对易受侵蚀的农田实施水土保持计划,以获得作物价格支持,**免耕面积从** 1990 年的 **700 万公顷增加到** 2000 年的近 **2 100 万公顷**(5 100 万英亩),十年内翻了三倍。

10）The retirement of 35 million acres under the CRP，together with the adoption of conservation practices on 37 percent of all cropland，reduced soil erosion in the United States from 3.1 billion tons in 1982 to 1.9 billion tons in 1997.

The retirement of 35 million acres under the CRP，together with the adoption of conservation practices on 37 percent of all cropland，**reduced soil erosion** in the United States from 3.1 billion tons in 1982 to 1.9 billion tons in 1997.

翻译：在 CRP 计划下，3 500 万英亩**土地的退耕**，加上对 37%的农田采取保护措施，**使美国的水土流失量**从 1982 年的 31 亿吨**减少**到 1997 年的 19 亿吨。

11）The state adopted boundaries to urban growth twenty years ago，requiring each community to project its growth needs for the next two decades and then，based on the results，draw an outer boundary that would accommodate that growth.

The state adopted boundaries to urban growth twenty years ago，**requiring each community to project its growth needs** for the next two decades **and** then，based on the results，**draw an outer boundary** that would accommodate that growth.

翻译：20 年前，**该州对城市增长采用了边界法**，要求每个社区预测未来 20 年的**增长需求**，然后根据结果，**划定一个**能够适应这种增长的**外部边界**。

12）There are several limiting factors，but results from a recent experiment suggest that in areas of the ocean where other nutrients are plentiful，iron may be one of the most important and unrecognized variables controlling phytoplankton production.

There are several limiting factors，but results from a recent experiment **suggest that** in areas of the ocean where other nutrients are plentiful，**iron may be one of the most important and unrecognized variables** controlling phytoplankton production.

翻译：有几个限制因素，但最近一项实验的**结果表明**，在其他营养物质丰富的海洋区域，**铁可能是**控制浮游植物生产**最重要的和未被认识的变量之一**。

13）Physical characteristics of aquatic environments at different depths such as salt level，light，inorganic nutrients，degree of acidity，and pressure all play key roles in the distribution of organisms.

Physical characteristics of aquatic environments at different depths such as salt level，light，inorganic nutrients，degree of acidity，and pressure **all play key roles** in the distribution of organisms.

翻译：不同深度水环境的**物理特征**，如盐分、光照、无机营养物、酸度和压力等，都对生物的分布**起着关键作用**。

14）First，it means that photosynthesis，the process by which plants use the energy of sunlight to produce the organic carbon compounds necessary for life，can only occur in surface waters where the light intensity is sufficiently high.

First，**it means that photosynthesis**，the process by which plants use the energy of sunlight to produce the organic carbon compounds necessary for life，**can only occur in surface waters** where the light intensity is sufficiently high.

翻译： 首先，**这意味着光合作用**，即植物利用阳光的能量产生生命所需的有机碳化合物的过程，**只能发生在**光照强度足够高的**地表水中**。

15）Tropical lakes and oceans show pronounced permanent stratification of their physical properties，with warm，well-oxygenated，and lighted surface water giving way to frigid，dark，deep water almost devoid of oxygen.

Tropical lakes and oceans show pronounced permanent stratification of their physical properties，**with** warm，well-oxygenated，and lighted **surface water giving way to** frigid，dark，**deep water** almost devoid of oxygen.

翻译：热带湖泊和海洋表现出物理性质的**明显的永久分层**，温暖、氧气充分、明亮的**表层水让位于**寒冷、黑暗、几乎没有氧气的**深水**。

16）Distinguished film stars，particularly those with theater backgrounds（as most have），routinely return to the live dramatic stage despite the substantially greater financial rewards of film work and invariably prefer stage acting because of the immediate audience response theater provides，with its corresponding sensations of excitement and presence.

Distinguished film stars，particularly those with theater backgrounds（as most have），**routinely return to the live dramatic stage** despite the substantially greater financial rewards of film work **and invariably prefer stage acting** because of the immediate audience response theater provides，with its corresponding sensations of excitement and presence.

翻译：杰出的影星，尤其是那些有戏剧表演背景的影星（大多数影星都是这样），尽管电影工作的经济回报大大增加，但**他们通常还是会重返现场戏剧舞台，而且总是更喜欢舞台表演**，因为剧院能为观众提供即时的反应，伴随着相应的兴奋感和存在感。

17）As a result of widespread access to goods produced by full-time specialists and the development of more intensive agriculture close to urban centers，Mesopotamian city-states were able to support numerous nonfood producers，possibly as high a proportion as 20 percent of the total population.

As a result of widespread access to goods produced by full-time specialists and the **development of more intensive agriculture** close to urban centers，**Mesopotamian city-states were able to support numerous nonfood producers**，possibly as high a proportion as 20 percent of the total population.

翻译：由于广泛获得由全职专家生产的**商品**，以及在靠近城市中心的地方发展**更为密**

集的农业，美索不达米亚城邦能够支持众多的**非食品生产者**，其比例可能高达总人口的 20%。

18）Termite evolution has several obvious trends, from primitive species, which live in small hidden colonies, to groups of millions strong, the builders of enormous mounds that allow for heat and gas exchange.

Termite evolution has several obvious trends, from primitive species, which live in small hidden colonies, **to groups of millions strong,** the builders of enormous mounds that allow for heat and gas exchange.

翻译：**白蚁的进化有几个明显的趋势**，从生活在隐蔽的小群落中的**原始物种**，到**数百万的群体**，这些群体是可以进行热量和气体交换的巨大土堆的建造者。

19）Moreover, when planetesimals, small, solid objects formed in the early solar system that may accumulate to become planets, condense within a forming star system, they are inevitably made from heavy elements because the more common hydrogen and helium remain gaseous.

Moreover, **when planetesimals,** small, solid objects formed in the early solar system that may accumulate to become planets, **condense within a forming star system, they are inevitably made from heavy elements** because the more common hydrogen and helium remain gaseous.

翻译：此外，**当星子**（在太阳系早期形成的可能聚集变成行星的小型固体物）**在形成的恒星系统中凝聚时，它们不可避免地由重元素组成**，因为更常见的氢和氦仍然是气态的。

20）The set of elements used by life based on some other element might be somewhat different from that used by carbon-based life on Earth.

The set of elements used by life based on some other element **might be somewhat different** from that used by carbon-based life on Earth.

翻译：以其他元素为基础的生命所使用的**一组元素可能**与地球上以碳为基础的生命所使用的元素**有些不同**。

21）The identification of the transforming material was a crucial step in the history of biology, accomplished over a period of several years by Oswald Avery and his colleagues at what is now Rockefeller University.

The identification of the transforming material was a crucial step in the history of biology, accomplished over a period of several years by Oswald Avery and his colleagues at what is now Rockefeller University.

翻译：**对转化物质的识别是生物学史上的关键一步**，由奥斯瓦尔德·艾弗里和他的同事在现在的洛克菲勒大学花了几年时间完成的。

22）They treated samples of the transforming extract in a variety of ways to destroy different types of substances proteins, nucleic acids, carbohydrates, and lipids and tested the treated samples to see if they had retained transforming activity.

They treated samples of the transforming extract **in a variety of ways** to destroy different types of substances proteins, nucleic acids, carbohydrates, and lipids **and tested the treated samples** to see if they had retained transforming activity.

翻译: **他们用各种方法处理**转化提取物**样品**,以破坏不同类型物质的蛋白质、核酸、碳水化合物和脂质,**并测试处理后的样品**,看它们是否保留了转化活性。

23) There is a songbird, called the white-crowned sparrow, whose song development follows this general script while providing some variations that are instructive about the interplay of internal influences and learning in birdsong.

There is a songbird, called the white-crowned sparrow, **whose song development follows this general script while providing some variations** that are instructive about the interplay of internal influences and learning in birdsong.

翻译: **有一种名为白冠麻雀的鸣禽**,**它的歌声发展遵循这一总纲,同时提供了一些变化**,这些变化对鸟鸣中内在影响和学习的相互作用具有指导意义。

24) For example, the white-crown found year-round in the San Francisco area sings a particular regional variant or dialect of the basic white-crown song and begins singing within six weeks or so of birth and may progress to fully crystallized song as early as three months after birth, meaning about September.

For example, **the white-crown** found year-round in the San Francisco area **sings a particular regional variant** or dialect of the basic white-crown song **and begins singing within six weeks** or so of birth **and may progress to fully crystallized song as early as three months after birt**h, meaning about September.

翻译: 例如,全年在旧金山地区发现的**白冠鸟演唱**白冠鸟基本歌曲**一种特定的地区变体**或方言,**它们在出生后6周左右开始歌唱,进展到完全成熟的歌曲是在出生后3个月**,这意味着大约在9月。

25) Young white-crowns, like many species, will extend this practice by counter singing, meaning that a male, upon hearing the song of a nearby male of its species, will repeat the exact song that he has heard, thus setting off a back-and-forth duel, like two children in an argument, each of them saying, I'm still here.

Young white-crowns, like many species, **will extend this practice by counter singing**, meaning that a male, upon hearing the song of a nearby male of its species, will repeat the exact song that he has heard, thus setting off a back-and-forth duel, like two children in an argument, each of them saying, I'm still here.

翻译: 像许多物种一样,**年轻的白冠会通过对唱来扩展这种做法**,这意味着雄性在听到附近同类雄性的歌声时,会重复他所听到的确切的歌声,从而引发一场来回的决斗,就像两个孩子在争吵,他们每个人都说,我还在这里。

26) We know that there is often a so-called sensitive period for animal learning, a kind of window in which an animal is able to acquire certain skills or information.

We know that there is often a so-called sensitive period for animal learning, a kind of window in which an animal is able to acquire certain skills or information.

翻译: 我们知道,动物学习往往有一个所谓的敏感期,在这个时期,动物能够获得某些技能或信息。

27) Meanwhile, white-crowns that are raised in nature through part of their sensitive period and then taken to the laboratory will begin singing the following winter in the dialect of the area in which they were hatched.

Meanwhile, **white-crowns** that are raised in nature through part of their sensitive period and then taken to the laboratory **will begin singing the following winter in the dialect of the area** in which they were hatched.

翻译: 与此同时,部分敏感期在自然环境中被培育的然后被带到实验室的**白冠将在第二年冬天开始用**孵化地的**方言唱歌**。

28) The seeds are rich in B vitamins and iron, contain on average two times the protein but less starch than cereals, and can be eaten, sometimes pods and all, while they're still green.

The seeds are rich in B vitamins and iron, **contain** on average **two times the protein but less starch than cereals**, **and can be eaten**, sometimes pods and all, **while they're still green.**

翻译: 这些种子富含维生素 B 和铁,蛋白质平均含量是谷类的两倍,但淀粉含量却比谷类少,而且可以在它们还是绿色的时候食用,有时还可以吃豆荚。

29) Legumes are characterized by a long period of sequential ripening, during which a single plant may have ripe pods, green pods, and flowers, all at the same time, which means that a stand of legumes can be harvested again and again over several weeks.

Legumes are characterized by a long period of sequential ripening, during which a single plant may have ripe pods, green pods, and flowers, all at the same time, which means that a stand of legumes can be harvested again and again over several weeks.

翻译: 豆科植物的特点是连续成熟的时间长,在此期间,一株植物可能同时长出成熟的豆荚、绿色豆荚和花朵,这意味着一片豆科植物可以在几个星期内一次又一次地收获。

30) When cereals and legumes are eaten together, they provide all eight of the

essential amino acids，a fact that the ancestors of early agriculturalists undoubtedly understood at least on a practical level and their descendants took advantage of that knowledge.

When cereals and legumes are eaten together，they provide all eight of the essential amino acids，a fact that the ancestors of early agriculturalists undoubtedly understood at least on a practical level and their descendants took advantage of that knowledge.

翻译：当谷物和豆类一起食用时，它们提供了所有8种必需氨基酸，这一事实无疑是早期农学家的祖先至少在实践层面上所了解的，并且他们的后代运用了这一知识。

31）Many of them are propagated asexually by using a plant part such as a bulb rather than sexually through seeds，so they are more complicated to grow than cereals and legumes，and this may account for their typically late addition to agricultural assemblages.

Many of them are propagated asexually by using a plant part such as a bulb rather than sexually through seeds，**so they are more complicated to grow** than cereals and legumes，**and this may account for their typically late addition to agricultural assemblages.**

翻译：它们中的许多是通过植物的一部分如球状茎进行无性繁殖，而不是通过种子进行有性繁殖，因此它们的生长比谷类和豆类更为复杂，这可能是它们通常较晚添加到农业组合中的原因。

32）It should be noted，however，that recent research in Israel suggests that figs may have been domesticated at a site near Jericho in the Jordan Valley at about the same time as the first experiments with cereals and legumes，and some archaeologists believe that in New Guinea，tubers may have been domesticated long before other crops were imported.

It should be noted，however，**that** recent **research** in Israel **suggests that figs may have been domesticated** at a site near Jericho in the Jordan Valley **at about the same time as the first experiments with cereals and legumes，and some archaeologists believe that** in New Guinea，**tubers may have been domesticated long before other crops were imported.**

翻译：然而，值得注意的是，最近在以色列的研究表明，无花果可能是在约旦河谷耶利哥附近的一个地点驯化的，与第一次对谷物和豆类进行试验的时间差不多，一些考古学家认为在新几内亚，块茎可能早在其他作物进口之前就已经被驯化了。

33）In the years since，the combined forces of a longer insect-breeding season and forest management practices that left forests overcrowded gave way to similar epidemics farther south.

In the years since，**the combined forces** of a longer insect-breeding season and forest management practices that left forests overcrowded **gave way to similar epidemics farther** south.

翻译：在此后的几年里，更长的昆虫繁殖季节和导致森林过度拥挤的森林管理措施的**共同作用让位于更南部的类似流行病**。

34）In the short term，the Alaskan spruce beetle epidemic supplied a lot of people with firewood，but only by destroying tons of otherwise valuable timber and threatening the livelihoods of loggers.

In the short term，**the Alaskan spruce beetle epidemic supplied a lot of people with firewood，but only by destroying tons of otherwise valuable timber and threatening the livelihoods of loggers.**

翻译：在短期内，**阿拉斯加云杉甲虫的流行为许多人提供了柴火，但只是通过摧毁成吨的本来很有价值的木材，并威胁到伐木工人的生计**。

35）Psychologists who study the acquisition of motor skills in children find it useful to distinguish between gross motor development，that is，motor skills which help children to get around in their environment such as crawling and walking，and fine motor development，which refers to smaller movement sequences like reaching and grasping.

Psychologists who study the acquisition of motor skills in children **find it useful to distinguish between gross motor development**，that is，motor skills which help children to get around in their environment such as crawling and walking，**and fine motor development**，which refers to smaller movement sequences like reaching and grasping.

翻译：研究儿童运动技能习得的**心理学家发现区分粗大运动发育**（即帮助儿童在爬行和行走等环境中走动的运动技能）**和精细运动发育**（即伸手和抓握等较小的运动序列）**是很有用的**。

36）Because infant memory is initially highly dependent on context，that is，the similarity between the situation where information is encoded（stored in memory）and where it is recalled，infants who have experience moving about the environment and who learn to spatially encode information become less dependent on context for successful recall.

Because infant memory is initially highly dependent on context，that is，the similarity between the situation where information is encoded（stored in memory）and where it is recalled，**infants who have experience moving about the environment and who learn to spatially encode information become less dependent on context for successful recall.**

翻译：**由于婴儿的记忆最初高度依赖于上下文**，即信息被编码（存储在记忆中）和回忆位置之间的相似性，**经历过在环境中移动和学习空间编码信息的婴儿在成功回忆时对上下文的依赖性降低**。

37) Renowned psychologist Jean Piaget argued that the development of reaching and grasping was a key aspect of development because it formed an important link between biological adaptation and intellectual adaptation.

Renowned psychologist **Jean Piaget argued that the development of reaching and grasping was a key aspect of development because it formed an important link between biological adaptation and intellectual adaptation.**

翻译: 著名心理学家**让·皮亚杰认为,伸手和抓握的发展是发育的一个关键方面,因为它在生物适应和智力适应之间形成了重要的联系**。

38) An individual with longer horns had a better chance of circumventing its opponents' horns and fatally wounding them than one with shorter horns, and females probably preferred to mate with winners of these contests rather than with losers, either because they liked what they saw in the male or because they liked the territory that the male could defend from competitors.

An individual with longer horns had a better chance of circumventing its opponents' horns and fatally wounding them than one with shorter horns, **and females probably preferred to mate with winners of these contests** rather than with losers, either **because** they liked what they saw in the male or **because** they liked the territory that the male could defend from competitors.

翻译: **角较长的个体**比角较短的个体**更有可能绕过对手的角并造成致命伤害,雌性个体可能更喜欢与这些比赛的获胜者交配**,而不是与失败者交配,要么是**因为**它们喜欢看到雄性动物身上的东西,要么是**因为**它们喜欢雄性动物能够抵御竞争对手的领地。

39) Because of their young ages, Theodosius' sons and grandsons could not rule without older advisors and supervising regents upon whom they naturally became dependent and from whom they were unable to break away after reaching maturity.

Because of their young ages,Theodosius' sons and grandsons could not rule without older advisors and supervising regents upon whom they naturally became dependent and from whom they were unable to break away after reaching maturity.

翻译: **由于年纪尚小,狄奥多西的儿子和孙子无法在没有年长的顾问和监督摄政王的情况下进行统治**,他们自然而然地依赖这些年长的顾问和摄政王,即使成年后也无法脱离他们。

40) They argue that the whole issue of the Upper Paleolithic Revolution stems from a profound Eurocentric bias and a failure to appreciate the depth and breadth of the African archaeological record.

They argue that the whole issue of the Upper Paleolithic Revolution **stems from** a profound Eurocentric **bias and a failure** to appreciate the depth and breadth of the

African archaeological record.

翻译：他们认为，旧石器时代晚期革命的**整个问题源于**深刻的欧洲中心主义**偏见，和**对于非洲考古记录的深度和广度的理解**失败**。

41）The extraordinary range of rock art in Australia adds great weight to the idea that artistic creativity was part and parcel of the intellectual capacity of modern humans that migrated out of Africa around 70 kya.

The extraordinary range of rock art in Australia **adds great weight to the idea** that artistic creativity was part and parcel of the intellectual capacity of modern humans that migrated out of Africa around 70 kya.

翻译：澳大利亚**岩石艺术的种类繁多**为艺术创造力是现代人智力的重要组成部分这**一观点增色不少**；这些现代人在 7 万年左右以前脱离非洲移居别处。

42）The fact that these people almost certainly arrived in Australia before 60 kya and were，in any case，completely isolated from any evolutionary events that may have occurred in Europe around 40 kya makes this argument compelling.

The fact that these people almost certainly arrived in Australia before 60 kya and were，in any case，completely isolated from any evolutionary events that may have occurred in Europe around 40 kya **makes this argument compelling.**

翻译：这些人几乎是在 6 万年前到达澳大利亚的，并且在任何情况下，都与 4 万年前后发生在欧洲的任一进化事件完全隔绝的事实**使得这一论点具有说服力**。

43）Recent evidence that in Africa the transition from the Middle Paleolithic to the Upper Paleolithic was also marked by enormous progress strengthens the European evidence.

Recent **evidence** that in Africa the transition from the Middle Paleolithic to the Upper Paleolithic was also marked by enormous progress **strengthens the European evidence.**

翻译：最近的（表明在非洲，从旧石器时代中期到旧石器时代晚期的转变也有巨大的进步的）**证据加强了欧洲的证据**。

44）However，one predator-avoidance mechanism，the ability to break off their tails when they are seized by predators，does not differ among lizards with different foraging modes.

However，**one predator-avoidance mechanism**，the ability to break off their tails when they are seized by predators，**does not differ** among lizards with different foraging modes.

翻译：然而，**一种回避捕食者机制**，即当它们被捕食者抓住时能够折断尾巴的能力，在具有不同觅食模式的蜥蜴之间**没有差异**。

45) Sit-and-wait lizards and active foragers differ in their relative emphasis on the two ways that most animals use adenosine triphosphate（ATP）, a molecule that transports energy within cells for activity, and in how long that activity can be sustained.

Sit-and-wait lizards and active foragers differ in their relative emphasis on the two ways that most animals use adenosine triphosphate（ATP）, a molecule that transports energy within cells for activity, **and in how long that activity can be sustained.**

翻译：**坐以待毙的蜥蜴和活跃的觅食蜥蜴在**大多数动物使用三磷酸腺苷的**两种方式的相对重视程度**(三磷酸腺苷是一种在细胞内传递能量进行活动的分子)**以及这种活动可以持续多久方面不同**。

46) The fact that the Cambrian explosion marks the only major diversification of body plans in the geological record presents us with two important and related questions：Why, so long after the origin of eukaryotes, did the pace of evolution suddenly accelerate dramatically at the beginning of the Cambrian, and why hasn't there been another period of similarly explosive diversification since then.

The fact that the Cambrian explosion marks the only major diversification of body plans in the geological record **presents us with two important and related questions：Why,** so long after the origin of eukaryotes, **did the pace of evolution suddenly accelerate dramatically** at the beginning of the Cambrian, **and why hasn't there been another period of similarly explosive diversification** since then.

翻译：寒武纪的爆发标志着地质记录中唯一主要的身体形态多样化的**事实向我们提出了两个重要的相关问题：为什么**真核生物起源这么久之后，**进化的速度**在寒武纪初期突然急剧加快？**为什么从那时起没有另一个**类似爆炸性多样化的**时期**?

47) Some scientists believe that the Cambrian explosion marks the point at which organisms developed certain kinds of genes that control body form and that could be combined in different ways, allowing the evolution of a great diversity of forms over time.

Some scientists believe that the Cambrian explosion marks the point at which organisms developed certain kinds of genes that control body form and that could be combined in different ways, allowing the evolution of a great diversity of forms over time.

翻译：**一些科学家认为，寒武纪的爆发标志着一个时间点**，在这个时间点有机体发展出控制身体形态并且可以不同的方式结合在一起的基因，从而随着时间的推移进化出多种多样的形态。

48) Or it may be that while more body plans may have been possible at some early point in evolution, it was not possible to evolve into those other body plans from the body plans that evolved in the Cambrian.

Or **it may be that** while more body plans may have been possible at some early point in evolution，**it was not possible to evolve into those other body plans from the body plans that evolved in the Cambrian.**

翻译：或者，虽然在进化的早期可能有更多的身体计划，**但不可能从寒武纪进化的身体计划演变成其他身体计划**。

49）Peasants attached wheels to their plows，which made it easier for oxen to pull them through the heavier，wetter soil of northern Europe，and made it possible for a plow to move more quickly down a row provided it had a speedy animal pulling it.

Peasants attached wheels to their plows，which made it easier for oxen to pull them through the heavier，wetter soil of northern Europe，and made it possible for a plow to move more quickly down a row provided it had a speedy animal pulling it.

翻译：农民**把轮子固定在犁上**，这样牛就可以更容易地把犁拉过北欧较重、较湿的土壤，而且如果犁上有一只快速的动物拉着它，它就可以更快地沿着一排犁向下移动。

注：provided 可以做连词，表示"如果"

50）Whether an increase in population across western Europe，particularly in the north，stimulated innovations or whether such innovations contributed to a rise in population，the cumulative effect of these changes in agriculture was apparent in the tenth century.

Whether an increase in population across western Europe，particularly in the north，**stimulated innovations or whether such innovations contributed to a rise in population，the cumulative effect of these changes** in agriculture **was apparent** in the tenth century.

翻译：无论整个西欧，特别是北部**人口的增加是否刺激了创新**，还是这些创新是否促进了人口的增长，这些农业变化的累积效应在 10 世纪是**显而易见的**。

51）The southwestern United States region also changed from a moist area with numerous lakes，where saber-tooth cats，giant ground sloths，and mammoths roamed，to a semiarid environment unable to support a diverse fauna of large mammals.

The southwestern United States region also changed from a moist area with numerous lakes，where saber-tooth cats，giant ground sloths，and mammoths roamed，**to a semiarid environment** unable to support a diverse fauna of large mammals.

翻译：美国西南部地区也从一个拥有许多湖泊的潮湿地区（那里有剑齿猫、巨大的地面树懒和猛犸象）**变成了一个半干旱的**无法维持多样化的大型哺乳动物群的**环境**。

52）The advantage for laying eggs on land was primarily to avoid the aquatic larval (pre-adult) stage during which immature amphibians live exclusively in water with its inherent risk of predators and drying of ponds.

The advantage for laying eggs on land **was primarily to avoid the aquatic larval（pre-**

adult) **stage** during which immature amphibians live exclusively in water with its inherent risk of predators and drying of ponds.

翻译: 在陆地上产卵的**优势主要是避免水生幼体（成虫前）阶段**，在此阶段，未成熟的两栖动物只生活在水中，其固有的捕食者风险和池塘干涸风险。

53) The task，often，is to identify an individual tree that may be not much thicker than your arm from the appearance of its bark，out of a total list of several hundred (or thousand) possibilities which may well include some that have not been described before，so that there is nothing to refer back to.

The task，often，**is to identify an individual tree** that may be not much thicker than your arm **from the appearance of its bark**，out of a total list of several hundred (or thousand) possibilities which may well include some that have not been described before，so that there is nothing to refer back to.

翻译: 通常，**任务是从树皮的外观上**，从几百（或几千）种可能性的列表中，**识别一棵可**能比你的手臂粗不了多少的**树**；这些列表很可能包括一些以前没有描述过的树，这样就没有什么可参考的了。

54) Scientists wondered for many years about what could have caused the dinosaurs' rapid disappearance at the end of the Cretaceous period，coming up with a great variety of theories and scenarios.

Scientists wondered for many years about **what could have caused the dinosaurs' rapid disappearance** at the end of the Cretaceous period，coming up with a great variety of theories and scenarios.

翻译: 多年来，**科学家们一直想知道是什么导致了恐龙**在白垩纪末期**的迅速消失**，他们提出了各种各样的理论和设想。

55) By contrast，knowledge born of hindsight may involve error when directed at past moments in time，as in evaluating the skill of decision makers who had no crystal ball and so could not possibly have known what is known now.

By contrast，**knowledge** born of hindsight **may involve error when directed at past moments in time**，as in evaluating the skill of decision makers who had no crystal ball and so could not possibly have known what is known now.

翻译: 相比之下，事后诸葛亮所产生的**知识在针对过去可能会出现的错误**，比如在评估决策者的技能时，他们没有水晶球，因此不可能知道现在所知道的。

56) Mathematical equations can sometimes tell such a convincing tale and they can seemingly radiate reality so strongly，that they become entrenched in the vernacular of working physicists，even before there's data to confirm them.

Mathematical equations can sometimes tell such a convincing tale and they can

seemingly radiate reality so strongly，that they become entrenched in the vernacular of working physicists，even before there's data to confirm them.

翻译：**数学方程式有时能讲述这样一个令人信服的故事，它们似乎能如此强烈地辐射进现实**，甚至在有数据证实它们之前，它们就已经深深扎根于在职物理学家的日常用语中。

57）Scientists seldom use such language when talking about their colleagues to a journalist，but this issue generates strong feelings，perhaps because it smudges the sharp line separating the animal kingdom from the plant kingdom.

Scientists seldom use such language when talking about their colleagues to a journalist，**but this issue generates strong feelings**，perhaps because it smudges the sharp line separating the animal kingdom from the plant kingdom.

翻译：**科学家在向记者谈论他们的同事时很少使用这样的语言**，但这个问题产生了强烈的感情，也许是因为它模糊了动物王国和植物王国的分界线。

58）The researchers also wanted to know whether extra beetles would impose a double cost by both damaging flowers and deterring bees，which might not bother to visit（and pollinate）a flower laden with other insects and their feces.

The researchers also wanted to know whether extra beetles would impose a double cost by both damaging flowers and deterring bees，which might not bother to visit（and pollinate）a flower laden with other insects and their feces.

翻译：**研究人员还想知道，额外的甲虫是否会造成双倍的损失**，通过既破坏花朵，又吓阻蜜蜂，这些蜜蜂可能懒得去拜访（和授粉）长满其他昆虫及其粪便的花朵。

59）But they conclude that this iron was probably not oxidized，producing the hematite，until about 300 million years later，after tectonic forces crumpled the sea floor into mountains and drove oxygen-laden water down into the rock.

But they conclude that this iron was probably not oxidized，producing the hematite，**until about 300 million years later**，after tectonic forces crumpled the sea floor into mountains and drove oxygen-laden water down into the rock.

翻译：**但他们得出结论，这种铁可能没有被氧化**，产生赤铁矿，**直到大约 3 亿年后**，在构造力将海底挤压成山脉，并将含氧的水冲入岩石之后。

60）Given that western Australia hosts the archetypal examples of BIFs in that early time，the Dales Gorge formation probably records fundamental processes that also affected other BIFs at some time on their history.

Given that western Australia hosts the archetypal examples of BIFs in that early time，**the Dales Gorge formation probably records fundamental processes** that also affected other BIFs at some time on their history.

翻译：考虑到西澳大利亚州在早期就拥有 BIF 的原型，**戴尔斯峡谷的形成可能记录了一些**在历史上影响其他 BIF 的**基本过程**。

61）He hopes to greatly increase the efficiency of silicon solar panels by combining silicon with one or two other semiconductors，each selected to efficiently convert a part of the solar spectrum that silicon doesn't convert efficiently.

He hopes to greatly increase the efficiency of silicon solar panels by combining silicon with one or two other semiconductors，each selected to efficiently convert a part of the solar spectrum that silicon doesn't convert efficiently.

翻译：他希望大大提高硅太阳能电池板的**效率**，通过将硅与其他一到两种半导体相结合，每种半导体被选择用来有效地转换硅不能有效转换的部分太阳光谱。

62）This kind of real-world manipulation of nature is called "experimental evolution，" and it is growing increasingly popular among scientists working with organisms that reproduce quickly enough for humans to be able to see the outcome within our lifetimes.

This kind of real-world manipulation of nature is called "experimental evolution，" and it is growing increasingly popular among scientists working with organisms that reproduce quickly enough for humans to be able to see the outcome within our lifetimes.

翻译：这种对自然界的真实操纵被称为"实验进化"，它越来越受到科学家们的欢迎，这些科学家们正在研究那些繁殖速度快到足以让人类在有生之年看到结果的生物体。

第七章

模式化

经过了足够多的难句语法分析和层次分析就会发现,这些难句的结构是有很明显的模式的。如果对于这些难句的模式及处理方法非常熟悉并且在阅读时能够快速识别并应用的话,我们的阅读速度和准确度都会有很大的提升。接下来,我们就来认识一些最常见的难句模式。

一 主干句型

句子的主干部分的识别是最为重要的,下面我们一起来看看几种难句中比较常见的主干类型。

1. 结构: 修饰成分,主干

这种句型的难点在于,主干信息之前先出现大量的修饰信息,容易因为信息量太大给主干信息造成干扰。不过,好在这些修饰成分与主干之间会使用逗号隔开,这样给我们主干信息的辨别提供了很有利的信号。

1) Since most of the metatarsus develops in utero and is fully grown by the time the moose is one to two years old, the pattern of increasing bone length with increasing age can't have a physiological explanation.

模式:状语从句,主句

(**Since** **most of the metatarsus develops in utero and is fully grown**) (by the time the moose is one to two years old), **the pattern** of increasing bone length with increasing age **can't have a physiological explanation.**

翻译: 由于大多数跖骨发育于子宫并且在麋鹿1—2岁时已完全生长,因此随着年龄的增长而骨长的增加模式无法通过生理解释。

2) Though the word "ecosystem" is overused as a way to make simple situations seem more complex, it is merited here, because large social systems cannot be understood as a simple aggregation of the behavior of some nonexistent "average" user.

模式：状语从句，主句

（Though the word "ecosystem" is overused as a way to make simple situations seem more complex），it is merited here，（because large social systems cannot be understood as a simple aggregation of the behavior of some nonexistent "average" user）.

翻译：尽管"生态系统"这个词被过度使用,它使简单的情况看起来更复杂,但它在这里是值得的,因为大型社会系统不能被理解为一个简单的、不存在的"普通"用户行为的简单集合。

3) In contrast to ancient DNA findings from central Europe, the people from Treilles lacked a key genetic variant that allows the body to digest lactose into adulthood.

模式：介词短语，主句

In contrast to ancient DNA findings from central Europe，the people from Treilles lacked a key genetic variant that allows the body to digest lactose into adulthood.

翻译：与远古的中欧DNA发现不同,特瑞尔人缺乏一种关键的基因变体,这种基因变体使身体能够在成年后消化乳糖。

4) By measuring the thickness of the strata, and making some educated estimates about how quickly they might have formed, John Grotzinger and his colleagues reckon the lake could have endured for anything from centuries to millennia.

模式：介词短语，主句

By measuring the thickness of the strata，and making some educated estimates about how quickly they might have formed，John Grotzinger and his colleagues reckon the lake could have endured for anything from centuries to millennia.

翻译：通过测量地层的厚度,并对它们的形成速度做出一些有根据的估计,约翰·格罗辛格和他的同事们认为,这个湖泊可能存在了几个世纪到几千年。

5) Instead of trying to figure out the ideal conditions for each and every one of the millions of organisms out there in the environment, to allow them to grow in the lab, we simply grow them in their natural environment where they already have the conditions they need for growth.

模式：介词短语，主句

Instead of trying to figure out the ideal conditions for each and every one of the millions of organisms out there in the environment，to allow them to grow in the lab，**we simply grow them in their natural environment**（where they already have the conditions）（they need for growth）.

翻译：没有试图弄清楚环境中数百万生物中每一种的理想条件，来让它们在实验室里生长，我们仅仅让它们在已经具备生长所需条件的自然环境中生长。

6）As part of the general process of the transformation of authority whereby there has been a reluctance to uncritically accept traditional sources of public knowledge，the demand has been for all authority to make explicit the frames of value which determine their decisions.

模式：介词短语 + 从句，主句

As part of **the general process of the transformation of authority**（whereby there has been a reluctance to uncritically accept traditional sources of public knowledge），**the demand has been for all authority to make explicit the frames of value**（which determine their decisions）.

翻译：作为权威转变的一般过程的一部分，在这个过程中人们不愿意不加批判地接受传统的公共知识来源，要求所有的权威确定其决定的价值框架。

在阅读到上述模式的句型时，要形成正确的预期，即**核心信息在修饰成分之后的主干**。如果修饰成分的信息过于冗余或者难以理解，可以直接跳过，看主干信息，尤其对于像句子6）中这种"短语 + 从句，主句"结构。这个句型中，从句是用来修饰前面的短语的，按照我们前面所讲的句子层次来看，它属于第三层的信息，基本属于非常次要的补充信息，可忽略。**忽略从句之后，不仅没有损失信息，反而会使原句子的信息更加清晰。**

2. 结构：主语　长修饰语　谓语

这种句型最大的难点是其与汉语思维的冲突。汉语中在大多数情况下，主语与谓语都是紧密相邻的，但英语中因为后置定语的存在，主语与谓语往往会存在一定间隔，尤其当主语的后置定语过长时，更是如此。在这种情况下，**主干信息会被长修饰语的信息冲散**，导致很大一部分习惯汉语主干模式的人很难迅速抓到主干信息，甚至抓错主干信息。不过，如果通过强化训练，我们熟悉了这种句式的存在后，情况就会好很多。主谓之间长修饰语的句型又可以详细分为以下两种情况：

- 主语，修饰语，谓语

这种情况，其实在汉语中也比较常见，和我们前面在特殊结构里面提到的插入成分是属于同一种现象，因为有逗号的存在，所以比较容易识别。处理的方法也比较清晰，就是**快速扫过两个逗号中间的信息，重点放在两个逗号前后的主干信息。**

1）Numerous such studies，especially of Y chromosomes，which are transmitted via the paternal line，suggest that actual farmers，not just their ideas，spread westward over the millennia，eventually reaching the British Isles.

Numerous such studies，especially of Y chromosomes，which are transmitted via the paternal line，**suggest**（**that actual farmers**，not just their ideas，**spread westward over the millennia**，eventually reaching the British Isles）.

分析：这种主谓分离的情况，不仅存在于主句的主干，**也会出现在从句的主干**。只要是主干，无论是主句还是从句，都可能被隔离开，因此阅读时的"**主干意识**"是非常重要的；两个逗号中间插入的信息既可以是简单的短语，也可以是从句，甚至可以是短语＋从句。

翻译：许多这样的研究，特别是通过父系传播的 Y 染色体的研究表明，真正的农民，包括他们的想法，在几千年中向西扩散，最终到达不列颠群岛。

2）Some of this research，most notably in Germany，suggests that male farmers entering central Europe mated with local female hunter-gatherers—thus possibly resolving the contradiction between the Y chromosome and mtDNA results.

Some of this research，most notably in Germany，**suggests that male farmers** entering central Europe **mated with local female hunter-gatherers**—thus possibly resolving the contradiction between the Y chromosome and mtDNA results.

分析：主句主干插入短语

翻译：一些在德国的研究表明进入中欧的男性农民与当地的女性狩猎采集者交配，从而可能解决了 Y 染色体和线粒体 DNA 结果之间的矛盾。

3）The second problem，which became obvious as a result of unmanned spacecraft looking at the planets and their satellites in the Solar System，is that long-runout landslides occur on our Moon and on four other moons in our Solar System that have no atmospheres.

The second problem，（which became obvious as a result of unmanned spacecraft/ looking at the planets and their satellites in the Solar System），**is that long-runout landslides occur on our Moon and on four other moons in our Solar System**（**that have no atmospheres**）.

分析：主句主干插入从句

翻译：第二个问题，由于无人驾驶的航天器观察太阳系中的行星及其卫星而变得明显，那就是在我们的月球和太阳系中没有大气层的其他四个卫星上发生了长时间的滑坡。

4）When O'Donnell，with support from the National Science Foundation's Directorate for Biological Sciences，looked at the brains in related species of wasps spanning the social spectrum，he found that living in a society did indeed affect the size of their brains.

When O'Donnell，with support from the National Science Foundation's Directorate for Biological Sciences，**looked at the brains** in related species of wasps spanning the social spectrum，**he found that living in a society did indeed affect the size of their brains**.

分析：从句主谓之间插入介词短语

翻译：奥唐纳在国家科学基金会生物科学理事会的支持下，研究了社会范围内黄蜂相关物种的大脑，他发现生活在一个群体里确实影响了它们大脑的大小。

5）Thomas McCord of the Bear Fight Center in Winthrop，Washington，who was not involved in any of the three studies，agrees that the asteroid belt probably hosts some small refuges from the outer solar system，but says there is no reason to believe Ceres is a stranger there.

Thomas McCord of the Bear Fight Center in Winthrop，Washington，（who was not involved in any of the three studies），**agrees that the asteroid belt probably hosts some small refuges** from the outer solar system，**but says there is no reason to believe Ceres is a stranger there**.

分析：主句主干插入定语从句

翻译：华盛顿温思罗普的 Bear Fight Center 的托马斯·麦考德没有参与这三项研究中的任何一项，他认同小行星带可能收容了一些来自外太阳系的小难民，但他不相信谷神星在那里是个陌生者。

- 主语　长修饰语　谓语（无逗号）

这种情况要比上一种情况识别起来更加困难一点，因为没有逗号的标记。并且，这种句型与汉语的句型相差最大，在汉语中几乎没有类似的情况。当我们阅读时发现主语后面的修饰信息过于冗长时（从句或多个短语），我们要意识到**这些信息并不是最重要的信息**，不要被其干扰以至于忽略了主干信息，或者我们**也可先跳过这些修饰语，找出谓语动词后，再回头补充这些修饰信息**。

1）Models that treated flapping birds like fixed-wing airplanes estimate that they save energy by drafting off each other，but currents created by airplanes are far more stable than the oscillating eddies coming off of a bird.

Models（that treated flapping birds like fixed-wing airplanes）**estimate that they save energy by drafting off each other**，**but currents/created by airplanes/are far more stable** than the oscillating eddies coming off of a bird.

分析：主句主谓之间有定语从句

翻译：那些把拍打着翅膀的鸟当作固定翼飞机对待的模型推测它们通过相互牵引来节省能量，但是飞机产生的气流远比鸟身上的振荡涡流稳定。

2）But the millions of hectares of this Eurasian species that inhabit western North America have displaced native plant species and reduced forage for both wild and domestic animals，costing hundreds of millions of dollars annually.

But the millions of hectares of this Eurasian species（that inhabit western North America）**have displaced native plant species and reduced forage for both wild and domestic animals**，costing hundreds of millions of dollars annually.

分析：主句主谓之间有定语从句

翻译：但是位于北美洲西部的数百万公顷欧亚物种已经取代了本地植物物种，从而减少了野生动物和家养动物的饲料，导致每年付出数亿美元的代价。

3）While the rote act of photographing a whole object led a person to dismiss it from memory，the slight uptick in focus required to zoom-in on a detail caused the same person to absorb the scene as if there were no camera present at all.

（**While the rote act** of photographing a whole object **led a person to dismiss it from memory**），**the slight uptick in focus**/required to zoom-in on a detail/ **caused the same person to absorb the scene**（as if there were no camera present at all）.

分析：主句主谓之间有多个短语

翻译：虽然机械地拍摄一个完整的物体会把它从记忆中抹去，但放大一个细节所需的注意力的轻微上移会使同一个人就像根本没有相机一样吸收这个场景。

4）Those who argue that apes aren't capable of language—and that the apes who've been trained in sign language are merely engaging in rote memorization，not true language acquisition—point to a lack of intentionality as one of the reasons why.

Those（who argue/that apes aren't capable of language—/and that the apes（who've been trained in sign language）are merely engaging in rote memorization，not true language acquisition—）**point to a lack of intentionality as one of the reasons why.**

分析：主句主谓之间有定语从句和插入成分；插入成分的主谓之间有定语从句

翻译：那些认为猿类没有语言能力——受过手语训练的猿类只是死记硬背，而不是真正的语言习得——的人指出，缺乏意向性是原因之一。

5）A new study of ancient DNA from 5,000-year-old skeletons found in a French cave suggests that early farmers entered the European continent by at least two different routes and reveals new details about the social structures and dairying practices of some of their societies.

A new study/of ancient DNA from 5,000-year-old skeletons/found in a French cave/**suggests that early farmers entered the European continent by at least two different routes and reveals new details about the social structures and dairying practices** of some of their societies.

分析：主句主谓之间有多个短语

翻译：在法国一个洞穴中发现的5 000年前骨骼的古老DNA的新研究表明，早期农民至少通过两条不同的路线进入欧洲大陆，并揭示了一些社会结构和乳品业运作的新细节。

6) Knowledge that is gathered later，such as from accident scene investigations，forensic tests，or the arbitrary discovery of an oddly misused product，is deemed irrelevant in evaluating the quality of the decisions made in the moment，that is，before a focal mishap occurred.

Knowledge（that is gathered later，/such as from accident scene investigations，forensic tests，or the arbitrary discovery of an oddly misused product，）**is deemed irrelevant in evaluating the quality of the decisions**/made in the moment，/that is，before a focal mishap occurred.

分析：主句主谓之间有定语从句

翻译：后来收集到的知识，例如事故现场调查、法医检验或一种奇怪的误用产品的意外发现，被认为与当时评估所做决定的质量无关，也就是说，在焦点事故发生之前。

7) Molecular evidence and comparisons of the biological gear the algae use to harvest light convince him that both red and green algae descend from one endosymbiotic event，when a eukaryote cell engulfed a photosynthesizing cyanobacterium and gained the ability to make its own food.

Molecular evidence and comparisons/ of the biological gear（the algae use to harvest light）**convince him that both red and green algae descend from one endosymbiotic event**，（when a eukaryote cell engulfed a photosynthesizing cyanobacterium and gained the ability to make its own food）.

分析：主句主谓之间有短语和定语从句；定语从句 the algae use to harvest light 的连词被省略了

翻译：分子证据和藻类用来采光的生物装置的比较让他相信红藻和绿藻都是从一个内共生事件中产生的，当真核细胞吞噬了一个光合作用的蓝藻，并获得了自己制造食物的能力。

8) Hypotheses explaining the exceptional success of exotic species are based upon ways in which a species' new range differs from its native range：fewer insects and diseases，less competitive environments，and competitors that are more susceptible to chemicals produced by the invader.

Hypotheses/explaining the exceptional success of exotic species/**are based upon ways in which a species' new range differs from its native range**：fewer insects and diseases，less competitive environments，and competitors（that are more susceptible to chemicals/produced by the invader）.

分析：主句主谓之间有多个短语

翻译：解释外来物种异常成功的假设是基于一个物种的新范围不同于其原生范围的

方式：更少的昆虫和疾病，更少的竞争环境，以及更易受入侵者产生的化学物质影响的竞争对手。

9）Work on this issue by linguists like Bill Darden of the University of Chicago has encouraged many linguists in their belief that Indo-European was a single language as recently as 5,500 years ago and that its daughter languages could not have come into existence until after this date.

10）**Work on this issue**/by linguists like Bill Darden of the University of Chicago/ **has encouraged many linguists in their belief**（that Indo-European was a single language as recently as 5,500 years ago）and（that its daughter languages could not have come into existence until after this date）.

分析：主句主谓之间有多个短语

翻译：芝加哥大学的比尔·达顿等语言学家在这个问题上的研究使许多语言学家相信，印欧语系早在5500年前就已经是一种单一的语言了，并且印欧语系的子语系直到这个时间之后才可能存在。

11）Whether behaviors observed in plants which look very much like learning, memory, decision-making, and intelligence deserve to be called by those terms or whether those words should be reserved exclusively for creatures with brains.

Whether behaviors/ observed in plants（which look very much like learning, memory, decision-making, and intelligence）**deserve to be called by those terms or whether those words should be reserved exclusively for creatures with brains**.

分析：主谓之间有短语和定语从句

翻译：在植物中观察到的与学习、记忆、决策和智力非常相似的行为是否应该用这些术语来称呼，或者这些术语是否应该专门留给有大脑的生物。

12）In a 2009 study by economists Gavin Cassar and Justin Craig, hundreds of entrepreneurs who were starting new businesses were asked to estimate the likelihood that their businesses would be successful; Years later, those whose businesses has failed were asked to recall, when they were getting started, what they had thought their chances of success were.

In a 2009 study by economists Gavin Cassar and Justin Craig/, **hundreds of entrepreneurs**（who were starting new businesses）**were asked to estimate the likelihood**（**that their businesses would be successful**）; Years later, **those**（whose businesses has failed）**were asked to recall**,（when they were getting started）, **what they had thought their chances of success were.**

分析：主句主谓之间有定语从句

翻译：2009年，经济学家加文·卡萨尔和贾斯汀·克雷格进行了一项研究，要求数百名创业者预估自己创业成功的可能性;几年后,那些创业失败的人被要求回忆他们刚刚起步的时候,认为自己成功的机会有多少。

不管是哪种情况,对于这种句型最需要强化的还是**主干意识**,养成**"看到主语后,优先找谓语"**的习惯。

二 从句嵌套

除了主干上存在难句模式,从句上也有。从句中最复杂的也是最难的点就是从句嵌套了,主要有以下两种形式:

1. 结构:连词1(连词2+从句2)从句1

这种从句的嵌套比较简单,因为虽然是从句内部又出现了一个新的从句,但是因为**该从句并没有切断原来从句的主干信息**,所以造成的困扰并不大,阅读时按语序直译理解即可,注意做好停顿。

1) In support of this, in trials in which the two individuals tested were a male and a female, Spinks and his colleagues found that while aggression was still uncovered in the low-resource, arid population, the level of aggression decreased dramatically when compared to aggression in same-sex interactions.

In support of this, in trials (in which the two individuals tested were a male and a female), **Spinks and his colleagues found** that (while aggression was still uncovered in the low-resource, arid population), **the level of aggression decreased dramatically** (when compared to aggression in same-sex interactions).

分析:that引导的宾语从句"the level of aggression decreased dramatically"嵌入了一个while引导的状语从句

翻译:为了支持这一点,在两名受试者分别是一雄一雌的实验中,斯宾克斯和他的同事们发现,虽然攻击性在低资源、稀少的群体中仍然被发现,但与同性交往中的攻击性相比,攻击性的程度显著降低。

2) Reznick has shown that if you bring the fish into the lab and let them breed there, the guppies from the sites with many predators become sexually mature when they are younger and smaller than do the guppies from the predator-free sites.

Reznick has shown that (if you bring the fish into the lab and let them breed there, **the guppies from the sites with many predators become sexually mature**)(**when they are younger and smaller**)(**than do the guppies from the predator-free sites**).

分析:that引导的宾语从句 the guppies from the sites with many predators become sexually mature 嵌入了 if 引导的状语从句修饰

翻译: 瑞斯尼克已经证明,如果你把鱼带到实验室,让它们在那里繁殖,相比那些没有捕食者地方的孔雀鱼,那些有很多捕食者地方的孔雀鱼在它们更年轻、更小的时候会性成熟。

2. 结构: 连词1 主语 (连词2+从句2) 谓语

这种从句嵌套的情况要比上面的更难,因为从句内部嵌入的从句割裂了原来句子的主语和谓语。在处理这种情况时,和之前"主语 长修饰语 谓语"这种模式一样,一定要有**主干意识**,不要被这些修饰成分干扰,或者我们**也可先跳过这些修饰语**,找出谓语动词后,再回头补充这些修饰信息。

1) A major development was the discovery,again about 3000 B. C. E.,that if copper,which had been known in Mesopotamia since about 3500 B. C. E.,was mixed with tin,a much harder metal,bronze,would result.

A major development was the discovery,again about 3000 B. C. E.,`that` (`if` **copper**,`which` had been known in Mesopotamia since about 3500 B. C. E.,**was mixed with tin**),**a much harder metal**,bronze,**would result.**

分析: that 引导的从句"a much harder metal,bronze,would result"修饰 discovery;if 引导的条件状语从句内部嵌入了 which 引导的定语从句,并且该定语从句割裂了 if 从句的主语"copper"和谓语"was",遇到类似的情况可以跳过 which 定语从句的信息,直接看完 if 从句的主干。

翻译: 一个主要的进展是发现同样是公元前 3000 年左右,如果从公元前 3500 年开始在美索不达米亚就知道的铜与锡混合,一种更硬的金属,青铜,就会产生。

三 从句串联

结构: 连词1+从句1+连词2+从句2+连词3+从句3……

从句串联就是一个从句结束后接着一个新的从句,就像火车头后面的一节一节车厢一样。由这种方式构成的句子,虽然长,但是语法结构并不复杂,阅读时按语序处理即可,注意停顿,消化完前面的信息之后再继续。

1) As the calcium ion concentrations dissipate over time,if the second touch don't happen quickly,the final concentration after the second trigger won't be high enough to close the trap,and the memory is lost.

(`As` the calcium ion concentrations dissipate over time,) (`if` the second touch don't happen quickly,) the final concentration after the second trigger won't be high enough to close the trap，and the memory is lost.

分析： as 和 if 引导的状语从句共同修饰主干

翻译： 随着时间的推移，钙离子浓度逐渐消失，如果第二次接触没有很快发生，第二次触发后的最终浓度将不足以关闭陷阱，记忆也会丢失。

2）When exoplanet hunters announced in January of 2014 that they had found a tribe of "mini-Neptunes" and the lightest planet ever detected outside our solar system，they highlighted more than just the diversity of exoplanets.

(When exoplanet hunters announced in January of 2014 (that they had found a tribe of "mini-Neptunes" and the lightest planet/ever detected outside our solar system))，they highlighted more than just the diversity of exoplanets.

分析： when 引导的状语从句中包含一个 that 引导的宾语从句

翻译： 当 2014 年 1 月，系外行星猎手宣布他们发现了一群"迷你海王星"以及太阳系外迄今为止最轻行星时，他们强调的不仅仅是系外行星的多样性。

3）But lignin is most abundant in the parts of the seaweed that are most mechanically stressed，which suggests to Martone that there could be some environmental stimulation that increases production of the polymer in the organism.

But lignin is most abundant in the parts of the seaweed (that are most mechanically stressed)，which suggests to Martone (that there could be some environmental stimulation) (that increases production of the polymer in the organism).

分析： 定语从句 that are most mechanically stressed 修饰前面的 parts，而不是 the seeweed

翻译： 但是木质素在海藻中受到机械压力最大的部分是最为丰富的，这向马托内表明，可能有一些环境刺激，这些刺激增加了生物体内聚合物的产生。

4）Spinks and his colleagues examined whether populations from arid areas were more xenophobic than those from wet environments，as one might predict based on our discussion of natural selection，resources，and xenophobia.

Spinks and his colleagues examined (whether populations from arid areas were more xenophobic than those from wet environments，) (as one might predict/based on our discussion of natural selection，resources，and xenophobia.)

分析： whether 引导宾语从句；as 引导方式状语从句修饰 whether 引导的宾语从句

翻译： 斯宾克斯和他的同事研究了来自干旱地区的群体是否比来自潮湿环境的群体更具有排外性，正如我们基于自然选择、资源和仇外心理的讨论所预测的那样。

5）China would gain foreign investment and energy infrastructure，while the British firm could meet its environmental obligations at lower cost because credits earned overseas are often less expensive than reducing emissions at home.

China would gain foreign investment and energy infrastructure，（ while the British firm could meet its environmental obligations at lower cost）（ because credits earned overseas are often less expensive than reducing emissions at home）.

分析：while 引导的状语从句修饰主句；because 引导的状语从句修饰 while 从句

翻译：中国将获得外国投资和能源基础设施，而这家英国公司可以以较低的成本履行其环保义务，因为在海外获得的信誉成本通常比在国内减少排放要低。

6）Closing its trap requires a huge expense of energy，and reopening the trap can take several hours，so Dionaea only wants to spring closed when it's sure that the dawdling insect visiting its surface is large enough to be worth its time.

Closing its trap requires a huge expense of energy，and reopening the trap can take several hours，（ so Dionaea only wants to spring closed） when it's sure（ that the dawdling insect visiting its surface is large enough to be worth its time）.

分析：so 引导的状语从句修饰主句；when 引导的状语从句修饰 so 从句的主干；that 引导的是宾语从句

翻译：关闭诱捕口需要耗费大量的能量，而重新打开诱捕口可能需要几个小时，因此，捕蝇草只会在其确定虫子够大和时间合理的情况下闭合。

7）Because star clusters can be identified and studied in other galaxies at distances where individual stars can no longer be distinguished，they give astronomers insight into star-formation processes across a broad expanse of space and time.

Because star clusters can be identified and studied in other galaxies/at distances（ where individual stars can no longer be distinguished），they give astronomers insight into star-formation processes/across a broad expanse of space and time.

分析：Because 引导的状语从句修饰主句；where 引导的定语从句修饰 distance

翻译：由于星团可以在其他星系中被识别和研究（在单个恒星已经无法被区分的距离内）因此它们让天文学家能够洞察跨越广阔时空的恒星的形成过程。

8）The true contact area is much smaller than its apparent value，and is proportional to the compressive force between the surfaces，in much the same way that the contact area between a car tire and the road increases when you load your car.

The true contact area is much smaller/ than its apparent value，and is proportional to the compressive force/ between the surfaces，/in much the same way（ that the contact area between a car tire and the road increases)（when you load your car）.

分析：that 引导的是定语从句,修饰 way；when 引导的状语从句修饰 that 从句的主干

翻译：真实的接触面积比它的表面值小得多,并且与表面之间的压缩力成正比,这与汽车轮胎和路面之间的接触面积在装载汽车时会增加的方式大致相同。

9）Adult tobacco hookworms—a species of moth—can remember things that it learned as a caterpillar, which means that despite the dramatic nature of metamorphosis, some elements of the young insect's nervous system remain intact through the process.

Adult tobacco hookworms—a species of moth—<u>can remember things</u> （ that 1 it learned as a caterpillar）, which means （ that 2 despite the dramatic nature of metamorphosis, some elements of the young insect's nervous system remain intact through the process）.

分析：that 1 引导的定语从句修饰 things；which 引导的定语从句修饰整个主句；that 2 引导的是宾语从句,顺译

翻译：成年的烟草钩虫——一种蛾子——能够记住它作为毛毛虫学到的东西,这意味着尽管有着戏剧性的蜕变性质,幼年昆虫的神经系统的一些元素在这个过程中仍保持完整。

10）While technological changes can be painful for workers whose skills no longer match the needs of employers, Lawrence Katz, a Harvard economist, says that no historical pattern shows these shifts leading to a net decrease in jobs over an extended period.

（ While technological changes can be painful for workers）（ whose skills no longer match the needs of employers）, <u>Lawrence Katz</u>, a Harvard economist, <u>says</u> （ that no historical pattern shows these shifts leading to a net decrease in jobs over an extended period）.

分析：while 引导状语从句,修饰主句；whose 引导定语从句,修饰 workers；that 引导宾语从句

翻译：哈佛经济学家劳伦斯·卡茨说,虽然技术变革对那些技能不再符合雇主需求的工人来说可能会很痛苦,但没有任何历史模式显示这些变化会导致长期内就业净减少。

11）These objects are a dark reddish color that suggests they are covered in carbon-rich gunk—just the sort of residue that might have been left behind on an icy object that had its outermost layers vaporized in the bright sunlight of the inner solar system.

These objects are a dark reddish color 〔that 1〕 suggests 〔(they are covered in carbon-rich gunk〕—just the sort of residue (〔that 2〕 might have been left behind on an icy object) 〔that 3〕 had its outermost layers vaporized in the bright sunlight of the inner solar system).

分析：that 1 是定语从句,修饰 colour；suggests 后的宾语从句省略了连词；that 2 是定语从句,修饰 residue；that 3 是定语从句,修饰 an icy object。

翻译：这些物体是深红色,表明它们被富含碳的黏糊糊的东西所覆盖——这是一种可能在最外层被内部太阳系亮光蒸发掉的冰之物体上留下的残留物。

12) Auersperg and colleagues reasoned that if a cockatoo must complete a chain of actions to receive a substantial reward at the end，and if each action leads only to the possibility of achieving the next action，then the bird could be unlikely to attain the final goal by mere chance.

Auersperg and colleagues reasoned 〔that〕 (〔if〕 a cockatoo must complete a chain of actions to receive a substantial reward at the end)，and (〔if〕 each action leads only to the possibility of achieving the next action)，then the bird could be unlikely to attain the final goal by mere chance.

分析：that 引导宾语从句；两个 if 引导的条件状语从句并列,修饰宾从的主干

翻译：奥尔施佩格和同事们推断,如果一只凤头鹦鹉必须完成一系列行动,最终获得实质性的奖励,如果每一项行动只导致实现下一项行动的可能性,那么鸟就不可能仅仅是偶然地实现最后目标。

13) The same barely-better-than-guessing accuracy is also found in experiments investigating how well speed daters can assess who wants to date them and who does not，how well job candidates can judge which interviewers were impressed by them and which were not，and even how well teachers can predict their course evaluations.

The same barely-better-than-guessing accuracy is also found in experiments/ investigating 〔how〕 well speed daters can assess (〔who〕 wants to date them) and (〔who〕 does not)〕，〔〔how〕 well job candidates can judge (〔which〕 interviewers were impressed by them) and (〔which〕 were not)〕，and (even 〔how〕 well teachers can predict their course evaluations).

分析：本句中所有的从句均是宾语从句；由三个 how 所连接的宾语从句是动词 investigating 的宾语；由 who 和 which 所连接的宾语从句分别属于动词 assess 和 judge 的宾语

翻译: 与猜测差不多的准确性也被发现在速配者评估谁想和他们约会,谁不想的调查中;求职者判断哪些面试官对他们印象深刻,哪些没有印象;甚至教师预测他们的课程评价的实验中。

14) Then participants in the no-outcome condition estimate the likelihood of a home team victory, whereas participants in the outcome condition are instructed to disregard their knowledge of how the game turned out and then make this same likelihood judgment while imagining themselves to be in the shoes of no-outcome participants.

Then participants in the no-outcome condition estimate the likelihood of a home team victory, [whereas participants in the outcome condition are instructed to disregard their knowledge of (how the game turned out) and then make this same likelihood judgment while imagining themselves to be in the shoes of no-outcome participants].

翻译: 然后,在不知结果情况下的参与者预估主队获胜的可能性,而知晓结果状态下的参与者被指示忽略他们对比赛结果的了解,然后想象在自己处于无结果参与者的位置时做出类似的可能性判断。

15) She found that the growth rates of the two species were nearly the same in the season (2007 - 2008) with close to average annual rainfall but that the invasive pinweed plants exhibited a greater growth rate than did the native heronbill plants in the season (2004 - 2005) when there was much more rainfall than in a typical year.

She found [that 1 the growth rates of the two species were nearly the same in the season (2007 - 2008)/with close to average annual rainfall] but (that 2 the invasive pinweed plants exhibited a greater growth rate)[than did the native heronbill plants in the season (2004 - 2005)](when there was much more rainfall than in a typical year).

分析: that 1 和 that 2 都是宾语从句;than 状语从句,顺译即可;when 引导定语从句,修饰 in the season (2004 - 2005)

翻译: 她发现,这两种植物的生长速度在接近平均年降雨量的季节(2007—2008 年)里几乎相同,但在降雨量比典型年份大得多的季节(2004—2005),入侵的凤尾草植物的生长展现出比本地太阳花植物更快的生长速度。

16) Colautti notes that the purple loosestrife found in North America contains far more genetic variability than the purple loosestrife indigenous to Europe, Asia, Africa, and parts of Australia, which suggests that there were multiple introductions of the

plant from different continents to the eastern seaboard of the United States.

Colautti notes (that 1 the purple loosestrife/found in North America/contains far more genetic variability than the purple loosestrife indigenous to Europe，Asia，Africa，and parts of Australia)，which suggests (that 2 there were multiple introductions of the plant from different continents to the eastern seaboard of the United States).

分析：that 1 和 that 2 均是宾语从句；which 引导定语从句，修饰整个宾语从句

翻译：科洛蒂指出，在北美发现的珍珠菜比原产于欧洲、亚洲、非洲和澳大利亚部分地区的珍珠菜具有更大的遗传变异性，这表明，是多次从不同大陆向美国东海岸引入了这种植物。

17）To be sure，there is contrary evidence showing that people can be roughly realistic in anticipating the altruism of others，but an increasing body of evidence suggests that when people are contemplating whether they should rely on the kindness of strangers，they suspect those strangers will prove more selfish than actually is the case.

To be sure，there is contrary evidence/showing (that 1 people can be roughly realistic in anticipating the altruism of others)，but an increasing body of evidence suggests (that 2 when people are contemplating whether they should rely on the kindness of strangers)，they suspect those strangers will prove more selfish (than actually is the case).

翻译：可以肯定的是，有相反的证据表明，人们可以大致现实地预测他人的利他，但越来越多的证据表明，当人们在考虑是否应该依赖陌生人的善良时，他们怀疑那些陌生人比实际情况更自私。

18）He developed a theory，based on archeological discoveries，that those basalt columns were astronomical observatories and had been used three hundred years before the Christian era to determine the Borana lunar calendar，which is still in use among shepherds in Ethiopia and Kenya.

He developed a theory，based on archeological discoveries，(that those basalt columns were astronomical observatories and had been used three hundred years before the Christian era/to determine the Borana lunar calendar)，(which is still in use among shepherds in Ethiopia and Kenya).

分析：that 引导的从句修饰 theory；which 引导定语从句，修饰 the Borana lunar calendar

翻译：他根据考古发现发展了一种理论。这个理论是：这些玄武岩柱是天文观测站，

并且被使用在公元前三百年来确定博拉纳农历;博拉纳农历仍在埃塞俄比亚和肯尼亚的牧羊人中使用。

四　固定搭配

应对长难句时,除了主干意识,还要有很强的固定搭配意识。所谓的固定搭配就是经常会一起出现的单词组,我们需要**看到这个词组的前半部分就能够预测到后半部分的内容,这样就可以避免被冗长的修饰信息干扰句子结构。**

1) The controversy is ⌈less⌉ about the remarkable discoveries of recent plant science ⌈than⌉ about how to interpret and name them.

The controversy is less about the remarkable discoveries of recent plant science than about how to interpret and name them.

分析:看到比较级就要想到比较对象,即使 than 与后面的信息被省略了也要根据上下文推理;"less A than B"还有一层意思是"与其说 A,不如说是 B"

翻译:这场争论**与其说**是关于最近植物科学的重大发现,**不如说**是关于如何解释和命名这些发现。

2) For both male vs. male and female vs. female, when the pair of individuals were from different colonies, fear of strangers and aggression toward such strangers was much more pronounced in the common mole rats from the arid environment, where resources were limited, than it was in the common mole rats from the wet environment.

For both male vs. male and female vs. female,(when the pair of individuals were from different colonies,)**fear** of strangers **and aggression** toward such strangers **was much** ⌈more⌉ **pronounced in the common mole rats from the arid environment**, where resources were limited, ⌈than⌉ **it was in the common mole rats from the wet environment.**

分析:more...than...

翻译:对于雄性对雄性和雌性对雌性两组而言,当每对中的个体来自不同的群体时,来自资源有限的干旱环境中的鼹鼠对陌生人的恐惧和对陌生人的攻击要比来自潮湿环境的鼹鼠更为明显。

3) The team realized not only do both rocks carry the same geochemical signature, but in comparing the Mariana and Nuvvuagittuq, they also discovered the rocks and the geochemistry of both sequences change in the exact same way.

The team realized ⌈not only⌉ **do both rocks carry the same geochemical signature,** ⌈but⌉

in comparing the Mariana and Nuvvuagittuq, **they** |also| **discovered the rocks and the geochemistry of both sequences change in the exact same way.**

分析：看到 not only，就得想到 but also，而且重点在 but also 后面的信息里

翻译：研究小组意识到，这两种岩石不仅具有相同的地球化学特征，而且在比较 Mariana 和 Nuvvuagittuq 时，他们还发现这两种层序的岩石和地质化学变化的方式完全相同。

4）Even more ominous for workers, they foresee dismal prospects for many types of jobs as these powerful new technologies are increasingly adopted not only in manufacturing, clerical, and retail work but in professions such as law, financial services, education, and medicine.

Even more ominous for workers, they foresee dismal prospects for many types of jobs（as these powerful new technologies are increasingly adopted |not only| in manufacturing, clerical, and retail work |but| in professions such as law, financial services, education, and medicine）.

分析：看到 not only，就得想到 but also，而且重点在 but（also）后面的信息里

翻译：对工人来说更为不祥的是，他们预见到许多类型的工作前景暗淡，随着这些强大的新技术不仅越来越多地被应用于制造业、文书业和零售业，而且在法律、金融服务、教育和医药等行业也越来越多地被采用。

5）This question is important not just because parasites can have major ecological and evolutionary impacts, but also because disease outbreaks can have devastating impacts in agricultural systems and on species of conservation concern.

This question is important |not just| because parasites can have major ecological and evolutionary impacts, |but also| because disease outbreaks can have devastating impacts in agricultural systems and on species of conservation concern.

分析：not just... but also... = not only... but also...

翻译：这个问题之所以重要，不仅因为寄生虫会对生态和进化产生重大影响，而且因为疾病暴发会对农业系统和物种保护产生毁灭性影响。

6）The company would then accrue credits for the difference between the "baseline" emissions that would have been released if some power plants had burned coal to generate electricity and the essentially zero emissions discharged by the wind farm.

The company would then accrue credits for the difference |between| the "baseline" emissions（that would have been released）（if some power plants had burned coal to generate electricity）$\boxed{\text{and}}$ the essentially zero emissions discharged by the wind farm.

分析：between...and...

翻译：然后,该公司将从某些发电厂烧煤发电产生的"基准排放"和风力发电场的零排放量之间的差异中获益。

7）Biologists have found that natural selection will find the optimal balance between the metabolic costs of developing particular areas of the brain and the benefits yielded.

Biologists have found that natural selection will find the optimal balance $\boxed{\text{between}}$ the metabolic costs of developing particular areas of the brain $\boxed{\text{and}}$ the benefits yielded.

分析：between...and...

翻译：生物学家发现,自然选择将在开发大脑特定区域的代谢成本和产生的效益之间找到最佳平衡。

第八章

综合练习与解析

练习一

要求：分析句子并翻译，注意句首【句子分析符号：主干（从句）意群/意群】。

1) Unable to deal with her complexity，her inherent challenge to every expectation of race and sex，history in the early 20th century all but forgot her.

2) By prohibiting mixed uses and mandating inordinate amounts of parking and unreasonable setback requirements，most current zoning laws make it impossible—even illegal—to create the sort of compact walkable environment that attracts us to older neighborhoods and historic communities all over the world.

3) Given the potential of these products to reduce the environmental impact of farming，it's ironic that traditional advocates for sustainable agriculture have led a successful campaign to blacklist GMOs irrespective of their applications.

4) Appearing at hundreds of freedom rallies and mass meetings during the early 1960s，they were the movement's singing newspaper—reporting and defining the actions and issues from the civil rights war zones where they were frequently arrested.

5) Conceived by television writer Gene Roddenberry as part American Western，part science fiction，and part contemporary morality play，Star Trek languished for two and a half years before being canceled as a ratings flop in January 1969.

6) Created in the optimistic afterglow of John F. Kennedy's inauguration of the space race，Star Trek's exploration of the "final frontier" was a theme that resonated with millions of idealistic and awestruck Americans who looked at the Apollo moon landings as crowning，positive achievement for humankind.

7) Fascinated by the difference between the world of appearances and the world of reality, in the visual and literary arts, the Bloomsberries (as they were sometimes called) experimented with brush and pen to express above all the subjective qualities of their work.

8) Unlike traditional power plants, which disguise themselves as other types of buildings, the JFK design is as honest as it is bold.

9) At the end of the Heian era, when political and military upheaval destroyed the leisurely culture in Kyoto, men, and martial virtues, took over the vernacular as well as official culture.

10) For the painters, who opened themselves up to the currents swirling around on the (European) Continent since the final days of Impressionism, this translated into an emphasis on line, mass, contour, and the rhythms they create.

11) In the winter of 1997, when the warm Gulf Stream edged shoreward toward the coast of Cape Hatteras, pressing against cold water rushing south in the Labrador Current, giant bluefin gathered in the warmth along the boundary.

12) The following year, when the Gulf Stream moved offshore and the chilly Labrador Current filled the waters of coastal Cape Hatteras, bluefin wintered in waters unknown to people.

13) Without trying to pretend that I'm an expert on it, because that's something you have to devote your whole life to, it's a second language that something in my heart was really drawing me toward.

14) In a culture that has undergone dramatic and far-reaching change in the last thirty years, Star Trek sweetens the often bitter alienation of contemporary change with the type of familiarity and constancy that only a show with a thirty-year history can offer.

15) For South Asian and Asian-American musicians, producers and disc jockeys who have been building their own scene in New York, the latest East-West hybrids are not just occasion for musical connections and experiments.

16) At the center of a network of influential women who ran the Women's Committee of the Democratic Party led by Molly Dewson, ER worked closely with the women who had dominated the nation's social reform struggles for decades.

17) In this woman who raised seven children during the day, and wrote at night, her prolific output fueled by an abiding passion for justice, Gornick finds the archetype of the feminist movement she knew in the 1970s, with its creative energy, its excitement at having identified the problem to be solved.

18) As a testament to the significance these stories held for the writers who collected them, many of these interviews became the raw material for later works of important fiction.

19) Although the largest giant redwood in existence does not hold any records for being the oldest, tallest or broadest tree in the world, nothing can match its sheer volume.

20) While these men and women promoted the art and literature they created in Harlem between 1924 and 1929, the Renaissance they are credited with starting was much more than an intellectual movement.

21) When these seekers from far-flung comers of the world began filling the vacant but plentiful housing Harlem had to offer, these railroad porters, domestic house cleaners, former tenant fanners, and immigrants brought their music, their literature, and their stories with them uptown to Harlem.

22) When he wrote or talked of New Orleans, of being out there with his horn or following the parades or listening to mentors like Joe Oliver, Armstrong never failed to project a joy so profound that it became an antidote to the blues of daily living.

23) If any one work by the Bloomsbury painters sums up adequately the era's avant-garde break with London's Victorian taste in art, and the influence of the French Post-Impressionists on British artists, it would be Vanessa Bell's 1915 oil on canvas of Mary St. John Hutchinson.

24) While Europeans were sailing close to the coastlines of continents before developing navigational instruments that would allow them to venture onto the open ocean, voyagers from Fiji, Tonga, and Samoa began to settle islands in an ocean area of over 10 million square miles.

25) When Donna House, a Navajo ethnobotanist, steps gingerly through the barbed wire fence into her backyard—a former alfalfa field along the Rio Grande now brimming with native plants framed by a distant mesa—there is a sense of homecoming, of reunion, of land returning to its origins.

26) When Bombay Dreams, the musical about making it in the Indian film capital known as Bollywood, was imported from London to Broadway in 2004, it introduced some listeners to the madcap eclecticism of *filmi*, the song-and-dance numbers that punctuate Bollywood sprawling musicals.

27) If a stage performance at its best makes us experience a certain inevitability, leading us to think of the actor's interpretation of the play, "This must be so," then a CD-ROM has the power to make us think, "It could be so different."

28）But，perhaps because the waning days of the twentieth century and the first days of the twenty-first have defined a new "age of invention," one as dynamic and transforming as the one that occurred over a hundred years ago，interest in Edison has recently skyrocketed.

29）Because that dimming can be mimicked by other phenomena，such as the pulsations of a variable star or a large sunspot moving across a star's surface，the Kepler scientists won't announce the presence of a planet until they have seen it transit at least three times—a wait that may be only a few days or weeks for a planet rapidly circling close to its star but years for a terrestrial twin.

30）While the cod，haddock，flounder，and plaice who dwell year-round in the North Sea and the Gulf of Mexico are cold-blooded，their body temperatures rising and falling in synchrony with the surrounding water，thus limiting their geographic range，swordfish and bluefin，exquisitely adapted to live in the vastness of the sea，are free from the boundaries imposed by temperature.

31）One of the most striking of the transparent glass buildings that are appearing like ghostly apparitions in cities around the world，the Rose Center for Earth and Space at the American Museum of Natural History in Manhattan marks a new age in glass architecture.

32）A traditional "old school" Indian，as she sometimes jokingly refers to herself，as well as an environmental scientist，she has worked for or consulted with the Nature Conservancy，the federal Fish and Wildlife Service，the National Park Service，the Navajo Nation and others，helping to protect rare and endangered plants that have cultural，as well as ecological，significance.

解析

1—7 的句式均是：短语(分词短语/介词短语等)，主干

1）**Unable to deal with her complexity,**/her inherent challenge to every expectation of race and sex，/**history in the early 20th century all but forgot her.**

难点：all but 几乎；差不多

翻译：无法应付她的复杂性,她对种族和性别的每一个预期的内在挑战,20 世纪初的历史几乎都忘记了她。

2）By prohibiting mixed uses/and mandating inordinate amounts of parking and unreasonable setback requirements，/**most current zoning laws make it impossible**—even illegal—**to create the sort of compact walkable environment**（that attracts us to older neighborhoods and historic communities all over the world）.

难点: 破折号插入成分可先忽略

翻译: 通过禁止混合使用,批准过多的停车场地和不合理的屋顶平台要求,大多数现行的分区法使得创造那种吸引我们到世界各地的老社区和历史社区的紧凑的步行环境是不可能的,甚至是不合法的。

3) **Given the potential of GMO products** to reduce the environmental impact of farming, **it's ironic (that traditional advocates for sustainable agriculture have led a successful campaign to blacklist GMOs** irrespective of their applications).

难点: given 鉴于;irrespective of 不管,不顾;that 连接的是主语从句

翻译: 鉴于转基因减少了农业对环境影响的潜力,具有讽刺意味的是,可持续农业的传统倡导者成功地将转基因生物列入黑名单,而不管其用途如何。

4) **Appearing at hundreds of freedom rallies and mass meetings**/during the early 1960s, **they were the movement's singing newspaper**—reporting and defining the actions and issues/from the civil rights war zones (where they were frequently arrested).

难点: 这里的 singing newspaper 指的是"用唱歌的方式来报道"

翻译: 在 20 世纪 60 年代早期,出现在数百个自由集会和群众集会上,他们用唱歌的方式来报道这些运动——报道和界定他们经常被捕的民权运动地区的行动和问题。

5) Conceived by television writer Gene Roddenberry as part American Western, part science fiction, and part contemporary morality play,/**Star Trek languished for two and a half years**/before being canceled as a ratings flop in January 1969.

难点: conceive...as 认为……是;三个 part... 并列;ratings 收视率;flop(电影、戏剧、聚会等)不成功

翻译: 被电视剧作家吉恩·罗登伯里认为是部分美国西部片,部分科幻片以及部分当代道德剧,《星际迷航》在萎靡不振了两年半后的 1969 年 1 月因收视率惨淡而被取消前。

6) Created in the optimistic afterglow of John Kennedy's inauguration of the space race, **Star Trek's exploration of the "final frontier" was a theme** (**that resonated with millions of idealistic and awestruck Americans**) (who looked at the Apollo moon landings as crowning, positive achievement for humankind).

难点: resonate with 与……共鸣

翻译: 在约翰·肯尼迪关于太空竞赛的就职演讲的乐观余晖中创作的,《星际迷航》对"最后的边疆"的探索是一个引起了数以百万计的理想主义和惊叹的美国人共鸣的主题,他们把阿波罗登月视为人类至高无上的成就。

7) **Fascinated by the difference** between the world of appearances and the world of reality, in the visual and literary arts, **the Bloomsberries** (as they were sometimes called) **experimented with brush and pen/to express above all the subjective qualities of their work**.

难点：in the visual and literary arts 是主句的状语，修饰 experiment with...；above all 最重要地

翻译：被表象世界和现实世界之间的差异所吸引，在视觉艺术和文学艺术中，布鲁姆斯伯里（正如他们被称呼的那样）尝试用笔刷和笔来表达他们作品的最重要的主观品质。

8—13 句的结构均是：**短语，从句，主干**；其中，从句修饰前面的短语

8) **Unlike traditional power plants，**（which disguise themselves as other types of buildings，）**the JFK design is as honest as it is bold.**

难点：as honest as (it is) bold 诚实又大胆（诚实的程度和大胆的程度一样）

翻译：与传统的发电厂伪装成其他类型的建筑不同，肯尼迪机场的设计既诚实又大胆。

9) **At the end of the Heian era，**（when political and military upheaval destroyed the leisurely culture in Kyoto，）**men**，and martial virtues，**took over the vernacular as well as official culture.**

难点：A，and B，结构中，B 是对于 A 的次要补充，而非平等的并列

翻译：在平安时代末期，当时政治和军事动乱摧毁了京都的悠闲文化，男人和军事美德，接管了方言和官方文化。

10) **For the painters，**（who opened themselves up to the currents/swirling around on the〔European〕Continent/since the final days of Impressionism，）**this translated into an emphasis on line，mass，contour，and the rhythms**（they create）.

难点：open oneself to 乐于接受；对……开放；swirl 打旋；current 潮流

翻译：对于那些愿意接受自印象主义末期以来在欧洲大陆上涌动的潮流的画家来说，这意味着他们强调线条、质量、轮廓和他们创造的节奏。

11) **In the winter of 1997，**（when the warm Gulf Stream edged shoreward toward the coast of Cape Hatteras，/pressing against cold water/rushing south in the Labrador Current，）**giant bluefin gathered in the warmth along the boundary.**

难点：pressing 的逻辑主语是 Gulf Stream；rushing 的逻辑主语是 cold water

翻译：1997 年冬天，当时温暖的墨西哥湾流逐渐向哈特拉斯角海岸移动，紧贴着拉布拉多海流中向南涌动的冷水，巨大的蓝鳍金枪鱼聚集在沿着边界的温暖区域里。

12) **The following year，**（when the Gulf Stream moved offshore/and the chilly Labrador Current filled the waters of coastal Cape Hatteras，）**bluefin wintered in waters unknown to people.**

难点：waters（大片）水域；winter 过冬

翻译：第二年，当时墨西哥湾流向近海移动，寒冷的拉布拉多海流充满了哈特拉斯角沿岸的水域，蓝鳍金枪鱼在人们所不知道的水域过冬。

13) Without trying to pretend that I'm an expert on it，（because that's something

you have to devote your whole life to,）**it's a second language**（**that something in my heart was really drawing me toward**）.

难点：devote. . . to. . . 将……致力于……

翻译：不用假装我是这方面的专家，因为这是我一生都要致力于的东西，它是一门使我内心充满兴趣的第二语言。

14—18 句主干结构是：短语(从句)，主干

14）In a culture（that has undergone dramatic and far-reaching change in the last thirty years）, ***Star Trek* sweetens the often bitter alienation of contemporary change/ with the type of familiarity and constancy**/（that only a show with a thirty-year history can offer）.

难点：用表示味觉的 bitter 和 sweeten 来表达感觉

翻译：在一个过去三十年里经历了戏剧性和深远变化的文化中，《星际迷航》用一种只有三十年历史的剧集才能提供的熟悉和恒久使苦涩的当代文化由疏远变得甜蜜。

15）For South Asian and Asian-American musicians, producers and disc jockeys（who have been building their own scene in New York）, **the latest East-West hybrids are not just occasion for musical connections and experiments.**

难点：scene 活动领域;界;坛;圈子

翻译：对于一直在纽约建造他们自己的圈子的南亚及亚裔美国音乐家、制作人和 DJ 来说，最新的东西方混合不仅仅是音乐联系和实践。

16）**At the center of a network of influential women**（who ran the Women's Committee of the Democratic Party led by Molly Dewson）, **ER worked closely with the women**（who had dominated the nation's social reform struggles for decades）.

翻译：在一个由莫莉·道森领导的民主党妇女委员会的有影响力的女性组成的网络中心，ER 与那些几十年来主导国家社会改革斗争的女性密切合作。

17）**In this woman**（who raised seven children during the day, and wrote at night）, her prolific output fueled by an abiding passion for justice, **Gornick finds the archetype of the feminist movement**（she knew in the 1970s）, with its creative energy, its excitement at having identified the problem to be solved.

难点：her prolific output fueled by an abiding passion for justice 是一个短语,是句子"her prolific output was fueled by an abiding passion for justice"的省略

翻译：在这个白天养育七个孩子，晚上写作的妇女身上，她对正义的持久热情推动了她丰富的作品，戈尼克发现了她在 20 世纪 70 年代所知道的女权运动的原型，有创造性的精力，以及发现解决问题时的兴奋。

18）**As a testament to the significance** these stories held/for the writers（who collected them）, **many of these interviews became the raw material** for later works of important fiction.

难点: a testament to... 对于……的证据;定语从句 these stories held 省略了连词 that; hold significance for... 对……有重要意义

翻译: 作为这些材料对于收集他们的作者的重要证据,很多采访后来变成了重要的小说的素材。

19—30 句的结构是：从句,主干

19)（Although the largest giant redwood in existence does not hold any records for being the oldest，tallest or broadest tree in the world），**nothing can match its sheer volume.**

难点: nothing can match... 是一个最高级的表达方式

翻译: 尽管现存最大的巨型红杉没有任何世界上最古老、最高或最宽的树的记录,但没有什么能比得上它的体积。

20) While these men and women promoted the art and literature（they created in Harlem between 1924 and 1929），**the Renaissance**（they are credited with starting）**was much more than an intellectual movement.**

难点: much more than 远不止是……; credit...with... 认为……有……品质;认为是……的功劳

翻译: 尽管这些人推动了他们在 1924 年至 1929 年间在哈莱姆区创作的艺术和文学,但他们开创的文艺复兴远不止是一场知识分子运动。

21)（When these seekers from far-flung comers of the world began filling the vacant but plentiful housing Harlem had to offer），**these railroad porters，domestic house cleaners，former tenant fanners，and immigrants brought their music，their literature，and their stories with them** uptown to Harlem.

难点: far-flung 遥远的; comer 到场者;定语从句 Harlem had to offer 省略了连词 that

翻译: 当这些来自世界遥远角落的人们开始填补哈莱姆区大量空置的住房时,这些铁路搬运工、家庭清洁工、前房客和移民把他们的音乐、文学和故事带到了哈莱姆住宅区。

22)（When he wrote or talked of New Orleans, of being out there with his horn or following the parades or listening to mentors like Joe Oliver），**Armstrong never failed to project a joy** so profound（that it became an antidote to the blues of daily living）.

难点: horn（乐器）号; project 展现; so...that... 如此……以至于……; an antidote to... 是……的解药; blue 忧郁

翻译: 当阿姆斯特朗写下或谈到新奥尔良,谈到他在外面吹号,谈到他在游行,或谈到他在听像乔·奥利弗这样的导师讲话时,他总能表现出喜悦,这种喜悦是如此的深刻以至于成了日常忧郁生活的解药。

23）（**If any one work** by the Bloomsbury painters **sums up** adequately **the era's avant-garde break** with London's Victorian taste in art，a**nd the influence** of the French Post-Impressionists on British artists），<u>**it would be Vanessa Bell's 1915 oil on canvas of Mary St. John Hutchinson**</u>.

难点：oil 油画；on canvas 和 of Mary St.John Hutchinson 均修饰 oil

翻译：如果有任何一幅布鲁姆斯伯里画家的作品能充分总结出这个时代与伦敦维多利亚时代艺术品位的前卫突破，以及法国后印象派画家对英国艺术家的影响，那将是凡妮莎·贝尔 1915 年创作的玛丽·圣约翰·哈钦森画布油画。

在 23—30 句中，在"从句，主干"这个结构中，从句中的成分又有较长修饰语，导致信息量过大，这时可以忽略从句中的修饰语，只看从句主干和主句信息

24）**While Europeans were sailing close to the coastlines of continents** before developing navigational instruments（that would allow them to venture onto the open ocean），**voyagers from Fiji，Tonga，and Samoa began to settle islands** in an ocean area of over 10 million square miles.

难点：从句部分信息过多，that 引导的定语从句是琐碎信息，可忽略

翻译：当在开发使他们能够冒险进入开阔海域的航海仪器之前，欧洲人在靠近大陆海岸线的地方航行时，来自斐济、汤加和萨摩亚的航海家开始在面积超过 1 000 万平方英里的海洋中定居岛屿。

25）（**When Donna House**，a Navajo ethnobotanist，**steps gingerly through the barbed wire fence into her backyard**—a former alfalfa field along the Rio Grande now brimming with native plants framed by a distant mesa—）<u>**there is a sense of homecoming，of reunion，of land returning to its origins.**</u>

难点：gingerly 小心翼翼地；through 穿过；brim with 充满；frame 形成……的边框；破折号中的内容可跳过；句尾的三个 of 短语并列，修饰 sense

翻译：当纳瓦霍民族植物学家唐娜·霍斯小心翼翼地穿过带刺的铁丝网走进她的后院——曾经里奥格兰德沿岸的一片紫花苜蓿地，现在被远处的岩滩围成一片充满本地植物的地方——有一种回家的感觉，有一种团圆的感觉，有一种土地回归原始的感觉。

26）（**When *Bombay Dreams***，the musical about making it in the Indian film capital known as Bollywood，**was imported from London to Broadway in 2004**），<u>**it introduced some listeners to the madcap eclecticism of *filmi***</u>，the song-and-dance numbers（that punctuate Bollywood sprawling musicals）.

难点：make it 成功；number 歌舞；when 从句中的主语和谓语之间有插入成分，可忽略；filmi 在句尾有同位语对其进行解释说明

翻译：当 2004 年《孟买之梦》——一部关于在印度电影之都宝莱坞成功的音乐剧——从伦敦引进百老汇时，这部音乐剧向一些听众介绍了 filmi 中疯狂的折衷主义，filmi 是宝

莱坞风情万种的音乐剧中穿插的歌舞表演。

27）（If a stage performance at its best makes us experience a certain inevitability，leading us to think of the actor's interpretation of the play，"This must be so，"）then **a CD-ROM has the power to make us think，"It could be so different."**

难点：at its best 在最好的状态；think of 认为；leading us to...非谓语短语修饰从句，导致从句部分整体较长

翻译：如果一个达到最佳状态的舞台表演让我们体验到某种必然性，让我们认为演员对这部戏的解读："这一定是这样"，那么一张光盘就能够让我们思考："它可能会如此不同。"

28）But，**perhaps because the waning days of the twentieth century and the first days of the twenty-first have defined a new "age of invention,"** one as dynamic and transforming as the one（that occurred over a hundred years ago），**interest in Edison has recently skyrocketed.**

难点：age 时代；the waning days 和 the first days 并列做从句的主语；as...as...结构；one 指代 age；that 从句修饰 the one

翻译：但是，也许是因为 20 世纪的落幕和 21 世纪的初期定义了一个新的"发明时代"，一个像一百多年前那样充满活力和变化的时代，最近人们对爱迪生的兴趣直线上升。

29）（Because **that dimming can be mimicked by other phenomena**，such as the pulsations of a variable star or a large sunspot moving across a star's surface），**the Kepler scientists won't announce the presence of a planet**（until they have seen it transit at least three times）—a wait（that may be only a few days or weeks for a planet rapidly circling close to its star but years for a terrestrial twin）.

难点：信息量较大，注意抓主干信息

翻译：因为这种变暗可以被其他现象所模仿，比如变星的脉动或者一个巨大的黑子在恒星表面移动，开普勒的科学家们在看到一颗行星至少经过三次之前不会宣布它的存在——对于一颗在其恒星附近快速旋转的行星来说，等待的时间可能只有几天或几周，而对于一颗陆地孪生行星来说，等待的时间可能是几年。

30）[**While the cod，haddock，flounder，and plaice**（who dwell year-round in the North Sea and the Gulf of Mexico）**are cold-blooded**，their body temperatures rising and falling in synchrony with the surrounding water，thus limiting their geographic range]，**swordfish and bluefin**，exquisitely adapted to live in the vastness of the sea，**are free from the boundaries imposed by temperature.**

难点：从句的主干与主句的主干均有长修饰语干扰；"their body temperatures rising and falling in synchrony with the surrounding water，thus limiting their geographic range"是对 cold-blooded 的进一步解释

翻译：虽然常年生活在北海和墨西哥湾的银鳕鱼、黑线鳕鱼、比目鱼和鲽都是冷血动物，它们的体温与周围的海水同步升降，从而限制了它们的地理范围，但是鳗鱼和蓝鳍金枪鱼非常适应生活在浩瀚的大海中，不受温度的边界限制。

31—32 句的结构是：同位语，主干

31）One of the most striking of the transparent glass buildings（that are appearing like ghostly apparitions in cities around the world），**the Rose Center for Earth and Space at the American Museum of Natural History in Manhattan marks a new age in glass architecture.**

难点：句首的名词短语是同位语，不是主语

翻译：全世界城市中像幽灵一样的透明玻璃建筑中最显著之一的，位于曼哈顿的美国自然历史博物馆的地球和太空的玫瑰中心标志着玻璃建筑进入了一个新时代。

32）A traditional "old school" Indian，as she sometimes jokingly refers to herself，as well as an environmental scientist，**she has worked for or consulted with the Nature Conservancy**，the federal Fish and Wildlife Service，the National Park Service，the Navajo Nation and others，helping to protect rare and endangered plants（that have cultural，as well as ecological，significance）.

难点：refer to 提及，称呼；as she sometimes jokingly refers to herself 是个插入成分，可忽略；A traditional "old school" Indian 是同位语

翻译：作为一名传统的"老派"印度人，正如她有时玩笑般地称呼自己一样，以及一名环境科学家，她曾为自然保护协会、联邦鱼类和野生动物管理局、国家公园管理局、纳瓦霍民族和其他机构工作或提供咨询，帮助保护具有文化价值以及生态意义的珍稀濒危植物。

练习二

要求：分析句子并翻译，注意主干【句子分析符号：主干（从句）意群/意群】。

1）The study of disease，for the physician，demands the study of identity，the inner worlds that patients，under the spur of illness，create.

2）Her home ground，or habitat—a word she prefers to landscape—stretches far into the horizon，to the cottonwoods along the river presided over by the steep，rocky mesa.

3）Moreover，the light and weather in that part of the world，so much farther north than Atlantic City，is much gloomier and more dramatic than that of the Jersey coast.

4）The work of Ha Jin，who has lived in the United States for more than 20 years and now teaches creative writing at Boston University, has been greeted with similar wonderment.

5) String theory, which nowadays dominates the research programs and main funding of theoretical physics in many western universities, was not so much discovered as invented in order to solve a vexing explanatory deficit.

6) Massive boulders, shipped from as far away as the Northwest Territories, echo the curvaceous form of the museum building, its rough-hewn limestone surface meant to recall a cliff face sculptured by the wind.

7) Fry felt, moreover, that nineteenth-century British artists in general, and Victorian painters in particular, had lost their way by becoming preoccupied with attempts at highly detailed and, in some cases, photographically accurate representations of reality.

8) Goethe's color theory, his Farbenlehre (which he regarded as the equal of his entire poetic opus), was, by and large, dismissed by all his contemporaries and has remained in a sort of limbo ever since, seen as the whimsy, the pseudoscience, of a very great poet.

9) Spalding, born in 1984 in Portland, Oregon, to a single mother of African American, Asian, Native American, and Hispanic heritage, belongs to a growing movement of young musicians who have taken a less traditional approach to the music.

10) Brent Berlin, an ethnobiologist at the University of Georgia, discovered this when he read pairs of names, each consisting of one bird and one fish name, to a group of 100 undergraduates, and asked them to identify which was which.

11) The art of stripping, which is carried out from mid-June to mid-August (while the sap is rising), lies in making longitudinal and then horizontal cuts on the trunk in order to release strips or sheets without damaging the inner bark.

12) Louis-Jacques-Mande Daguerre, a Frenchman known for his elaborate and whimsical stage design in the Paris theater, began building on the work of Joseph Nicephore Niepce to try to produce a fixed image.

13) But knowing where exactly our food comes from—geographically, culturally, and genetically—is of paramount importance to the rather small portion of our own species that regularly concerns itself with the issue of food security.

14) With arched eyebrow, lips slightly pursed, and cool self-assurance, Mrs. Hutchinson sits noticing something to her left, and the viewer, disarmed at first perhaps by the flatness of the composition and the coarse brushwork, feels as much as sees the various tones of the few colors in the portrait—ochre, green, and pink, and,

where the whites of the eyes should be，teal.

15）Thus the giant trees，what I have come to love and admire about Sarapiqui ［rain forest］when I stop at a ridge above the forest canopy，are supported precariously upon a thin，fragile tissue of microbes and organic matter，matter that is turned over，transformed by millipedes，sowbugs，ants，and millions of other tiny creatures.

16）While Jin has always been polite to his interviewers，it seems quite clear that Nan Wu，the poet who is the protagonist of A Free Life，speaks for his creator in response to a magazine editor who asks "Can you imagine your work becoming part of our language?

解析

1—16 句结构均是：主语，修饰，谓语

1）**The study of disease**，for the physician，**demands the study of identity，the inner worlds** that patients，under the spur of illness，create.

难点：主句和从句中的主语和谓语都被插入成分分割裂了

翻译：疾病的研究对于医生来说，需要研究身份，研究病人在疾病刺激下产生的内心世界。

2）**Her home ground**，or habitat——a word she prefers to landscape——**stretches far into the horizon，to the cottonwoods** along the river presided over by the steep，rocky mesa.

难点：prefer A to B 比起 B 更喜欢 A；preside over 主持（这里是拟人的用法，意思就是河边主要都是 mesa）

翻译：她的家园，或者说栖息地——相比风景而言她更喜欢用这个词——远远地延伸到地平线，直至沿着由陡峭的岩石平顶山所控制的河边的棉林。

3）Moreover，**the light and weather** in that part of the world，so much farther north than Atlantic City，**is much gloomier and more dramatic** than that of the Jersey coast.

难点：that of the Jersey coast 中的 that 指的是 the light and weather，在英语中，比较的对象一定要一致；另外 the light and weather 作为一个整体，是单数，所以用 that 而不是 these

翻译：此外，比大西洋城更北方的，世界上的那个地区的光线和天气，比泽西海岸的天气更为阴暗和戏剧性。

4）**The work of Ha Jin**，who has lived in the United States for more than 20 years and now teaches creative writing at Boston University，**has been greeted with similar wonderment.**

难点：greet...with... 用……迎接

翻译：在美国生活了 20 多年，现在在波士顿大学任教创造性写作的 Ha Jin 的作品也受到了相似的赞誉。

5）**String theory**，which nowadays dominates the research programs and main funding of theoretical physics in many western universities，**was not so much discovered as invented** in order to solve a vexing explanatory deficit.

难点：not so much A as B 与其说是 A，不如说是 B

翻译：当今主导西方许多大学理论物理研究项目和主要资助的弦理论与其说是被发现的倒不如说是被发明的，来解决令人困扰的解释性缺陷。

6）**Massive boulders**，shipped from as far away as the Northwest Territories，**echo the curvaceous form of the museum building**，its rough-hewn limestone surface meant to recall a cliff face sculptured by the wind.

难点：hew 劈；mean... to... 想要……成为，"its rough-hewn limestone surface meant to recall a cliff face sculptured by the wind" = "its rough-hewn limestone surface was meant to recall a cliff face sculptured by the wind"，但因为它在句中不是一个独立的句子，只是一个修饰成分，所以把 was 去掉后，由原来的句子降级为一个短语，但是意思本身没有变化

翻译：从西北地区运来的巨石，与博物馆建筑的曲线形状相呼应，它粗糙的石灰岩表面本意是来唤起被风雕刻的悬崖面。

7）**Fry felt**，moreover，that **nineteenth-century British artists** in general，and Victorian painters in particular，**had lost their way** by becoming preoccupied with attempts at highly detailed and，in some cases，photographically accurate representations of reality.

难点：be preoccupied with 全神贯注于，and Victorian painters in particular 用两个逗号隔开的并列成分，通常只是补充说明，相当于插入成分

翻译：此外，弗赖伊认为，19 世纪的英国艺术家，特别是维多利亚时期的画家，已经迷失，因为他们全神贯注于对现实的高度细节和在某些情况下像摄影一样精确的呈现。

8）**Goethe's color theory**，his *Farbenlehre*（which he regarded as the equal of his entire poetic opus），**was**，by and large，**dismissed by all his contemporaries and has remained in a sort of limbo** ever since，seen as the whimsy，the pseudoscience，of a very great poet.

难点：regard...as... 认为……是……；by and large 总体上，总的来说；limbo 处于不定状态

翻译：歌德的色彩理论，他的色彩学（他认为这与他整个诗作平等），大体上被所有同时代的人所排斥，从此一直处于一种不定的状态，被视为一个伟大诗人的奇想、伪科学。

9）**Spalding**，born in 1984 in Portland，Oregon，to a single mother of African American，Asian，Native American，and Hispanic heritage，**belongs to a growing**

movement of young musicians（who have taken a less traditional approach to the music）.

难点：born to... 由……生下来

翻译：于 1984 年出生在俄勒冈州波特兰市,母亲是一位有着非洲裔美国人、亚洲裔、美洲土著人和西班牙裔血统的单身母亲,斯伯丁属于那种兴起的年轻音乐家,他对音乐的态度不那么传统。

10）**Brent Berlin**，an ethnobiologist at the University of Georgia，**discovered this**（**when he read pairs of names**，each consisting of one bird and one fish name，**to a group of 100 undergraduates，and asked them to identify which was which**）.

难点：主句和从句都有两个逗号引入的插入成分

翻译：佐治亚大学的民族学学家布伦特·伯林发现了这一点,当他把由一只鸟和一条鱼组成的名字组读给 100 个研究生听并要求他们确定哪个是哪个时。

11）**The art of stripping**，which is carried out from mid-June to mid-August（while the sap is rising），**lies in making longitudinal and then horizontal cuts on the trunk in order to release strips or sheets without damaging the inner bark**.

难点：sap（植物体内运送养分的）液

翻译：在 6 月中旬至 8 月中旬(当树液上升时)进行的剥皮的艺术是在树干上进行纵向和横向切割,在不会损坏内部树皮的情况下剥下条状或片状(树皮)。

12）**Louis-Jacques-Mande Daguerre**，a Frenchman known for his elaborate and whimsical stage design in the Paris theater，**began building on the work of Joseph Nicephore Niepce to try to produce a fixed image.**

难点：build on... 以……为基础

翻译：以在巴黎剧院的精细且异想天开的舞台设计而闻名的法国人 Louis-Jacques-Mande Daguerre 开始在 Joseph Nicephore Niepce 的作品基础上努力创造一个固定的形象。

13）But **knowing where exactly our food comes from**—geographically，culturally，and genetically—**is of paramount importance to the rather small portion of our own species**（that regularly concerns itself with the issue of food security）.

难点：破折号可跳过;rather small portion of our own species 略带自嘲语气;that 从句修饰 rather small portion

翻译：但是,知道我们的食物来源——地理上、文化上和基因上——对于我们自己的物种中经常关注食品安全问题的一小部分来说是至关重要的。

14）With arched eyebrow，lips slightly pursed，and cool self-assurance，**Mrs. Hutchinson sits**/noticing something to her left，**and the viewer**，disarmed at first perhaps by the flatness of the composition and the coarse brushwork，**feels as much as sees the various tones of the few colors in the portrait**—ochre，green，and pink，and，where the whites of the eyes should be，teal.

难点：tone 色调；feel as much as sees... 感受到和看到一样多，可引申为，不仅可以看到，还能感受到

翻译：眉弓，嘴唇微微地撅起，冷静自信，哈钦森夫人坐在那里，注意她左边的东西；观画者，可能起初因平坦的构图和粗糙的笔触放下了戒心，赏画者不仅能看到，也能感受到画像里少数色彩的多样性——赭石、绿色和粉色，以及本应该是眼白部分的蓝绿色。

15）Thus **the giant trees**，what I have come to love and admire about Sarapiqui［rain forest］when I stop at a ridge above the forest canopy，**are supported precariously upon a thin，fragile tissue of microbes and organic matter**，matter（that is turned over，transformed by millipedes，sowbugs，ants，and millions of other tiny creatures）.

难点：主干之间的插入成分很长，可忽略

翻译：因此，当我停留在森林冠层上方的山脊上时，我开始喜欢和钦佩萨拉比基雨林的大树，被一个由微生物和有机物质组成的薄而脆弱的组织支撑着，这些有机物质被千足虫、潮虫、蚂蚁和数百万其他微小生物转化。

16）（**While Jin has always been polite to his interviewers**），**it seems quite clear**（that **Nan Wu**，the poet who is the protagonist of A Free Life，**speaks for his creator** in response to a magazine editor）（who asks "Can you imagine your work becoming part of our language?"）

难点：creator 指的是 Jin，也就是小说的作者

翻译：虽然金对采访者一向有礼貌，但似乎很明显，作为《自由生活》主角的诗人 Nan Wu 在回应杂志编辑的"你能想象你的作品成为我们语言的一部分吗？"这个问题时为其创作者发声。

练习三

要求：分析句子并翻译，注意主干【句子分析符号：主干（从句）意群/意群】。

1）Despite the seemingly sacred mission，political forces opposed to the use of federal money for WPA projects moved against sponsoring New Deal Democrats.

2）However，given that Marshall laid the foundation for today's racial landscape，his grand design of how race relations best work makes his life story essential for anyone delving into the subject.

3）The central idea of the public philosophy by which we live is that freedom consists in our capacity to choose our ends for ourselves.

4）People who say that sprawl is merely the natural product of marketplace forces at work fail to recognize that the game isn't being played on a level field.

5) As author Daniel Chiras says, more companies are recognizing that technologies that produce by-products society cannot absorb are essentially failed technologies.

6) In the black community, Anderson's accomplishments as a singer and the sense of pride and purpose she inspired brought her many honors.

7) The thing that had gone wrong with my sisters and myself, according to the extended family back home, was that we had settled in the United States of America where people got lost because they didn't have their family around to tell them who they were.

8) My mother and the other women I knew as a child, just before World War II began, were farm women, one or two generations removed from the real pioneer days, gentled and domesticated by the time I came among them.

9) That is because the technology used to make hordes of these menacing, computer-generated monsters move convincingly on screen turns out to be just what is needed to predict how crowds of humans move around inside buildings.

10) The variety of foods that we keep in our fields, orchards, and, secondarily, in our seed banks is critically important in protecting our food supply from plagues, crop diseases, catastrophic weather, and political upheavals.

11) The claim that capitalism has delivered us from excessive toil can be sustained only if we take as our point of comparison eighteenth- and nineteenth-century Europe and America—a period that witnessed what were probably the longest and most arduous work schedules in the history of humankind.

12) The driving forces behind the varied activities that made Harlem so vibrant in the twentieth century were sparked by the massive migration of black people from the rural South and the Caribbean.

13) Miss Anderson's power to move her listeners as can no other singer of her generation is not made less by the simple, almost unsmiling dignity which clothes her like a garment.

解析

1—13 句的结构均为：主语　长修饰语　谓语（修饰之前无逗号提示）

1) Despite the seemingly sacred mission, **political forces** opposed to the use of federal money for WPA projects **moved against sponsoring New Deal Democrats.**

难点: be opposed to...反对

翻译: 尽管这项使命看似神圣的,但反对将联邦资金用于 WPA 项目的政治力量反对赞助实施新政的民主党。

2）However，（given that Marshall laid the foundation for today's racial landscape），**his grand design** of how race relations best work **makes his life story essential** for anyone delving into the subject.

难点：given 鉴于，考虑到；lay the foundation for 为……打下基础；delve into 钻研，探索

翻译：然而，鉴于马歇尔为今天的种族环境奠定了基础，他对种族关系最大的贡献使他的生活故事对于任何研究这个问题的人来说都是必不可少的。

3）**The central idea** of the public philosophy（by which we live）**is**（**that freedom consists in our capacity to choose our ends for ourselves**）.

难点：本句的 by which we live ＝ by the public philosophy we live ＝ we live by the public philosophy；live by...philosophy 信奉……哲学；consist in... 存在于……中；end 目标

翻译：我们赖以生存的公共哲学的中心思想是，自由在于我们为自己选择目的的能力。

4）**People** who say that sprawl is merely the natural product of marketplace forces at work **fail to recognize**（**that the game isn't being played on a level field**）.

难点：at work 起作用；fail to ＝ don't；play on a level field 公平竞争

翻译：那些认为随意扩张仅仅是市场力量作用下的自然产物的人没有意识到这个游戏不是竞争公平的。

5）As author Daniel Chiras says, more companies are recognizing that technologies（that produce by-products（society cannot absorb）are essentially failed technologies）.

难点：定语从句 society cannot absorb 前省略了连词 that

翻译：正如作者丹尼尔·奇拉斯所说，越来越多的公司认识到，生产社会无法吸收的副产品的技术本质上是失败的技术。

6）In the black community，**Anderson's accomplishments** as a singer **and the sense of pride and purpose**（she inspired）**brought her many honors.**

难点：定语从句 she inspired 前省略了连词 that

翻译：在黑人社区，安德森作为一名歌手的成就以及她所激发的自豪感和目标感给她带来了许多荣誉。

7）**The thing**（**that had gone wrong with my sisters and myself**），according to the extended family back home，**was**（**that we had settled in the United States of America**）（where people got lost）（because they didn't have their family around to tell them who they were）.

难点：虽然从句很多，但基本都是串联式，按顺序直译即可

翻译：据老家的大家庭说，我和我的姐妹们的问题是，我们在美国定居，那里的人们迷

失了,因为他们没有家人在身边告诉他们自己是谁。

8) **My mother and the other women** (I knew as a child),(just before World War II begin),**were farm women**, one or two generations removed from the real pioneer days, gentled and domesticated by the time I came among them.

难点: by the time 到……为止; one or two generations removed from the real pioneer days 和 gentled and domesticated by the time I came among them 均是修饰前面的 farm woman

翻译: 我的母亲和我小时候认识的其他女人,就在第二次世界大战开始前,都是农妇,从真正的拓荒者时代经历了一两代人,直至我来到她们中间时,她们已经变得温文尔雅了。

9) That is (because the technology used to make hordes of these menacing, computer-generated monsters move convincingly on screen **turns out to be just what is needed to predict how crowds of humans move around inside buildings**).

难点: make...do... 使……做……; turn out to be 结果是

翻译: 这是因为,用来让成群结队的这些具有威胁性的、由计算机生成的怪物在屏幕上令人信服地移动的技术,正是预测人类如何在建筑物内走动所需要的技术。

10) **The variety of foods** (that we keep in our fields, orchards, and, secondarily, in our seed banks) **is critically important** in protecting our food supply from plagues, crop diseases, catastrophic weather, and political upheavals.

难点: in our fields, orchards 和 in our seed banks 并列; protect...from... 使……免受……; upheaval 巨变;动荡

翻译: 我们保存在田地、果园中,其次是种子库中的各种食物,对于保护我们的食物供应免受瘟疫、农作物病害、灾难性天气和政治动荡的影响是至关重要的。

11) **The claim** (that capitalism has delivered us from excessive toil) **can be sustained** (**only if we take as our point of comparison eighteenth- and nineteenth-century Europe and America**)—a period (that witnessed what were probably the longest and most arduous work schedules in the history of humankind).

难点: deliver...from... 把……从……中解救出来; toil 劳累的工作; take as our point of comparison eighteenth- and nineteenth-century Europe and America = take eighteenth- and nineteenth-century Europe and America as our point of comparison; 破折号后面的内容对 eighteenth- and nineteenth-century Europe and America 进行解释

翻译: 资本主义把我们从过度劳累中解救出来的说法,只有当我们把 18 世纪和 19 世纪的欧洲和美国作为比较的对象时才能得到支持,这一时期可能是人类历史上工作时间最长、最艰苦的时期。

12) **The driving forces** behind the varied activities (that made Harlem so vibrant in

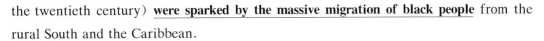

the twentieth century) **were sparked by the massive migration of black people** from the rural South and the Caribbean.

难点：A behind B 可引申为，A 是 B 的原因

翻译：使哈林文艺在 20 世纪如此充满活力的各种活动背后的驱动力，是由来自南部农村和加勒比地区的大批黑人移民引发的。

13）**Miss Anderson's power** to move her listeners（as can no other singer of her generation）**is not made less by the simple，almost unsmiling dignity**（which clothes her like a garment）.

难点：move 打动，感动；as can no other singer of her generation = as no other singer of her generation can（move），这是 as 引导的方式状语从句

翻译：安德森女士以她同时代没有其他歌手可以做到的方式感动听众的力量一点也不会被她那朴素、不苟言笑的像一件衣服一样包裹着她的尊严所减弱。

练习四

要求：分析句子并翻译，注意句尾【句子分析符号：<u>主干</u>（从句）意群/意群】。

1）Typically a clump of Mucuna occupies little more than a few square meters of habitat floor space，an area not even the girth of an average canopy tree of the tropical rain forest.

2）These stories are further evidence that there was a renaissance in Harlem，one that may have been completely missed by some of the intellectuals who first coined the phrase.

3）These prepared the way for his most spectacular demonstration，the demonstration in 1861 that color photography was possible，despite the fact that photographic emulsions were themselves black and white.

4）The result was a very different，less elastic sense of what might be called the ownership of time，an ownership that employers took quite seriously and were able to measure with increasing，almost fanatical precision by the mid-18th century.

5）Through Homer's eyes，it is a world in which people live in close contact with nature and natural forces，a world where landscape and ocean are viewed not as a paradise but as powers and presences that can be enjoyed and whose threats can sometimes be overcome.

6）Birds have developed a special kind of bone，called medullary bone，which females lay down in the marrow cavity of existing bones during the weeks before laying commences and use as a source of calcium when the eggshells are being formed.

7) Her years of using her gift in live performance had taught her how to make a listener feel a song, not just hear it, by making use of vibrato, trills, enunciation, dynamic variety (variations in loudness), and melisma, a gospel hallmark in which the vocalist sings several notes within the space of a single syllable.

8) They also hinged on a special financing scheme to pay recalcitrant developing countries for the cost of instituting deep cuts in emissions, an option that is an essential part of addressing the climate change problem, but one that is much harder to carry out.

9) Maguire and her team thought it was possible that they might discover anatomical differences in the brains of the memory champs, evidence that their brains had somehow reorganized themselves in the process of doing all that intensive remembering.

10) Sister Rosetta Tharpe, as she was professionally billed, was not supposed to be a highlight of the fall 1938 Cotton Club revue, a fast-paced variety show headlining Cab Calloway and the Nicholas Brothers, young dancers who thrilled audiences with their acrobatic elegance.

11) During her eight years advising the Nature Conservancy about conservation on Indian lands, House worked with the Tohono Oodham (the Papago) in southern Arizona, on whose lands grows Kearney's blue star, a wildflower that in the late 1980's federal botanists declared the rarest plant in Arizona, believing that it was down to its last eight specimens.

12) Cows that eat grass are commonly touted as the sustainable alternative to feedlot beef, a resource-intensive form of production that stuffs cows with a steady diet of grain fortified with antibiotics, growth hormones, steroids, and appetite enhancers that eventually pass through the animals into the soil and water.

13) Conversion of a mangrove forest to a shrimp pond changes a carbon sink into a carbon source, liberating the accumulated carbon back into the atmosphere—but 50 times faster than it was sequestered.

14) My sisters and I would roll our eyes, but in fact, we cared very much for those letters, "the favorite" bragging that she had gotten the original as opposed to one of three carbon copies.

15) After the war, Tubman settled in Auburn, N. Y., where she struggled economically the rest of her life, undertaking domestic work and public speaking to support herself and dedicating much of her energy to philanthropic efforts on behalf of the freed people.

16）Painter, curator, and instigator, Fry studied the sciences at Cambridge University in the 1880s, developing a habit of skepticism that would serve him well as he guided painters Vanessa Bell and Duncan Grant toward modernism in the years leading up to World War I.

17）For years, young jazz musicians adopted a near slavish devotion to sounding like players from jazz's golden age (anywhere between the nineteen-twenties and the arrival of the Beatles in America, in 1964), rejecting the pop, rock, and fusion experimentation that came in the nineteen-seventies and eighties.

18）The literary significance of this is that I believed in what essayist William Hazlitt called the "spirit of the age"—meaning that this age we were living in had a character all its own and could be related to other ages and periods, thus constituting a historical scene in which a period was known through its writers and its writers through their period.

19）However, for human visualization it is easiest to think in terms of a family of curved lines leaving the fish through a series of portholes spaced along the front half of the body, all curving round in the water and diving into the fish again at the tip of its tail.

20）It would give the most skilful [European] builder a shock to see craft having no more breadth of beam than three [arm] spans carrying a spread of sail so large as to befit one of ours with a beam of eight or ten spans, and which, though without means of lowering or furling the sail, make sport of the winds and waves during a gale.

21）Rosetta's first session reveals a young woman capable of finding and communicating the emotional core of a song through exquisite phrasing, inventive vocal technique, and guitar playing of originality, confidence, and grace.

22）It was left to women to write in Japanese, in the vernacular, while men reserved the supposedly more difficult Chinese for themselves, unaware that what they were writing was imitation Chinese literature, inferior to the original, and, above all, inferior to what contemporary women were writing in their native tongue.

解析

本练习中的所有句子，均是主干信息比较清晰明确，但是句尾部分出现大量的修饰语。

1—12句的结构：句尾同位语提供解释（斜体表示）

1）**Typically a clump of Mucuna occupies little more than a few square meters of habitat floor space**, *an area not even the girth of an average canopy tree of the tropical* *rain forest* .

难点：girth 围长,腰围,干围;little more than 不超过

翻译：通常,一丛鹭豆占据的栖息地面积不过就几平方米,这一面积甚至还不到热带雨林平均树冠树的周长。

2）**These stories are further evidence**（**that there was a renaissance in Harlem**）, *one that may have been completely missed by some of the intellectuals who first coined the phrase* .

难点：renaissance 文艺复兴;coin 创造;one 指的是 renaissance

翻译：这些故事进一步证明了哈林文艺曾有过一次文艺复兴,但最早创造这一短语的知识分子已经完全忽略了这一复兴。

3）**These prepared the way for his most spectacular demonstration**, *the demonstration in 1861 that color photography was possible*, *despite the fact that photographic emulsions were themselves black and white* .

难点：prepare the way for... 为……做准备

翻译：这为他最壮观的演示铺平了道路,1861 年的展示表明彩色摄影是可能的,尽管摄影乳胶本身是黑白的。

4）**The result was a very different**, **less elastic sense of what might be called the ownership of time**, *an ownership that employers took quite seriously and were able to measure with increasing*, *almost fanatical precision by the mid-18th century* .

难点：take...seriously 严肃对待

翻译：结果是对时间的所有权产生了一种完全不同的、不那么有弹性的感觉,这种所有权到 18 世纪中叶,雇主们对其相当重视,能够以越来越高的、近乎狂热的精确度来衡量。

5）Through Homer's eyes, **it is a world**（**in which people live in close contact with nature and natural forces**）, *a world where landscape and ocean are viewed not as a paradise but as powers and presences that can be enjoyed and whose threats can sometimes be overcome* .

难点：view...as... 把……视作;not...but... 不是……而是……

翻译：在荷马的眼中,这是一个人们与自然和自然力密切接触的世界,在这个世界里,风景和海洋不是天堂,而是可以享受的力量和存在,它们的威胁有时是可以克服的。

6）**Birds have developed a special kind of bone**, *called medullary bone*, *which females lay down in the marrow cavity of existing bones during the weeks before laying commences and use as a source of calcium when the* eggshells are being formed.

难点：commence 开始;句尾虽然长,但信息基本是串联的,按顺序理解即可

翻译：鸟类已经发展出一种特殊的骨头,称为脊髓骨,雌性在产蛋前的几周内,将其放

置在现有骨头的脊髓腔中，并在蛋壳形成时用作钙的来源。

7) **Her years of using her gift** in live performance **had taught her how to make a listener feel a song**, not just hear it, by making use of vibrato, trills, enunciation, dynamic variety（variations in loudness）, and melisma, *a gospel hallmark in which the vocalist sings several notes within the space of a single syllable*.

难点：gift 天赋；hallmark 特征

翻译：她多年来在现场表演中运用自己的天赋，学会了如何让听众感受到一首歌，而不仅仅是听到它，通过使用颤音、发音、动态变化（响度的变化）和花腔（一个福音的标志，演唱者在一个音节的空间内唱几个音符）。

8) **They also hinged on a special financing scheme/ to pay recalcitrant developing countries/for the cost of instituting deep cuts in emissions**, *an option that is an essential part of addressing the climate change problem*, *but one that is much harder to carry out*.

难点：hinged on 依赖，取决于；address 处理；one 指代 option

翻译：它们还依赖于一项特殊的融资计划，向顽固的发展中国家支付实施大幅减排的代价，这是解决气候变化问题的一个重要部分，但实施起来要困难得多。

9) Maguire and her team thought **it was possible**（**that they might discover anatomical differences in the brains of the memory champs**）, *evidence that their brains had somehow reorganized themselves in the process of doing all that intensive remembering*.

难点：it 是形式主语，真正的主语是 that 引导的从句

翻译：马奎尔和她的团队认为，他们有可能在记忆冠军的大脑中发现解剖学上的差异，这证明他们的大脑在进行所有强化记忆的过程中，以某种方式重组了自己。

10) **Sister Rosetta Tharpe**, as she was professionally billed, **was not supposed to be a highlight of the fall 1938 Cotton Club revue**, *a fast-paced variety show headlining Cab Calloway and the Nicholas Brothers*, *young dancers who thrilled audiences with their acrobatic elegance*.

难点：bill...as... 把……宣传为……

翻译：罗塞塔·撒普，正如她被专业宣传的一样，不应该成为 1938 年秋季棉花俱乐部的一个亮点，棉花俱乐部是一个快节奏的、以凯比·卡洛威和尼古拉斯兄弟为头条的表演，凯比·卡洛威和尼古拉斯兄弟是用优雅的特技来使观众振奋的年轻舞蹈演员。

11) During her eight years/advising the Nature Conservancy about conservation on Indian lands, **House worked with the Tohono Oodham（the Papago）in southern Arizona**, on whose lands grows Kearney's blue star, *a wildflower（that in the late 1980's federal botanists declared the rarest plant in Arizona*, *believing that it was down to its last eight specimens*.）

难点：down to 下降至……

翻译: 在为自然保护协会提供关于印第安土地保护建议的八年中,豪斯与亚利桑那州南部的托霍诺奥德姆合作,在那里的土地上生长着卡尼蓝星,这是一种野花,在20世纪80年代末,联邦植物学家宣布它是亚利桑那州最稀有的植物,相信它只剩下最后八个标本了。

12) <u>**Cows**</u> (*that eat grass*) **are commonly touted as the sustainable alternative to feedlot beef**, *a resource-intensive form of production* (*that stuffs cows with a steady diet of grain fortified with antibiotics, growth hormones, steroids, and appetite enhancers*) (*that eventually pass through the animals into the soil and water*).

难点: feedlot 饲养场;tout... as... 标榜,吹捧;stuff... with... 用……填满;fortify... with... 加入……来强化

翻译: 吃草的奶牛通常被吹捧为饲养场牛肉的可持续替代品,饲养场牛肉是一种资源密集型的生产方式,用添加抗生素、生长激素、类固醇和增食欲剂的强化的谷物稳定地喂养奶牛,这些抗生素、生长激素、类固醇和增食欲剂最终通过牲畜进入土壤和水。

13—20句的结构是:主干后面有非谓语动词(斜体表示);信息量虽大,但结构并不复杂,重点在于把握非谓语短语的逻辑主语

13) **Conversion of a mangrove forest** to a shrimp pond **changes a carbon sink into a carbon source**, *liberating the accumulated carbon back into the atmosphere—but 50 times faster than it was sequestered*.

难点: conversion of A to B 将A转化为B;liberating 的逻辑主语是前面整个句子所表达的事情(= which liberates the accumulated carbon back into the atmosphere)

翻译: 红树林改造成虾池把碳沉淀转变为碳源,将累积的碳释放回大气中,但速度比封存的快50倍。

14) **My sisters and I would roll our eyes, but in fact, we cared very much for those letters,** "*the favorite*" *bragging* (*that she had gotten the original as opposed to one of three carbon copies*).

难点: roll one's eyes 翻白眼;care for 在乎;the favorite 指最受宠的孩子;brag 吹嘘;as opposed to 而不是,相对于;bragging 的逻辑主语是 the favorite

翻译: 我和我的姐妹们都会翻白眼,但事实上,我们非常喜欢那些信,最受宠的那个孩子吹嘘她拿到了原件,而不是三份复写本中的一份。

15) After the war, **Tubman settled in Auburn, N. Y.,** (*where she struggled* economically the rest of her life, *undertaking domestic work and public speaking to support herself and dedicating much of her energy to philanthropic efforts on behalf of the freed people*).

难点: undertaking 和 dedicating 的逻辑主语都是 Tubman;dedicate... to... 将……奉献于

翻译：战后,塔布曼定居在纽约州的奥本,在那里她在经济上挣扎了一辈子,靠从事家务工作和公开演讲来养活自己,并将大部分精力奉献给代表被解放的人民的慈善事业。

16）Painter, curator, and instigator, **Fry studied the sciences** at Cambridge University in the 1880s, *developing a habit of skepticism（that would serve him well）（as he guided painters Vanessa Bell and Duncan Grant toward modernism in the years leading up to World War I.）*

难点：developing 的逻辑主语是 Fry

翻译：画家、策展人和发起人弗赖伊于 19 世纪 80 年代在剑桥大学学习科学,养成了怀疑主义的习惯,这对他很有帮助,当他在第一次世界大战前的几年引导画家瓦内萨·贝尔和邓肯·格兰特走向现代主义时。

17）For years, **young jazz musicians adopted a near slavish devotion to sounding like players from jazz's golden age**（anywhere between the nineteen-twenties and the arrival of the Beatles in America, in 1964）, *rejecting the pop, rock, and fusion experimentation（that came in the nineteen-seventies and eighties）.*

难点：a devotion to...对……的献身;sounding like players from jazz's golden age 整体做 to 的宾语,年轻音乐家的献身对象;rejecting 的逻辑主语是 young jazz musicians

翻译：多年来,年轻的爵士乐音乐家采取近乎奴性的献身到听起来像爵士乐的黄金时代的歌手(20 世纪 20 年代到 1964 年披头士乐队来到美国的任何时间),他们拒绝流行音乐,摇滚乐和 20 世纪 70 年代和 80 年代的音乐融合物。

18）**The literary significance** of this **is that I believed in** what essayist William Hazlitt called the **"spirit of the age"**—*meaning that this age we were living in had a character all its own and could be related to other ages and periods, thus constituting a historical scene（in which a period was known through its writers and its writers through their period）.*

难点：a period was known through its writers and its writers through their period＝a period was known through its writers and its writers were known through their period

翻译：这一点的文学意义在于,我相信散文家威廉·哈兹里特所说的"时代精神",也就是说,我们生活的这个时代有自己的特点,并且可以与其他时代和时期相联系,从而构成了一个历史场景,在这个场景中,一个时期是通过它的作者被了解而它的作者又通过他们的时期被了解。

19）However, for human visualization **it is easiest to think in terms of a family of curved lines** *leaving the fish through a series of portholes spaced along the front half of the body, all curving round in the water and diving into the fish again at the tip of its tail.*

难点：for human visualization 没有用逗号停顿;in terms of 从……角度/方面看;a family of 一群；leaving、curving 和 diving 的逻辑主语均是 lines；space 以一定的间隔排列；paced along... 修饰 portholes

翻译：然而，对于人类的视觉化来说，最容易从一系列曲线的角度去想，这些曲线通过沿着鱼前半部分身体上以一定间隔排列得像一组舷客，在水里弯曲绕成一圈，然后再次在鱼的尾端回到鱼体内。

20）**It would give the most skilful〔European〕builder a shock**/**to see craft** *having no more breadth of beam than three*〔*arm*〕*spans carrying a spread of sail*/*so large as to befit one of ours with a beam of eight or ten spans*，*and*（*which*，*though without means of lowering or furling the sail*，*make sport of the winds and waves during a gale*）．

难点：it 是形式主语，to see... 是真正的主语；craft 船；beam 梁；spans 跨度；so... as to... 如此……以至于……；befit 合适；means 方式，方法；make sport of 戏弄；gale 大风；having 和 carrying 的逻辑主语是 craft；which 定语从句修饰 craft

翻译：最有技术的(欧洲)建船者看到这样一艘船也会大吃一惊的，其横梁宽度不超过三个(臂)跨度，携带的船帆如此之大，以至于适合我们中的一个拥有八个或十个跨度的横梁，并且，这种船帆虽然没有降下或卷起帆的方法，却能在大风中劈波斩浪。

21—22 句共同结构：句尾有较长的形容词短语修饰(斜体)；与前面非谓语和同位语情况类似，重点是找到修饰对象。虽然信息量大，但本身句式结构不是非常复杂，都是串联的方式。

21）Rosetta's first session reveals a young woman/capable of finding and communicating the emotional core of a song/through exquisite phrasing，inventive vocal technique，and guitar playing of originality，confidence，and grace.

难点：capable of... 修饰 a young woman

翻译：通过精湛的措辞，创造性的声乐技巧，吉他的原创性，自信和优雅的演奏，罗赛塔的第一场就揭示了一个年轻的女人能够找到和传达一首歌的情感核心。

22）**It was left to women to write in Japanese**，in the vernacular，（**while men reserved the supposedly more difficult Chinese for themselves**，unaware）that（what they were writing）was imitation Chinese literature，inferior to the original，and，above all，inferior to（what contemporary women were writing in their native tongue）．

难点：in the vernacular = in Japanese；unware 修饰 men；inferior to... 修饰 imitation Chinese literature

翻译：让女性用日语、本国语言写作，而男性则把据说更难的中文留给自己，却不知道自己写的是模仿中国文学，不如原创的，尤其重要的是还不如当代女性用母语写作。

练习五

要求：分析句子并翻译，标记连词【句子分析符号：主干(从句)意群/意群】。

1) What began in the early 1990s as a place with a few hundred curious visitors has now become a tourism destination that attracts 10.000 penguin peepers a year.

2) What was needed—and what Cristofori invented—was an instrument as large and robust as the big harpsichords that would also allow the dynamic-range that before had only been available on the flimsy clavichords.

3) What is illusory is the widely held assumption that humans have toiled miserably throughout history, only to be freed from labor by 20th-century technology.

4) But leisure was something that manual workers did not know they possessed until after they had exchanged agricultural jobs for industrial ones.

5) Equally important, leisure is no longer folded continuously into the contours of the year in a pattern that reflects the rhythms of season and holiday.

6) The museum's directors were initially reluctant to give the green light to such an experimental system of glass construction because nothing like it had been used here in the United States.

7) The sufficiency or insufficiency of food was a powerful motivator of human action, sometimes on a national or even continent-wide scale, with consequences that could take decades to unfold.

8) One can only wonder whether he foresaw the extraordinary potential of the contralto singer whom he had agreed to manage, or the remarkable relationship they would enjoy.

9) In fact, Edison derided scientists who spent their lives "studying the fuzz on a bee" as morally suspect and complained when one of his sons began to pursue theoretical physics.

10) And yet if leisure indeed became a right, it was one that people virtually stopped fighting for during the manufacturing boom that followed World War II, when "workers" became better known as "consumers".

11) If behavioral complexity is one consequence of mental power, then we might expect to uncover among dinosaurs some signs of social behavior that demand coordination, cohesiveness and recognition.

12) If that sounds like pure eco-nut talk, try the question he puts to potential clients when he undertakes any of his architectural projects: "I ask, 'How do we love all children, all species, all time?'"

13) After a day of McDonough's instruction in much more than architecture, one sees that his utopianism is grounded in a unified philosophy that—in demonstrable and practical ways—is changing the design of the world.

14) Decca had recorded songs by gospel singer Mahalia Jackson in May 1937, but they did so poorly that the label dropped her and didn't venture back into the gospel field until it took a chance on Rosetta seventeen months later.

15) Justice Marshall gave a clear signal that while legal discrimination had ended, there was more to be done to advance educational opportunity for blacks and to bridge the wide canyon of economic inequity between blacks and whites.

16) While none of the stories in *A Renaissance in Harlem* are fictional in the strictest sense of the word, many of them are literary versions crafted by writers who struggled to accurately tell the stories they found in creative ways.

17) All the women were required to withdraw to the periphery, where, Vivian Gornick writes in her new book on Stanton, *The Solitude of Self*, "They could see but not be seen, hear but not be heard".

18) Though a decidedly unnerving discovery, this was very much of a piece with the results of mathematical models of many physical and biological systems that exhibit the phenomena popularized under the heading "chaos theory".

19) In the case of traffic, the physicists found that given a certain combination of vehicle density and vehicle flow rate along a highway, the solution to their equations undergoes a sudden phase shift from freely moving traffic to what they call synchronized traffic.

20) The physicists had noticed that if one simulated the movement of cars and trucks on a highway using the well-established equations that describe how the molecules of a gas move, some distinctly eerie results emerged.

21) This deviation from standard casting brings a new force to the musical—which itself changed musicals forever by introducing plot and narrative development into what had previously been considered a frivolous genre.

22) Helmholtz was very conscious of "color constancy"—the way in which the colors of objects are preserved, so that we can categorize them and always know what we are looking at, despite great fluctuations in the wavelength of the light illuminating them.

23) It is not clear when a redwood stops expanding, because there is no definite record of any giant redwood dying of old age and they continue to grow indefinitely until a natural disaster, such as a lightning strike, or storm-force wind, occurs.

24) Whether the sheep or the goat was the first animal to be domesticated remains an open question, though the balance of probabilities favors the goat—an animal which has been greatly maligned through the ages, for its destructive browsing habits as well

as its pungent smell.

25) So it is, too, on the National Mall in Washington, D.C., where House is the guiding force behind a landscape of cornfields, meadows, forest and wetlands—complete with 3,500 specially introduced ladybugs—outside the Smithsonian Institution's National Museum of the American Indian.

26) Peacock speculates that ceremonies and legends depicting the prairie turnip as sacred may reflect the tribes' need to conserve the plant, which the nomadic Blackfoot may have had difficulty harvesting as they moved from one site to the next.

27) For me, as a physician, nature's richness is to be studied in the phenomena of health and disease, in the endless forms of individual adaptation by which human organisms, people, adapt and reconstruct themselves.

28) It plagued the art world when the printing process allowed the mass reproduction of great works of art, and its effects can still be seen whenever one overhears a museum-goer express disappointment that the Van Gogh he sees hanging on the wall is nowhere near as vibrant as the one on his coffee mug.

29) Stanton, Gornick argues, is the model for this revolutionary feminism, because she was the one who always refused to scale back her just demands out of political expediency, who remained faithful to the radical vision of foil equality.

30) Stanton's radical demand for equality for both blacks and women lost her, moreover, the friendship of many feminist women, who were willing to postpone the suffrage fight to be on good terms with powerful men and to preserve solidarity with the abolitionist cause.

31) If read with the care Humez's introduction to the documentary section of her book prescribes, the collection of Tubman sources she has assembled provides the basis for a far fuller and more complex portrait than has hitherto been available.

32) Color constancy, for him, was a special example of the way in which we achieve perceptual constancy generally, make a stable perceptual world from a chaotic sensory flux—a world that would not be possible if our perceptions were merely passive reflections of the unpredictable and inconstant input that bathes our receptors.

33) He formalized the notions of primary colors and color mixing by the invention of a color top (the colors of which fused, when it was spun, to yield a sensation of grey), and a graphic representation with three axes, a color triangle, which showed how any color could be created by different mixtures of the three primary colors.

34) By the time it became a state, eighteen years later, the Territory, as it was known, was populated by white settlers from other parts of the country, as well as a

number of emancipated slaves and forcibly resettled Native Americans，who braved drought，harsh economic times，and often brutal and complicated racial interactions to make the Territory their home.

35）In a very real sense，the forests of wild foragers and the orchards of traditional farmers in such centers of crop diversity are the wellsprings of diversity that plant breeders，pathologists，and entomologists return to every time our society whittles the resilience in our fields and orchards down to its breaking point.

36）The first of San Francisco's road signs were only just being erected，hammered up by an enterprising insurance underwriter who hoped to win clients by posting directions into the countryside，where drivers retreated for automobile "picnic parties" held out of the view of angry townsfolk.

37）The story of this conflict is the story of how we view ourselves in relation to animals，whether we can replace the assumption of "dominion" that has been so destructive to us and the natural world with a worldview that recognizes that we live in a state of reciprocity with the birds and the beasts—that we are not only the product of nature but also part of it.

38）With no formal education or apprenticeship to any watchmaker，Harrison nevertheless constructed a series of virtually friction-free clocks that required no lubrication and no cleaning，that were made from materials impervious to rust，and that kept their moving parts perfectly balanced in relation to one another，regardless of how the world pitched or tossed about them.

解析

本部分的句子虽然长,但是本身结构并不复杂,几乎都是用连词将一连串的句子串联到一起,就像火车头拉车厢一样。虽然信息量大,但信息间关系比较清晰,阅读时注意适当地停顿消化信息即可。同时,我们也能意识到,从句本身或者长句子本身不可怕,可怕的是句子结构的混乱,尤其像练习二三中的主干结构被打散,所以最重要的还是主干意识。

1）What began in the early 1990s as a place with a few hundred curious visitors has now become a tourism destination（that attracts 10.000 penguin peepers a year）.

翻译: 从20世纪90年代初开始只有几百名好奇的游客的地方,现在已经成为一个旅游目的地,每年吸引10 000位企鹅窥视者。

2）What was needed—and what Cristofori invented—was an instrument as large and robust as the big harpsichords（that would also allow the dynamic-range）（that before had only been available on the flimsy clavichords）.

难点：as...as...结构

翻译：需要的是——克里斯托福里发明的是——一种像大竖琴一样大而坚固的乐器，它能够展现出以前只在脆弱的古钢琴上才有的动态范围。

3）|What| is illusory is the widely held assumption（|that| humans have toiled miserably throughout history，only to be freed from labor by 20th-century technology）.

翻译：虚幻的是一个普遍持有的假设，认为人类在整个历史上都在痛苦地劳作，只有被 20 世纪的技术从劳动中解放出来。

4）But leisure was something |that| manual workers did not know（they possessed）（|until after| they had exchanged agricultural jobs for industrial ones）.

难点：定语从句 they possessed 前省略了 that；exchange A for B 用 A 交换 B

翻译：但是，休闲是直到体力劳动者在把农业工作换成工业工作之后才知道自己拥有的东西。

5）Equally important，leisure is no longer folded continuously into the contours of the year in a pattern（|that| reflects the rhythms of season and holiday）.

翻译：同样重要的是，休闲不再以反映季节和假期节奏的模式不断地折叠到一年的轮廓中。

6）The museum's directors were initially reluctant to give the green light to such an experimental system of glass construction（|because| nothing like it had been used here in the United States）.

难点：give green light to 通过

翻译：博物馆的负责人最初不愿意给这样一个玻璃建筑实验系统亮绿灯，因为在美国像这样的系统没有被使用过。

7）The sufficiency or insufficiency of food was a powerful motivator of human action，sometimes on a national or even continent-wide scale，with consequences（|that| could take decades to unfold）.

翻译：粮食的充足或不足是人类行动的有力动力，有时在全国甚至整个大陆范围内采取行动，其后果可能需要几十年才能展开现出来。

8）One can only wonder |whether| he foresaw the extraordinary potential of the contralto singer（|whom| he had agreed to manage），or the remarkable relationship（they would enjoy）.

难点：定语从句 they would enjoy 省略了 that

翻译: 人们只能好奇他是否预见到了他愿意合作的女低音歌手的非凡潜力,或者他们彼此享受到的美妙关系。

9) In fact, Edison derided scientists (who spent their lives "studying the fuzz on a bee") as morally suspect and complained (when one of his sons began to pursue theoretical physics).

难点: deride...as... 嘲笑……是……

翻译: 事实上,爱迪生嘲笑那些一生"研究蜜蜂上的绒毛"的科学家在道德上不可信,并抱怨他的一个儿子开始追求理论物理学。

10) And yet (if leisure indeed became a right), it was one (that people virtually stopped fighting for during the manufacturing boom) (that followed World War II), (when "workers" became better known as "consumers").

难点: one 指代 right

翻译: 然而,如果休闲确实成为一种权利,那它就是一个人们在第二次世界大战后制造业繁荣时期实际上停止了为之奋斗的一种权利,当时"工人"更多地被称为"消费者"。

11) (If behavioral complexity is one consequence of mental power), then we might expect to uncover among dinosaurs some signs of social behavior (that demand coordination, cohesiveness and recognition).

难点: uncover among dinosaurs some signs of social behavior = uncover some signs of social behavior among dinosaurs,因为 some signs of social behavior 有定语从句修饰,所以放到 among dinosaurs 后面

翻译: 如果行为复杂性是精神力量的结果,那么我们可能会期望在恐龙中发现一些需要协调、凝聚力和认可的社会行为的迹象。

12) (If that sounds like pure eco-nut talk), try the question (he puts to potential clients) (when he undertakes any of his architectural projects): "I ask, 'How do we love all children, all species, all time?'"

难点: 定语从句 he puts to potential clients 前省略了 that;nut 怪人;all time 一直

翻译: 如果这听起来像是纯粹的生态怪人的谈话,那么看看当他接手任何一个建筑项目时他向潜在客户提出的问题:"我们如何一直爱所有的孩子,爱所有的物种?"

13) After a day of McDonough's instruction in much more than architecture, one sees (that his utopianism is grounded in a unified philosophy) (that—in demonstrable and practical ways—is changing the design of the world).

难点: much more than 不仅仅;one 泛指人们;be grounded in... 基于……

翻译：在麦克多诺不仅仅是建筑学的一天教学之后，人们看到他的乌托邦主义是建立在一个统一的哲学基础上的，这种哲学以可证明和实用的方式正在改变世界的设计。

14）Decca had recorded songs by gospel singer Mahalia Jackson in May 1937，but they did so poorly（that the label dropped her and didn't venture back into the gospel field）（until it took a chance on Rosetta seventeen months later）.

难点：so...that... 如此……以至于……；label 唱片公司；take a chance on 冒险；碰运气

翻译：迪卡唱片公司曾在1937年5月录制过福音歌手马哈丽亚·杰克逊的歌曲，但它们的表现太差，以至于唱片公司把她放弃了，并且不敢冒险回到福音领域，直到17个月后，公司才在罗赛塔身上开始尝试。

15）**Justice Marshall gave a clear signal** [that（while legal discrimination had ended），**there was more to be done** to advance educational opportunity for blacks and to bridge the wide canyon of economic inequity between blacks and whites].

难点：advance 促进；bridge 连接

翻译：法官马歇尔明确表示，虽然法律歧视已经结束，但仍有更多工作要做，以促进黑人的受教育机会，并弥合黑人和白人之间巨大的经济不平等鸿沟。

16）（While none of the stories in *A Renaissance in Harlem* are fictional in the strictest sense of the word），many of them are literary versions crafted by writers who struggled to accurately tell the stories（they found）in creative ways.

难点：in the sense of 在……意义上；craft 精心制作；定语从句 they found 前省略了 that

翻译：虽然《哈林文艺复兴》里的故事在最严格的意义上都不是虚构的，但其中许多都是作家精心制作的文学版本，他们努力以创造性的方式准确地讲述他们所发现的故事。

17）**All the women were required to withdraw to the periphery**，（where，Vivian Gornick writes in her new book on Stanton，*The Solitude of Self*，**"They could see but not be seen，hear but not be heard"**）

难点：Vivian Gornick writes in her new book on Stanton，*The Solitude of Self* 是个插入成分

翻译：所有的女人都被要求撤退到外围，在外围，维维安·戈尼克在她关于斯坦顿的新书《自我的孤独》中写道，"她们能看到但不被看见，听到但不被听到。"

18）Though a decidedly unnerving discovery，**this was very much of a piece**/**with the results of mathematical models of many physical and biological systems**（that exhibit the phenomena/popularized under the heading "chaos theory"）.

翻译：尽管这是一个令人不安的发现,但这在很大程度上是一个与许多物理和生物系统的数学模型的结果,这些物理和生物系统展示了在"混沌理论"标题下普及的现象。

19）In the case of traffic, the physicists found（that **given a certain combination of vehicle density and vehicle flow rate** along a highway, **the solution to their equations undergoes a sudden phase shift** from freely moving traffic to what they call synchronized traffic）.

难点：given 给定的;from...to... 从……到……

翻译：就交通来说,物理学家发现,在沿公路的给定车辆密度和车辆流量的一定组合下,其方程的解会经历从自由移动的交通到所谓的同步交通的突然阶段性转变。

20）**The physicists had noticed** [that if **one simulated the movement of cars and trucks** on a highway/**using the well-established equations**（that describe how the molecules of a gas move）, **some distinctly eerie results emerged**].

难点：one 泛指人们;using the well-established equations 的逻辑主语是 one

翻译：物理学家们注意到,如果一个人用描述气体分子运动的建立方程模拟汽车和卡车在公路上的运动,就会出现一些明显的怪异结果。

21）**This deviation** from standard casting **brings a new force to the musical**—（which itself changed musicals forever/by introducing plot and narrative development/into what had previously been considered a frivolous genre）.

难点：deviation from 与……的偏离;casting 角色分配;演员挑选

翻译：这种偏离标准的演员挑选给音乐带来了新的力量——它本身通过将情节和叙事发展引入以前被认为是轻浮的流派,从而永远改变了音乐剧。

22）**Helmholtz was very conscious of "color constancy"**—the way（in which the colors of objects are preserved）,（so that we can categorize them and always know what we are looking at, despite great fluctuations in the wavelength of the light illuminating them）.

难点：illuminating them 的逻辑主语是 light

翻译：亥姆霍兹意识到"颜色的恒定性"——物体颜色的保存方式,以便我们能够对它们进行分类,并且始终知道我们在看什么,尽管照亮了它们的光的波长有很大的波动。

23）**It is not clear**（when a redwood stops expanding）,（because there is no definite record of any giant redwood dying of old age and they continue to grow indefinitely）（until a natural disaster, such as a lightning strike, or storm-force wind, occurs）.

难点：die of 死于……；until 从句的主干被插入成分分割

翻译：红木何时停止生长还不清楚，因为没有任何巨大红木死于衰老的确切记录，而且它们会持续无限期地增长，直到雷击或风暴等自然灾害发生。

24）（**Whether** the sheep or the goat was the first animal to be domesticated）**remains an open question**，（**though** the balance of probabilities favors the goat）—an animal（**which** has been greatly maligned through the ages，for its destructive browsing habits as well as its pungent smell）.

难点：an open question 尚未解决的问题；browse 吃草

翻译：第一个被驯养的动物是绵羊还是山羊，仍然是一个悬而未决的问题，尽管答案倾向于山羊——山羊它在过去的岁月里受到了极大的中伤，因为它破坏性的吃草习惯以及刺激性的味道。

25）**So it is**，too，**on the National Mall in Washington，D. C.**，（**where** House is the guiding force behind a landscape of cornfields，meadows，forest and wetlands—complete with 3,500 specially introduced ladybugs—outside the Smithsonian Institution's National Museum of the American Indian）.

难点：so it is＝it is so；complete with...包括，具有配套的……

翻译：华盛顿的国家广场也是如此，在那里，House 是美国国立印第安人博物馆外的玉米田、草地、森林和湿地景观背后的引导力量——包括 3 500 只被特别展示的瓢虫。

26）Peacock speculates（**that** ceremonies and legends depicting the prairie turnip as sacred **may reflect the tribes' need to conserve the plant**），（**which** the nomadic Blackfoot may have had difficulty harvesting）（**as** they moved from one site to the next）.

难点：depict...as... 把……描述为……

翻译：皮科克推测，把草原萝卜描绘为神圣的典礼和传说可能反映了部落保护这种植物的需要，当他们从一个地点迁移到另一个地点时，这种植物是游牧的黑脚族人难以收割的。

27）For me，as a physician，**nature's richness is to be studied in the phenomena of health and disease，in the endless forms of individual adaptation**（**by which** human organisms，people，adapt and reconstruct themselves）.

翻译：对我来说，作为一名医生，在健康和疾病现象中，在人类有机体（人）适应和重建自身的无休止的个体的适应形式中需要研究自然的丰富性。

28）**It plagued the art world**（**when** the printing process allowed the mass reproduction of great works of art），**and its effects can still be seen**（**whenever** one overhears a museum-goer express disappointment) (that the Van Gogh he sees hanging on the wall is nowhere near as vibrant as the one on his coffee mug).

难点：one 泛指人；nowhere near as...as... 不像……一样的……

翻译：这一现象困扰着艺术界,当印刷工艺可以大规模复制伟大艺术作品,并且它的影响仍然可以被看到,每当有人无意中听到博物馆的参观者失望地表示挂在墙上的梵高远不及咖啡杯上的梵高那么充满活力时。

29) **Stanton**, Gornick argues, **is the model for this revolutionary feminism**, because she was the one (who always refused to scale back her just demands out of political expediency), (who remained faithful to the radical vision of foil equality).

难点：scale back 缩减；just 正义的；out of 出于

翻译：戈尼克认为,斯坦顿是这种革命女权主义的典范,因为她一直拒绝出于政治权宜之计而降低她的公正要求,她始终忠于完全平等的激进愿景。

30) **Stanton's radical demand for equality** for both blacks and women **lost her**, moreover, **the friendship of many feminist women**, (who were willing to postpone the suffrage fight to be on good terms with powerful men and to preserve solidarity with the abolitionist cause).

难点：lost her, moreover, the friendship of many feminist women 中,moreover 是插入成分,可跳过；suffrage 选举权；on good terms with 与……关系好；cause 事业

翻译：而且,斯坦顿对黑人和妇女平等的激进要求使她失去了许多女性主义妇女的友谊,这些女性愿意推迟选举权斗争来与有权势的男性和睦相处以维护废奴事业。

31) If read with the care (Humez's introduction to the documentary section of her book prescribes), **the collection of Tubman sources** (she has assembled) **provides the basis for a far fuller and more complex portrait** (than has hitherto been available).

难点：定语从句 Humez's introduction to the documentary section of her book prescribes 省略了连词 that,修饰 care；prescribe 要求；定语从句 she has assembled 省略了连词 that,修饰 sources；hitherto 迄今,到目前为止

翻译：如果仔细阅读赫曼兹书中文献部分的引言,她所收集的塔布曼资料为一幅比迄今更完整、更复杂的肖像提供了基础。

32) **Color constancy**, for him, **was a special example of the way** (in which we achieve perceptual constancy generally, make a stable perceptual world from a chaotic sensory flux) —a world (that would not be possible) (if our perceptions were merely passive reflections of the unpredictable and inconstant input) (that bathes our receptors).

翻译：对他来说,色彩的恒常性是我们通常获得感知恒常性,从混乱的感觉流动中获得稳定的感知世界方式的一个特别例子——这个世界是不可能的,如果我们的感知仅仅是对沐浴着我们感受器的不可预测和不稳定输入的被动反映的话。

33) **He formalized the notions of primary colors and color mixing** by the invention of a **color top** (the colors of which fused, when it was spun, to yield a sensation of grey), **and a graphic representation with three axes**, a color triangle, which showed how any color could be created by different mixtures of the three primary colors.

难点：a color triangle 是 a graphic representation with three axes 的同位语,对其进行解释说明

翻译：他定义了三原色和颜色混合的概念,通过发明一种颜色顶部(在旋转时,这些颜色融合产生灰色感)和三轴图形(颜色三角形),它表明了如何通过三种原色的不同混合来创建任何颜色。

34) (By the time it became a state, eighteen years later), **the Territory**, (as it was known), **was populated** by white settlers from other parts of the country, **as well as a number of emancipated slaves and forcibly resettled Native Americans**, (who braved drought, harsh economic times, and often brutal and complicated racial interactions to make the Territory their home).

难点：by the time 到……为止(连词);brave 勇敢面对

翻译：18 年后,到它成为一个州时,Territory(正如我们所知)居住着来自国家其他地区的白人定居者,以及一些被解放奴隶和被迫重新安置的土著美洲人,他们勇敢地经受干旱、经济困难时期,而且经常是残酷复杂的种族互动,使 Territory 成为他们的家园。

35) In a very real sense, **the forests of wild foragers and the orchards of traditional farmers** in such centers of crop diversity **are the wellsprings of diversity** (that plant breeders, pathologists, and entomologists return to) (every time our society whittles the resilience in our fields and orchards down to its breaking point).

难点：wellspring 源泉,来源;every time 每次;whittle 削减

翻译：从非常真实的意义上讲,野生采猎者的森林和在这种作物多样性中心的传统农民果园,是多样性的源泉;每次在我们的社会将我们农田和果园的复原力降至其断裂点时,植物育种者、病理学家和昆虫学家都会返回到这个多样性源泉。

36) **The first of San Francisco's road signs were only just being erected, hammered up by an enterprising insurance underwriter** (who hoped to win clients by posting directions into the countryside), (where drivers retreated for automobile "picnic parties"/held out of the view of angry townsfolk).

167

难点：win clients 吸引客户；held out 的逻辑主语是"picnic parties"

翻译：旧金山的第一批路标仅仅是刚刚由一个有进取心的保险商敲打竖立，他希望通过向农村张贴路标来赢得客户的青睐，在乡村，司机们退回来参加在愤怒的市民的视线外举行的汽车"野餐会"。

37) **The story of this conflict is the story of**（how we view ourselves in relation to animals），whether **we can replace the assumption of "dominion"**（that has been so destructive to us and the natural world）**with a worldview** that recognizes（that we live in a state of reciprocity with the birds and the beasts）—（that we are not only the product of nature but also part of it）.

难点：replace...with... 用……替换，原句中给这个结构因为定语从句的修饰相隔甚远

翻译：这场冲突的故事是我们在与动物的关系中如何看待自己的故事，我们是否能够以一种认识到我们与鸟类和野兽互惠的状态生活，我们不仅是自然的产物，而且也是自然的一部分的世界观取代对我们和自然世界有如此破坏的"统治"的假设。

38) With no formal education or apprenticeship to any watchmaker, **Harrison nevertheless constructed a series of virtually friction-free clocks**（that required no lubrication and no cleaning），（that were made from materials impervious to rust），and（that kept their moving parts perfectly balanced in relation to one another, regardless of how the world pitched or tossed about them）.

难点：impervious to 不受……的影响；regardless of 无论，不管；三个 that 引导的定语从句并列，修饰 clocks

翻译：没有接受过任何钟表师的正规教育或指点，但哈里森打造了一系列几乎无摩擦的钟，不需要润滑和清洁，由不会生锈的材料制成的，并且使它们的运动零件彼此保持完美平衡，不管世界是如何将它们摇摆或是抛来荡去。

练习六

要求：分析句子并翻译，注意并列结构【句子分析符号：<u>主干</u>（从句）意群/意群】。

1) Treatment of subject, use of line and color, lack of shadowing, and the solidness of the background in relation to the figure are all in sync with the modernist modes that had been in style on the Continent, most notably in France.

2) A daguerreotype of Edgar Allan Poe, taken in 1848, depicts the writer with a

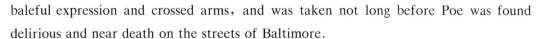

baleful expression and crossed arms, and was taken not long before Poe was found delirious and near death on the streets of Baltimore.

3) Male and female, mostly in their twenties, the Bloomsbury lot addressed each other by their first names, and, till the wee hours of the morning, reflected on how to spend their lives.

4) This meandering yet deeply affecting novel is at once a version of the classic saga of an immigrant family adjusting to life in the United States and a highly unconventional portrait of the artist as an immigrant, family man, and all-around ordinary guy.

5) Plants die in the rain forest, including the woody vines Morpho caterpillars feed upon and are evolutionarily specialized to exploit, and saprophytic fungi and bacteria attack the dead plant material.

6) At least before World War II broke out, my work in progress was very much the product of and a response to the social crises of the 1930s.

7) There was always a danger of swamping or capsizing in heavy seas, of having sails ripped apart or masts and booms broken by fierce winds, of smashing the hulls against unseen rocks or reefs.

8) Whole architectural histories can be read in the structural particulars he drew, civic histories in tomb inscriptions he transcribed, histories of religion and fashion in the ornaments he rendered.

9) The linchpins of the show are Aunt Eller, played by the gritty, droll comedienne Andrea Martin, who is American and nails it, and the feisty lovelorn Laurey, played by the fine-voiced, demure Josefina Gabrielle, who is English and doesn't.

10) They could be guided by internal compasses of magnetite chips embedded in their skulls, by the warmth, salinity, or motion of the current, by patterns of polarized light received by the pineal window in their heads, or by prey leaving their scent as an oily, odorous slick in the water.

11) With her partners, ER was a businesswoman who co-owned the Val-Kill crafts factory, a political leader who edited and co-published the *Women's Democratic News*, and an educator who co-owned and taught at a New York school for girls.

12) ER's mentors since 1903, they had battled on the margins of national politics since the 1880s for public health, universal education, community centers, sanitation programs, and government responsibility for the welfare of the nation's poor and neglected people.

13) Indeed, she and Kate Clifford Larson, in her first book, *Bound for the Promised Land*, have both done extensive and imaginative research in local historical sources that tell us almost more than we want to know about the Eastern Shore in the mid-19th century; in the papers of antislavery activists who interacted with Tubman; in the correspondence of an earlier Tubman biographer who in the 1940's interviewed individuals who had been alive long enough to remember her.

14) I wouldn't mind that being said, although one could also point out that work is also tied together by the unity of place, or by the failure of love to solve people's lives, or by the desperate wish to be back in our parents' arms, or to be home, or by the dreadful and persistent longing to know why we are on earth.

15) Some of these early alterations were likely made by the theater company to adapt a play to a particular occasion, others by a collaborator, others for the government censors, still others by the printer, but many of the most significant changes seem to bear the mark of Shakespeare himself.

16) It has long been possible to read the text of the play while listening to a recorded version, but now it is wonderfully easy to locate particular scenes and instantly hear them, to go back and listen again, and to stop and look at the glosses keyed to difficult words and phrases.

17) And it was such an idealistic America, defined by its purest spirits, from Audubon and Jefferson to Emerson and Thoreau to the Lincoln who had saved the Union, to the great democrats of philosophy John Dewey and William James, and to the Willa Cather, Theodore Dreiser, Sherwood Anderson, and Carl Sandburg who brought home the Middle West to me as the valley of democracy and the fountainhead of hope.

18) The seesaw brought cycles of intensely cold winters and easterly winds, then switched abruptly to years of heavy spring and early summer rains, mild winters, and frequent Atlantic storms, or to periods of droughts, light northeasterly winds, and summer heat waves that baked growing corn fields under a shimmering haze.

19) With this in mind, I have taken off my white coat, deserted, by and large, the hospitals where I have spent the last twenty-five years, to explore my subjects' lives as they live in the real world, feeling in part like a naturalist, examining rare forms of life; in part like an anthropologist, a neuroanthropologist, in the field—but most of all like a physician, called here and there to make house calls, house calls at the far borders of human experience.

20) Her striking voice, never more opulent than in those years; the range of her

programs, which included, in addition to spirituals, more popular numbers than she normally sang on concert programs; and the charm and radiance of her personality, so intimately bound up with her singing, made her an extraordinarily popular radio performer.

解析

1) Treatment of subject, use of line and color, lack of shadowing, and the solidness of the background in relation to the figure are all in sync with the modernist modes (that had been in style on the Continent, most notably in France).

难点：主语部分四项并列；in sync with 与……同步；in style 在流行中

翻译：主题的处理、线条和色彩的使用、阴影的缺乏以及背景与人物的牢固性都与欧洲大陆上，最突出的是法国，流行的现代主义模式同步。

2) **A daguerreotype of Edgar Allan Poe**, taken in 1848, **depicts the writer** with a baleful expression and crossed arms, **and was taken** (**not long before Poe was found delirious and near death on the streets of Baltimore**).

难点：not long before... 在……不久之前；daguerreotype（早期的）达盖尔银版照片

翻译：1848 年拍摄的一张的埃德加·爱伦·坡照片描绘了这个作家凶恶的表情和交叉的双臂；这张照片是坡在巴尔的摩街头被发现神志失常，临死前拍的。

3) Male and female, mostly in their twenties, **the Bloomsbury lot addressed each other by their first names, and**, till the wee hours of the morning, **reflected on how to spend their lives**.

难点：lot 群体；address 称呼

翻译：男性和女性，大多在他们 20 多岁时期，布鲁姆斯伯里这群人以名字称呼对方，直到凌晨，他们都在思考如何度过一生。

4) **This meandering yet deeply affecting novel is** at once **a version of the classic saga of an immigrant family** adjusting to life in the United States **and a highly unconventional portrait of the artist** as an immigrant, family man, and all-around ordinary guy.

翻译：这部耐人寻味而又影响深远的小说，立刻成为适应美国生活的移民家庭的经典传奇，也是一幅极具非传统的作为移民、居家男人和全能普通人的艺术家的肖像。

5) **Plants die in the rain forest**, including the woody vines (Morpho caterpillars feed upon and are evolutionarily specialized to exploit), **and saprophytic fungi and bacteria attack the dead plant material**.

难点：定语从句 Morpho caterpillars feed upon and are evolutionarily specialized to exploit 省略了前面的连词 that，修饰 he woody vines，在这个从句中 feed upon 和 are... 并列

翻译：植物在雨林中死亡,包括大闪蝶毛毛虫所吃的且进化上所依赖的木质藤蔓,腐生真菌和细菌攻击死去的植物。

6) At least before World War II broke out，<u>my work in progress was very much the product of and a response to the social crises of the 1930s.</u>

难点: the product of and a response to the social crises = the product of the social crises and a response to the social crises

翻译：至少在第二次世界大战爆发之前,我正在进行的工作在很大程度上是20世纪30年代社会危机的产物和对30年代社会危机的回应。

7) **There was always a danger** of swamping or capsizing in heavy seas，**of** having sails ripped apart or masts and booms broken by fierce winds，**of** smashing the hulls against unseen rocks or reefs.

难点: 三个 of 短语都是修饰 danger；having sails ripped apart or masts and booms broken by fierce winds = having sails ripped apart or having masts and booms broken by fierce winds，have something done...使······被······

翻译：总是有淹没或倾覆在汹涌的大海、帆被撕开、桅杆被强风吹破、船体撞在看不见的岩石或礁石上的危险。

8) Whole architectural histories can be read in the structural particulars（he drew），civic histories in tomb inscriptions（he transcribed），histories of religion and fashion in the ornaments（he rendered）.

难点: particular 细节；render 提供；本句省略较多,整个句子等同于：Whole architectural histories can be read in the structural particulars he drew; civic histories can be read in tomb inscriptions he transcribed; histories of religion and fashion can be read in the ornaments he rendered

翻译：从他所画的结构细节可以看出整个建筑史;市民的历史可以从他抄写的墓志中读到;宗教和时尚的历史可以从他提供的装饰品中读到。

9) **The linchpins of the show are Aunt Eller**，played by the gritty，droll comedienne Andrea Martin，（who is American and nails it，）**and the feisty lovelorn Laurey**，played by the fine-voiced，demure Josefina Gabrielle，（who is English and doesn't）.

难点: linchpin 关键人物；nail it 成功；doesn't = doesn't nail it,省略

翻译：表演的关键人物是爱勒姑姑和活泼可爱的失恋者劳瑞;爱勒姑姑由勇敢、滑稽可笑的喜剧演员安德列·马丁饰演,她是美国人并且成功出演了;劳瑞是由好嗓子、娴静的约瑟芬娜·加布里埃莱饰演,她是英国人但没有表演成功。

10) **They could be guided** by internal compasses of magnetite chips/embedded in their skulls， by the warmth，salinity，or motion of the current， by patterns of

polarized light/received by the pineal window in their heads, or [by] prey/leaving their scent as an oily, odorous slick in the water.

难点：四个 by 短语并列，列举被引导的方式；非谓语动词 embedded/received/leaving 分别修饰离它们最近的名词

翻译：它们可以通过嵌入头骨的磁铁矿芯片；通过水流的温度、盐度或运动；通过它们头部松果体窗口所接收的偏振光模式；或是通过将气味作为一种油性、有气味的浮油留在水中的猎物来引导。

11) With her partners, **ER was a businesswoman** (who co-owned the Val-Kill crafts factory), **a political leader** (who edited and co-published the *Women's Democratic News*), **and an educator** (who co-owned and taught at a New York school for girls).

翻译：与她的合伙人一起，ER 是一位共同拥有 Val-Kill 工艺厂的女商人，一位编辑并联合出版《妇女民主新闻》的政治领袖，以及一位共同拥有纽约一所女子学校并任教的教育者。

12) ER's mentors since 1903, **they had battled on the margins of national politics** since the 1880s/for public health, universal education, community centers, sanitation programs, and government responsibility for the welfare of the nation's poor and neglected people.

难点：ER's mentors since 1903 是 they 的同位语

翻译：自 1903 年以来 ER 的导师，从 19 世纪 80 年代起，他们在国家政治的边缘上进行了斗争，为了公共卫生、普及教育、社区中心、卫生项目以及政府对国家穷人和被忽视的人民的福利的责任进行斗争。

13) Indeed, **she and Kate Clifford Larson**, in her first book, *Bound for the Promised Land*, **have both done extensive and imaginative research** [in] local historical sources (that tell us almost more than we want to know about the Eastern Shore in the mid-19th century); [in] the papers of antislavery activists (who interacted with Tubman); [in] the correspondence of an earlier Tubman biographer (who in the 1940's interviewed individuals) (who had been alive long enough to remember her).

难点：三个 in 短语并列，列举她们研究的信息范围；in her first book, *Bound for the Promised Land*, 仅修饰 Kate Clifford Larson

翻译：事实上，她和凯特·克利福德·拉尔森在她的第一本书《奔向应许之地》中都做了广泛而富有想象力的研究，研究那些比我们想知道的要多的 19 世纪中叶东海岸的当地历史资料；研究与塔布曼互动的反奴隶制活动家的论文；研究在一位早期传记作家的通信，他在 1940 年采访了那些活得足够长能记得塔布曼的人。

14) <u>I wouldn't mind that being said</u>, (although one could also point out that work

is also tied together |by| the unity of place, or |by| the failure of love to solve people's lives, or |by| the desperate wish to be back in our parents' arms, or to be home, or |by| the dreadful and persistent longing to know why we are on earth).

翻译： 我不介意别人这么说，虽然人们也可以指出，这个作品被联系在一起，通过地方的统一，通过爱未能解决人们的生活，通过想回到父母怀抱、或回家的绝望愿望，或者通过想知道为甚我们在地球上既痛苦又持续的渴望。

15) **Some** of these early alterations were likely made by the theater company to adapt a play to a particular occasion, **others** by a collaborator, **others** for the government censors, **still others** by the printer, **but many** of the most significant changes seem to bear the mark of Shakespeare himself.

难点： bear the mark of 带有……的印记；整个句子等同于 Some of these early alterations were likely made by the theater company to adapt a play to a particular occasion; others were likely made by a collaborator; others were likely made for the government censors; still others were likely made by the printer, but many of the most significant changes seem to bear the mark of Shakespeare himself

翻译： 其中一些早期的改动很可能是剧院公司为了使一出戏适应某个特定的场合而做的；其他的很可能是合作者所为；另一些则可能是为政府审查人员准备的；还有一些可能是印刷者所做的，但许多最重要的变化似乎带有莎士比亚本人的印记。

16) It has long been possible to read the text of the play while listening to a recorded version, but now it is wonderfully easy |to| locate particular scenes and instantly hear them, |to| go back and listen again, and |to| stop and look at the glosses keyed to difficult words and phrases.

难点： it 做形式主语，真正的主语是后面的 to do...；key 键入；gloss 注释，评注

翻译： 长期以来，人们可以一边听录音一边阅读剧本，但现在很容易找到特定场景，然后立刻听到它们，或者回去再听一遍，或者停下来看看那些键入在难懂的字和短语中的注释。

17) And **it was such an idealistic America**, defined by its purest spirits, |from| Audubon and Jefferson |to| Emerson and Thoreau |to| the Lincoln who had saved the Union, |to| the great democrats of philosophy John Dewey and William James, |and to| the Willa Cather, Theodore Dreiser, Sherwood Anderson, and Carl Sandburg (who brought home the Middle West to me as the valley of democracy and the fountainhead of hope).

难点： bring home to... 使……深刻领会到；who brought home the Middle West to me as the valley of democracy and the fountainhead of hope = who brought home to me the Middle West as the valley of democracy and the fountainhead of hope

翻译：这是一个理想主义的美国,由它最纯粹的精神所定义,从奥杜邦和杰斐逊到爱默生和梭罗,到拯救联邦的林肯,到伟大的哲学民主派约翰·杜威和威廉·詹姆斯,以及到使我深深领会到中西部是民主的山谷和希望的源泉的薇拉·凯瑟、西奥多·德莱塞、舍伍德·安德森和卡尔·桑德堡。

18) **The seesaw brought cycles**/of intensely cold winters and easterly winds/, **then switched abruptly to years**/ of heavy spring and early summer rains, mild winters, and frequent Atlantic storms/, **or to periods**/ of droughts, light northeasterly winds, and summer heat waves (that baked growing corn fields under a shimmering haze).

翻译：波动带来了严寒的冬季和东风的循环,然后突然转变为多年的春季和初夏的大雨,温和的冬季,频繁的大西洋风暴,或变为干旱、东北风和闪烁的烟雾下烘烤着生长玉米田的夏季热浪时期。

19) With this in mind, **I have taken off my white coat**, **deserted**, by and large, **the hospitals** (where I have spent the last twenty-five years), **to explore my subjects' lives** (as they live in the real world), feeling in part like a naturalist, examining rare forms of life; in part like an anthropologist, a neuroanthropologist, in the field—but most of all like a physician, called here and there to make house calls, house calls at the far borders of human experience.

难点：by and large 大体上；here and there 在各处；house calls 上门诊治

翻译：考虑到这一点,我脱掉了我的白大褂,大体上,离开了我在过去25年里所待的医院,去探索我的病人在现实世界中的生活,部分感觉自己像一个博物学家,研究稀有的生命形式;部分像一个在野外的人类学家,一个神经人类学家——但最重要的是,像一个医生,在各处上门问诊,在人类经验的遥远边界问诊。

20) **Her striking voice**, never more opulent than in those years; **the range of her programs**, (which included, in addition to spirituals, more popular numbers than she normally sang on concert programs); **and the charm and radiance of her personality**, so intimately bound up with her singing, **made her an extraordinarily popular radio performer**.

难点：三个主语并列但每个主语都有较长的修饰语;in addition to spirituals 是插入成分,分裂了 which 从句中的主语与谓语

翻译：她那动人的嗓音,从未比那些年更华丽;她的节目范围,包括除了灵歌之外比通常的演唱节目更多的流行歌曲;她的人格魅力和光辉,与她的歌声紧密相连,使她成为一个非常受欢迎的广播表演者。

练习七

要求：分析句子并翻译，注意句子语序【句子分析符号：<u>主干</u>（从句）意群/意群】。

1）In effect，the livestock industry has successfully transferred to the general public one of its most basic operational costs：prevention of predator losses.

2）The industrial revolution completed with dramatic rapidity a process that had been going on for several centuries：the transformation of labor into a salable commodity.

3）The idea of building a canal to connect the Hudson with the Great Lakes there had been around for many years but always dismissed as hopelessly impracticable.

4）Somehow，somewhere，we lost sight of what success means and fashioned in its place a glorious，shining future where bigger is better，new is good，and old is to be replaced as quickly as possible.

5）Government should not affirm，through its policies or laws，any particular conception of the good life；The republican conception of freedom，unlike the liberal conception，requires a formative politics，a politics that cultivates in citizens the qualities of character that self-government requires.

6）There had to be some way，Helmholtz thought，of "discounting the illuminant"—and this he saw as an "unconscious inference" or "an act of judgement" (though he did not venture to suggest where such judgement might occur).

7）Glass can serve as a lens，revealing and bringing into focus the interior of buildings—as in the Rose Center，and in the award-winning Hillier Group design for the power plant that supplies electricity to New York's John R Kennedy International Airport.

8）To find，as Jean M. Humez seeks to do in *Harriet Tubman*：*The Life and the Life Stories*，"the private woman whose life has virtually disappeared behind the heroic public icon，" is no small challenge.

9）Should A sprint a little too fast and dash beyond antennae range，she slows until her partner catches up.

10）Another approach is to watch a star for the slight periodic dip in its brightness that will occur should an orbiting planet circle in front of it and block a fraction of its light.

11）So important were women to the native literature that when men set their hands to writing poetic diaries，as Tsurayuki did in the *Tosa Diary*，they often wrote under the persona of a woman.

12) Not that conformity to rules was at first obvious to anthropologists who were instead understandably dazzled by the variety in folk taxonomies.

13) Not until the beginning of the twentieth century did women reappear as an important force in Japanese literature，despite the existence of one or two significant *haiku* poets，for example Chiyo，in the Tokugawa Period.

14) Not since the early 1950s，when sleek，green-tinted glass buildings like New York City's Lever House rose amid the stone canyons of countless major cities，has glass elicited so much attention.

15) Hence not only were local postmasters well informed on local reading habits，they were privy to much of the news locally in circulation and often，monitors，even censors，of what newspapers local postal patrons would read and what mail they would receive.

解析

1—8 句中，句子中宾语位置与我们预期的宾语出现的位置不一致，需要注意。关于这一现象，前面特殊现象一章有详细的讲解，这里不加赘述。

1) In effect，**the livestock industry has successfully transferred** to the general public **one of its most basic operational costs**: prevention of predator losses.

难点: transferred to the general public one of its most basic operational costs = transferred one of its most basic operational costs to the general public，因为 costs 后有冒号进行解释说明，所以 transfer A to B 结构调整为 transfer to B A

翻译: 实际上，畜牧业已成功地向公众转移了其最基本的运营成本之一：防止捕食者损失。

2) **The industrial revolution completed** with dramatic rapidity **a process**（that had been going on for several centuries：the transformation of labor into a salable commodity）.

难点: completed with dramatic rapidity a process = completed a process with dramatic rapidity，因为 process 被定语从句修饰，所以将 process 位置向后调整，方便修饰

翻译: 工业革命以惊人的速度完成了几个世纪以来一直在进行的一个过程：劳动力转变成一种可销售的商品。

3) **The idea** of building a canal to connect the Hudson with the Great Lakes **there had been** around for many years **but always dismissed** as hopelessly impracticable.

难点: 原结构为，there had been the idea... around for many years but（the idea had been）always...，为了强调也为了平衡并列的谓语，将 idea 提前。这点无需掌握，因

177

为基本不影响理解；dismiss...as... 拒绝……因为……

翻译：修建一条运河把哈德逊河与五大湖连接起来的想法已经有多年了，但总是被拒绝是因为这个想法被认为是毫无希望的不切实际。

4）Somehow，somewhere，**we lost sight of what success means and fashioned** in its place **a glorious，shining future**（where bigger is better，new is good，and old is to be replaced as quickly as possible）.

难点：fashioned in its place a glorious，shining future = fashioned a glorious，shining future in its place，因为 future 被 sing 与从句修饰，所以位置向后调整；fashion 制做，创造；in it's place 取代它

翻译：不知何故，在某个地方，我们忘记了成功的意义，创造了一个越大越好，新就是好的，旧的将被尽快更换的光辉未来来取代它。

5）**Government should not affirm**，through its policies or laws，**any particular conception of the good life**；**The republican conception of freedom**，unlike the liberal conception，**requires a formative politics**，a politics that cultivates in citizens the qualities of character that self-government requires.

难点：not affirm，through its policies or laws，any particular conception of the good life = not affirm any particular conception of the good life through its policies or laws；a politics that...解释说明 a formative politics；cultivates in citizens the qualities of character = cultivates the qualities of character in citizens

翻译：政府不应通过其政策或法律确认任何特定的美好生活观念；与自由主义观不同的是，共和党的自由观要求形成性政治，一种在公民中培养自治所要求的品格的政治。

6）**There had to be some way**，Helmholtz thought，**of "discounting the illuminant"——and this he saw as an "unconscious inference" or "an act of judgement"**（though he did not venture to suggest where such judgement might occur）.

难点：Helmholtz thought 是插入成分，可跳过；this he saw as... = he saw this as...

翻译：亥姆霍兹认为，必须有某种方式来"低估光源"——他认为这是一种"无意识的推理"或"判断行为"（尽管他没有冒险提出这种判断可能在哪里发生）。

7）**Glass can serve as a lens，revealing and bringing into focus/the interior of buildings**——as in the Rose Center，and in the award-winning Hillier Group design/for the power plant（that supplies electricity to New York's John R Kennedy International Airport）.

难点：revealing and bringing into focus the interior of buildings = revealing and bringing the interior of buildings into focus；plant 工厂

翻译：玻璃可以充当镜头，显示和聚焦建筑物的内部，就像玫瑰中心以及由屡获殊荣的希利尔集团设计的为肯尼迪国际机场供电的发电厂一样。

8）**To find**，as Jean M. Humez seeks to do in *Harriet Tubman*：*The Life and the Life Stories*，"**the private woman**（whose life has virtually disappeared/behind the heroic public icon,）" **is no small challenge.**

难点：插入成分 as Jean M. Humez seeks to do in *Harriet Tubman*：*The Life and the Life Stories* 分离了 find 和其宾语

翻译：正如让·M·休梅兹在《哈丽特·塔布曼：生命与生活故事》中所寻求的那样，找到"（个人）实际生活上已经消失在英雄的公众偶像形象后的这个隐秘女人"并不是一个小挑战。

注：这句话有点抽象，其实意思就是，这个女人作为公众人物，人们过于熟悉她的英雄形象，而其英雄形象背后的、私下的、真实的形象很难被人们了解

9—15 句中，主语与谓语动词或助动词的位置与常规的位置不一致，需要注意。关于这一现象，前面特殊现象一章有详细的讲解，这里不加赘述。

9）（Should A sprint a little too fast and dash beyond antennae range,）she slows（until her partner catches up）.

难点：if 从句的虚拟语气的省略，Should A sprint a little too fast and dash beyond antennae range＝If A should sprint a little too fast and dash beyond antennae range

翻译：如果 A 冲刺的速度过快，冲出触角范围，她会放慢速度，直到伴侣赶上为止。

10）**Another approach is to watch a star for the slight periodic dip in its brightness**（that will occur should an orbiting planet circle in front of it and block a fraction of its light）.

难点：should an orbiting planet circle in front of it and block a fraction of its light＝if an orbiting planet should circle in front of it and block a fraction of its light

翻译：另一种方法是观察恒星亮度的轻微周期性下降，如果绕行的行星出现在它面前并阻挡它的一部分光芒时，那么恒星亮度的轻微周期性下降将发生。

11）**So important were women to the native literature**［**that**（when men set their hands to writing poetic diaries, as Tsurayuki did in the *Tosa Diary*,）**they often wrote under the persona of a woman**］.

难点：So important were women to the native literature ＝ Women were so important to the native literature，so…that…句式中，so 放句首时，句子要倒装

翻译：女性对本土文学如此重要以至于当男人们着手写诗篇日记时，他们常常以女人的身份写作，就像纪贯之在《土佐日记》中所做的那样。

12）**Not that conformity to rules was at first obvious to anthropologists**（who were instead understandably dazzled by the variety in folk taxonomies）.

难点：not 放句首表强调；conformity to… 与……一致

翻译：对于被民间分类的多样性所迷惑的人类学家们来说，对规则的遵守起初并不

明显。

13）**Not until the beginning of the twentieth century did** <u>women reappear as an important force in Japanese literature</u>，despite the existence of one or two significant *haiku* poets，for example Chiyo，in the Tokugawa Period.

难点：not 放句首，句子倒装，Not until the beginning of the twentieth century did women reappear... = Until the beginning of the twentieth century，women did not appear...

翻译：直到 20 世纪初,女性才重新成为日本文学的重要力量,尽管在德川时期有一两位重要的佛句诗人,例如千代。

14）**Not since the early 1950s**，（when sleek，green-tinted glass buildings like New York City's Lever House rose amid the stone canyons of countless major cities），**has glass elicited so much attention**.

难点：not 放句首，句子倒装，Not since the early 1950s... has glass elicited so much attention = Since the early 1950s... glass has not elicited so much attention；when 引导的从句修饰 1950s,相当于插入成分,可先忽略；the stone canyon 是比喻手法,指城市高楼之间

翻译：自从 20 世纪 50 年代初,像纽约市 Lever House 这样的时尚绿色玻璃建筑在无数大城市的高楼之中升起时,玻璃就没有引起如此多的关注了。

15）Hence not only were local postmasters well informed on local reading habits，<u>they were privy to much of the news</u> locally in circulation **and often monitors**，even censors，**of**（**what newspapers local postal patrons would read**）**and**（**what mail they would receive**）.

难点：not 放句首，句子倒装，not only were local postmasters well informed... = local postmasters were not only well informed...；be privy to 参与,知晓

翻译：因此,当地邮递员不仅对当地的阅读习惯了如指掌,而且他们了解当地发行的大部分新闻,并且经常监控甚至是审查当地邮政用户会读什么报纸,以及他们将收到什么样的邮件。

练习八

要求：分析句子并翻译,注意固定搭配【句子分析符号：主干（从句)意群/意群】。

1）Indeed，it was precisely because of its futuristic storyline that Star Trek was able to address many of the contemporary social problems that other programs shunned.

2）And it was Marshall，as the nation's first African American Supreme Court justice, who promoted affirmative action—preferences, set-asides, and other race-conscious policies—as the remedy for the damage remaining from the nation's history of slavery and racial bias.

3) Larson and Humez tend to conjecture less and instead to supply the reader with the considerable information they have collected—sometimes, it seems, more because they have found it than because it adds significantly to our understanding of Tubman's life.

4) The final 200 pages consider the contemporary stories and texts through which we know Tubman, with most of this space devoted to excerpts from the documents themselves.

5) The reader gains not just glimpses of Tubman, but sees how she confounded even those admirers who still could not comprehend a black woman who behaved like the bravest of men.

6) Its young mix of writers, thinkers, and artists stood at the vanguard of a shift in manners away from nineteenth-century formality and reticence and toward twentieth-century candor and playfulness.

7) Olin Downes, for example, never comfortable with extravagant praise, held to his gravity of manner in reviewing Anderson's first New York recital in 1939: "Miss Anderson sings music by classic masters, not as a lesson learned, or a duty carefully performed, but as an interpreter who has fully grasped and deeply felt the import of the song."

8) Bloomsbury's anti-Victorian revolt had, in fact, as much to do with getting back to Fry's perceptions of the great traditions in art as it did with youthful rebellion.

9) Smith raises the roof not so much with "colorblind" casting as by paying attention to how the characters might have looked if they were actual Oklahomans of the period.

10) Star Trek offers viewers the paradox of a program that combines provocative insight into changing cultural values with the reassuring comfort that the "known" universe of Starfleet, Kligons and phasers can nonetheless survive intact, and even grow.

11) What struck me from the first was the astonishment with which American writers confronted situations as new to themselves as to the Europeans who were often reading about America for the first time.

12) For the true writer, though, however close the events may be to her life, there is some distance, some remove, that allows for the shaping of the work.

13) Along the way, she often bridges the gap between the native world view—in

which human beings and nature are interrelated, and all plants, animals and mountains and other landforms are sacred—and the more scientific one, pollinating a deeper understanding between them.

14) Biologists have dubbed mountaintop habitat patches "sky islands" because the valleys in between are as uninhabitable as the sea for nonmobile alpine species.

15) Since this discovery, the main interest of DeVries and his team has been to discover how immune systems, in his fish and other living organisms, fight off invading foreign bodies, be they cold virus, cancer cells or ice crystals.

16) Nearly all of my patients, so it seems to me, whatever their problems, reach out to life—and not only despite their conditions, but also because of them, and even with their aid.

解析

1) Indeed, ~~it was~~ **precisely because of its futuristic storyline** ~~that~~ **Star Trek was able to address many of the contemporary social problems** that other programs shunned.

难点: it was/is...that...是强调句型,翻译为"正是……";address 处理;shun 回避

翻译: 事实上,正是因为它的未来主义故事情节,星际迷航能够解决许多其他节目回避的当代社会问题。

2) And ~~it~~ was **Marshall**, as the nation's first African American Supreme Court justice, ~~who~~ **promoted affirmative action**—preferences, set-asides, and other race-conscious policies—**as the remedy for the damage**/remaining from the nation's history of slavery and racial bias.

难点: it was/is....who...是强调句型,翻译为"正是……";affirmative action(鼓励雇用少数民族成员、妇女等的)反歧视行动,平权运动;preferences 和 set-asides 是两种针对种族歧视的政策

翻译: 正是马歇尔,作为美国第一位非洲裔最高法院的大法官,他提倡平权行动——偏好、搁置和其他有种族意识的政策——以弥补美国奴隶制和种族偏见历史遗留下来的损害。

3) **Larson and Humez tend to conjecture less and** instead to **supply the reader with the considerable information**(they have collected)—sometimes, it seems, more(because they have found it)than(because it adds significantly to our understanding of Tubman's life).

难点: more A than B 是 A 不是 B

翻译: 拉森和胡梅兹倾向于减少猜测,相反,向读者提供他们收集到的大量信息——有时似乎是因为他们发现了这些信息,而不是因为它大大增加了我们对塔布曼生活的

理解。

4）**The final 200 pages consider the contemporary stories and texts**（**through which we know Tubman**），with most of this space devoted to excerpts from the documents themselves.

难点：with most of this space devoted to excerpts from the documents themselves 是 with＋n＋v-ing/v-ed 结构，with 没有具体含义，表示伴随的状态

翻译：最后 200 页考虑了我们了解塔布曼的当代故事和文本，大部分篇幅都是从文件本身摘录的。

5）**The reader gains not just glimpses of Tubman，but sees how she confounded even those admirers**（who still could not comprehend a black woman）（who behaved like the bravest of men）.

难点：not just...but... 不但……而且……

翻译：读者不仅了解了塔布曼，还看到了她是如何让那些崇拜者感到困惑，他们仍然不能理解这个表现得像最勇敢的男人的黑人女人。

6）**Its young mix** of writers, thinkers, and artists **stood at the vanguard of a shift** in manners away from nineteenth-century formality and reticence and toward twentieth-century candor and playfulness.

难点：away from...and towards... 远离……朝向……；at the vanguard of 在……的前列

翻译：由年轻的作家、思想家和艺术家组成的年轻组合站在了从 19 世纪的拘谨和沉默寡言，到 20 世纪的坦率和玩乐方式转变的前列。

7）**Olin Downes**，for example，never comfortable with extravagant praise，**held to his gravity of manner**/ in reviewing Anderson's first New York recital in 1939/："**Miss Anderson sings music** by classic masters, not as a lesson learned, or a duty carefully performed，but **as an interpreter who has fully grasped and deeply felt the import of the song. "**

难点：not...but... 不是……而是……；the import of... 意思，含义

翻译：奥林·唐斯从不轻易赞美，在回顾安德森 1939 年在纽约举行的第一次独奏会时，坚持自己的严肃态度："安德森小姐演唱经典大师的音乐，不是作为一个学来的课程，也不是作为一种认真履行的职责，而是作为一个完全掌握并深切感受到这首歌的含义的诠释者。"

8）**Bloomsbury's anti-Victorian revolt had**，in fact，**as much to do with getting back to Fry's perceptions** of the great traditions in art **as it did with youthful rebellion**.

难点：have to do with... 与……有关联；as much A as B　A 与 B 一样

翻译：实际上，布鲁姆斯伯里反维多利亚起义与回到弗莱对艺术伟大传统的看法和年

轻人的反叛有着同样多的关系。

9）Smith raises the roof not so much with "colorblind" casting as by paying attention to how the characters might have looked（if they were actual Oklahomans of the period）.

难点：raise the roof 喧嚣；not so much with A as with B 与其说是 A，不如说是 B；casting 演员挑选

翻译：史密斯引起轰动与其说是通过"无视肤色"的演员挑选，不如说是通过关注角色可能的样子（如果他们真的是那个时期的俄克拉荷马拉人的话）。

10）**Star Trek offers viewers the paradox of a program** that combines provocative **insight** into changing cultural values **with the reassuring comfort**（that the "known" universe of Starfleet，Kligons and phasers can nonetheless survive intact，and even grow）.

难点：combine A with B 把 A 与 B 结合起来

翻译：《星际迷航》为观众提供了一个节目的悖论，该节目结合了不断变化的文化价值观的挑衅性见解与令人放心的安慰，即"已知"的星际舰队、克利贡和相位器宇宙仍然可以完整地生存，甚至成长。

11）**What struck me from the first was the astonishment**（**with which American writers confronted situations**/as new to themselves as to the Europeans）（who were often reading about America for the first time）.

难点：as...as...结构；as new to themselves as to the Europeans 修饰 situations

翻译：从一开始就让我震惊的是，美国作家面对新情况时的惊讶；这些新情况对他们来说就像第一次读到关于美国的书的欧洲人一样的陌生。

12）For the true writer，though，（however close the events may be to her life），**there is some distance**，some remove，**that allows for the shaping of the work.**

难点：however + 句子，意思是无论……；though + 逗号，意思是然而，但是；remove 差距，间距

翻译：然而，对于真正的作家来说，不管这些事件与她的生活多么接近，总有一些距离和有些间距，以便塑造作品。

13）Along the way，**she often bridges the gap between the native world view**—（in which human beings and nature are interrelated，and all plants，animals and mountains and other landforms are sacred）—**and the more scientific one**，pollinating a deeper understanding between them.

难点：between...and...的固定搭配意识；破折号可跳过

翻译：一直以来，她联合了原生世界观和更为科学的世界观之间的距离，使它们之间有更为深刻的理解；原生世界观是，人与自然相互联系，所有的植物、动物和山脉以及其他

地貌都是神圣的。

14) <u>Biologists have dubbed mountaintop habitat patches "sky islands"</u>（because the valleys in between are as uninhabitable as the sea for nonmobile alpine species）.

难点： 将山顶类比为大海上的岛屿

翻译： 生物学家将山顶栖息地称为"天空岛屿"，因为对于不可移动的高山植物物种来说，它们之间的山谷就像大海一样不适合居住。

15) Since this discovery，**the main interest** of DeVries and his team **has been to discover**（**how immune systems**，in his fish and other living organisms，**fight off invading foreign bodies**，be they cold virus，cancer cells or ice crystals）.

难点： be they cold virus，cancer cells or ice crystals 这里的 be 表示无论，不管，be it/they… 相当于 whether it is/they are…

翻译： 自从这一发现以来，德弗里斯和他团队的主要兴趣就是探索他的鱼和其他生物的免疫系统是如何抵御外来异物的入侵，不管是感冒病毒、癌细胞还是冰晶。

16) **Nearly all of my patients**，so it seems to me，whatever their problems，**reach out to life**—and not only despite their conditions，but often because of them，and even with their aid.

难点： so it seems to me = it seems so to me

翻译： 几乎我所有的病人，在我看来，不管他们有什么问题，都会拥抱生活——不仅不顾他们的病情，而且常常是因为病情，甚至在病情的帮助下。

练习九

要求： 分析句子成分并翻译【句子分析符号：<u>主干</u>（从句）意群/意群】。

1) In paintings such as Eastern Point and Cannon Rock the construction of the water has been reorganized into clear graphic shapes and strong directional lines that echo the Japanese printmaking that had such a lasting effect on his work.

2) Although many of the icons of early glass architecture rose in U.S. cities during the years after World War II，since the energy crisis of 1973 most of the advances in glass architecture have taken place in Europe.

3) Although television news programs helped focus the country on the rifts that had begun to percolate on campuses，in city streets，and around dining room tables，as a rule entertainment programming avoided conflict and controversy.

4) In recent decades the civic，or formative，aspect of our politics has given way to a procedural republic，concerned less with cultivating virtue than with enabling persons to choose their own values.

5) When she disgorges the nectar she adds to it fluids secreted from her salivary and now contracted hypopharyngeal glands, filled with enzymes to purify and preserve the honey.

6) Won't a sense of inevitable mystery underpinning our intricate lives serve us better than the notion that we will each be given a neat set of blanks to fill in—always?

7) How else to explain the fact that, every year, people shell out millions of dollars on extended warranties that they seldom get a chance to take advantage of?

8) Could it be that some dinosaurs traveled much as some advanced herbivorous mammals do today, with large adults at the borders sheltering juveniles in the center?

9) Do you know anyone who would wager a substantial sum even at favorable odds on the proposition that Homo sapiens will last longer than Brontosaurus!

解析

1) In paintings such as Eastern Point and Cannon Rock/**the construction of the water has been reorganized into clear graphic shapes and strong directional lines** (that echo the Japanese printmaking that had such a lasting effect on his work).

难点: In paintings such as Eastern Point and Cannon Rock 与主语之间没有逗号隔开

翻译: 在像 Eastern Point 和 Cannon Rock 这样的绘画作品中,水的结构被重新组织成清晰的图形形状和强烈的方向线,与对他的作品产生了如此持久影响的日本版画相呼应。

2) (Although many of the icons of early glass architecture rose in U. S. cities during the years after World War II), since the energy crisis of 1973 most of the advances in glass architecture have taken place in Europe.

难点: since the energy crisis of 1973 与主句之间没有用逗号隔开

翻译: 尽管许多早期玻璃建筑的标志性建筑在第二次世界大战后的几年里在美国城市兴起,但自 1973 年能源危机以来,玻璃建筑的大部分改进都发生在欧洲。

3) **Although television news programs helped focus the country on the rifts** (that had begun to percolate/on campuses,/in city streets,/and around dining room tables), as a rule/**entertainment programming avoided conflict and controversy**.

难点: as a rule 与主语之间没有逗号隔开

翻译: 尽管电视新闻节目有助于全国关注校园、城市街道和餐桌周围开始蔓延的裂痕,但通常,娱乐节目会避免冲突和争议。

4) In recent decades/**the civic, or formative, aspect of our politics has given way to a procedural republic,** concerned less with cultivating virtue/than with enabling persons to choose their own values.

难点：In recent decades 与主语之间没有逗号隔开；give way to... 让位于……；concerned less with... 修饰 a procedural republic；less A than B 不是A,而是B

翻译：近几十年来,我们政治的公民性或形成性方面已经让位给一个程序性的共和观念,它关注的不是培养美德,而是使人们能够选择自己的价值观。

5)（**When she disgorges the nectar**）**she adds to it fluids**/secreted from her salivary and now contracted hypopharyngeal glands/, filled with enzymes/to purify and preserve the honey.

难点：When she disgorges the nectar 与主语之间没有逗号隔开；adds to it fluids＝adds fluids to,因为 fluids 后面有长修饰,所以位置向后移动,方便修饰；salivary 和 contracted 并列,修饰 hypopharyngeal glands；contract 收缩；filled with enzymes to purify and preserve the honey 修饰 fluids

翻译：当她吐出花蜜时,她会添加从她唾液分泌的液体、现在收缩下咽腺体,这些液体充满了酶来净化和保存蜂蜜。

6)**Won't a sense of inevitable mystery**/ underpinning our intricate lives/**serve us better than the notion**（**that we will each be given a neat set of blanks to fill in**）?

难点：较长的疑问句也是优先找主干,只是其语序与陈述句不一样,多了一层障碍；underpin 支撑

翻译：一种支撑我们错综复杂生活的不可避免的神秘感,难道不会比我们每个人都会得到一组整洁的空白来填写的想法更好吗?

7)How else to explain the fact（that, every year, people shell out millions of dollars on extended warranties）（that they seldom get a chance to take advantage of）?

难点：shell out 支付；take advantage of 利用；warranty 保修期

翻译：否则,如何解释这样一个事实：每年,人们在延长保修期上花费数百万美元,而他们却很少有机会去利用这一点?

8)**Could it be**（**that some dinosaurs traveled much as some advanced herbivorous mammals do today**, with large adults at the borders sheltering juveniles in the center）?

难点：as... as... 结构；with large adults at the borders sheltering juveniles in the center 是 with＋n＋v-ing/v-ed 结构,其中 with 表示伴随的状态,无实际意义

翻译：是不是有些恐龙以今天的一些高级食草哺乳动物一样的方式出行,在边界上有大型成年恐龙保护在中间的幼崽?

9)**Do you know anyone**（who would wager a substantial sum even at favorable odds **on the proposition**）（**that Homo sapiens will last longer than Brontosaurus!**）

难点：wager... on... 在……打赌；at favorable odds 在有利的机会下

翻译：你知道有谁会在智人比雷龙存活更长这一命题上下一大笔赌注? 即使是在有利的赔率上。